Language in the Blood

Book 1

By **Angela Lockwood**

First published on Amazon KDP (ebook) August 2013

Amazon Createspace (print) August 2015

ISBN-13: 978-2746669000 (Angela Lockwood)

ISBN-10: 2746669005

To my husband Adam who, on a rainy day when I was bored to tears, told me 'just write a book!'.
I would like to thank my friend Penny Hunter for her input and editing, as one doesn't 'just write' a book.

Contents

Chapter 1: Cameron

I was born in Edinburgh in 1895 and had a normal upbringing. My dad worked at the McEwan's brewery in Fountainbridge and my mother did a bit of sewing for the women in the neighbourhood. We didn't have much spare, but I had a happy time growing up, often playing with other boys by the Water of Leith, doing what all boys do when they find themselves by the riverside and getting rows from our mums for coming home all wet and dirty.

I didn't excel at school and left at 14 to become an apprentice cooper at the brewery. My parents weren't too upset at my leaving school; whilst they would have been pleased to have a doctor or a lawyer in the family, my dad was proud of his work and was happy enough for me to follow in his footsteps. Work at the brewery was hard, but I liked the fact that my dad and I could walk there together and I already knew most of the men. My schoolfriend Wee Tam worked there too so we were still able to switch sandwiches like we'd done at school. I preferred his mum's sarnies, though I'd never have told mine that. Wee Tam on the other hand would eat anything and preferably in large quantities – he could eat for Scotland so we were all amazed that he stayed so small and weedy.

Most of my friends followed their dads into their respective trades too. Big Tam became an apprentice brickie and Fat Malckie went to help his dad out in their shop. The Malcolms had a small grocery where we would go and buy sweets if we had any money, which was probably the reason that Malckie was the only fat kid in my class. We were all jealous of him and his easy access to so many sweets, but we all liked him as he'd sometimes give us a few too. Only Hootie was more academically gifted and he got a bursary for a place at Edinburgh University to study law. We'd always made a lot of fun of Alistair Henderson as he wore spectacles and was just a bit too clever. We told him he looked like an owl and the name Hootie quickly stuck.

My friends and I signed up together when war broke out. We were all 18 and 19 and it seemed like the right thing to do. My dad said he was proud of me and warned me not to turn any girls' heads in my fancy new uniform, but he needn't have worried. I only had eyes for my Fiona, and had promised her we would get married when the war was won.

Bagpipes played as we boarded the steamer for France. On board, my friends and I, all part of the new pal's battalion of the Royal Scots Lothian Regiment, played cards and smoked, blissfully unaware of what was waiting for us on the other side. We didn't discuss the possibility of dying. We were young and naïve and besides, it was a different time back then; we didn't talk about our fears and feelings. We all went on that boat feeling sure we'd be back in a few months after we'd given the Germans a good drubbing.

***

The Two Tams, Big and Wee, Fat Malckie, Hootie and I had been friends since childhood and suddenly we found ourselves marching together as men through the fields of France towards the trenches near Loos. I was from a city with hilly streets and had never seen land that was so flat. The straight roads and fields seemed to go on forever. We went past some farm houses and a few sleepy villages, but I didn't think France was very interesting. A knot was forming in my stomach; in this terrain the enemy would be able to see us coming from miles away and there was nowhere to hide. Fortunately I had my pals there to distract me with their songs and silly banter.

'Lads! They've got cows here too!' shouted Big Tam.

'Nah, those are *vaches*,' said Hootie. Smart specky bastard knew a bit of French. I was surprised he'd signed up as he was in the middle of his studies. He'd told me he thought the war would be over quickly and he'd hate to miss the whole thing.

'Do you think they have beer?' asked Wee Tam as we passed a village. I knew he wasn't pretending to be worried; being able to go to the pub and drink beer was a big deal to him.

'First leave, we'll get you a pint,' I assured him.

As we marched through the French countryside singing songs, I thought of my Fiona. We'd known each other since I was about four and had grown up together. Our families lived in the same tenement and as I was two months older I always felt very protective of her. We'd play together on the back drying green, annoying the neighbours by chasing each other around the washing. When it was raining, she'd come down to our flat.

'Can me and Cameron play in the living room Mrs Blair?' she'd ask.

'Of course you can Fiona, but it is "Cameron and I",' my mother corrected, smiling.

'Sorry Mrs Blair.'

My mother adored her. Having three boys herself she loved having this wee girl in our home and was more indulgent when she was around. She trusted Fiona wouldn't let our games get too wild and raucous. We mostly played cowboys and Indians, as my younger brothers enjoyed being wild Indians and Fiona and I liked being the cowboy and the damsel in distress. My mum would let us play in the long hallway if we promised to keep James away from under her feet and not make too much noise. My wee brother James was only a toddler then, but he enjoyed whooping like an Indian.

When we were old enough to go, I'd walk Fiona to and from school and deal with any cheekiness from boys along the way. I knew Hootie was sweet on her too, but I was taller and more athletic, so I felt I didn't have to worry about him. Big Tam was another matter and I did get into a fight with him over her once. We were mucking about by the Water of Leith as usual when Tam suddenly blurted:

'See you, Cameron. Just because she lives in your building doesn't mean Fiona belongs to you.'

'What d'ye mean?' I asked. We must have been about fifteen and we were all beginning to notice that Fiona had become quite pretty with her long, golden-brown hair and curves forming in all the right places.

'I was thinking of asking her to the dance, you know. Ye dinnae own her,' he said, taunting me.

'I ken I dinnae own her, but I'd die afore I let you put your hackit mitts on her!'

At that, Big Tam launched himself at me and we proceeded to batter lumps out of each other. Even though Tam was bigger than me I managed to get on top of him and gave him a bloody nose. That earned me a lot of respect from the other boys and I didn't have much trouble after that.

A few days later, Tam and I were friends again and he'd got himself another date for the dance. It was at that dance that Fiona let me kiss her for the first time and I walked on air for the next few days. However, for three years she let me do nothing more than that. Her parents had brought her up well and so had mine and we were hardly ever left alone once our parents noticed we'd started to see each other with different eyes. Whenever we wanted to go for a walk, we had to take either my wee brother or her wee sister with us and her wee sister was a right pain in the neck, always wanting something and never giving us a moment's peace.

Everyone knew that eventually we'd get married. My father even lent me a bit of money to buy a small, very dark, sapphire ring so we could get engaged before I set off for war. We had a small engagement party before I left and had our pictures taken so she could have me on her bedside table and I could carry her with me in my wallet. She was clearly very proud of me and loved being seen out with me in my uniform.

***

Apart from Big Tam, who had always been more forward, none of us had done it with a girl. Big Tam had got talking to some of the older French soldiers – how I do not know, as he didn't speak a word of French; I guessed there must be a universal sign for 'where do I find the loose women?'. With only one night of leave in the last town before we reached the trenches, Big Tam wasn't going to let it go to waste.

He marched us all down to the local cathouse and instructed us to pick a girl each. Tam went upstairs with the prettiest one and the rest of us just stood there red-faced, staring at our feet. Tam had told us how much it would cost, so when one of the girls came up to me, I just handed her the money and tried to get out of the door as fast as I could. She gently pulled me back and led me up the stairs. She took off my clothes, pushed me on to the bed and then undressed in front of me. I was far too excited – I mean my first sight of *a naked woman*! – and when she sat on top of me and started to move with my manhood inside her it was over for me in a few seconds. She lay next to me and stroked my chest, murmuring a few French words. It sounded sweet, but she could have been calling me a silly twat for all I knew. After a few moments she got up and handed me my clothes. I dressed and went downstairs to wait for the others. I was pleased that I didn't have to wait long. When we walked back to camp, big Tam slapped us all on the back and told us jovially:

'Now you are going to war like men, not like the silly girls you were yesterday.'

We did all have a bit of a spring in our step now, which some of the older soldiers noticed with great glee.

'Look at them! The little buggers must've got lucky,' one of them shouted.

As we neared our camp, Wee Tam suddenly piped up. 'Any of you lads got any money left for a pint? I spend all mine on that hoor.'

'We'll go on the pish next leave, Tam,' Malckie told him reassuringly. 'I promise.'

On the 25 September 1915, Wee Tam and I saw our first and last battle and we never did get to have that pint.

***

As we waited for hours in the trenches, nerves finally set in. We were told to put our gas masks on and sit tight ready for orders. A few of the lads began to get nervous and some seemed to have trouble breathing. One or two of them began to rip their masks off.

'Keep them on,' barked the sergeant furiously, but for Wee Tam it was already too late. Our own gas had been blown back over our trenches and Tam had taken a good couple of lungfuls. We could do nothing but watch as he was taken away on a stretcher, gasping for air and screaming in agony. I was sure he was going to die. At around half past six in the morning, we were ordered over the top regardless. As we ran towards the German lines, tears streamed down my face.

Hardly any time had passed when a sharp pain in my shoulder stopped me in my tracks. Then a shot to the stomach dropped me to the ground. I cried in pain as I held my stomach and tried to stop the flow of blood. I lay, drifting deliriously in and out of consciousness, until nightfall. An animal must have been attracted by my open wounds as I felt something licking the blood, but I was too weak to push it away. It moved from my stomach to my shoulder wound, then – vicious and sudden – its sharp fangs penetrated my neck. I felt my life draining away as it bit deeper and I lost consciousness completely. When I came to again, a man was sitting close to me. He had his wrist above my mouth and I thought he must have been injured too, as his blood was dripping on to my lips. It tasted sweet and was strangely intoxicating and I found myself grabbing his wrist to drink more deeply. He pulled away his arm leaned in close and whispered in my ear:

'Take heed. The Germans are no longer your enemy. The sun and the whole of humanity is. Kill them or be killed. We will spend the day underground together and when the sun sets we will part ways.'

I was barely conscious and grateful someone was there with me so I let him bury us with sand and slept a dreamless sleep. When I woke up it was night and I was alone again.

I felt fine, like nothing had happened at all. My two wounds seemed to have healed miraculously, and if I hadn't found myself in the middle of the craters and barbed wire I'd have thought I'd dreamed getting shot and the strange visitation.

I decided to make my way back to the trench and instinctively decided I should leave my bloodied tunic and shirt behind. I soon found out that we had managed to capture the town of Loos and there I caught up with my unit. I told them I had become so tangled in barbed wire that it had taken me this long to wriggle free and that my clothing was still out there. They gave me a whisky and a blanket and seemed very pleased to see me back.

Hootie sat next to me and gave me one of his fags.

'You're really all right, Blairy?' he asked.

'I think so,' I said, drawing on my cigarette.

'You didn't see Big Tam and Malckie out there?' he asked me after a while.

'They didn't come back?' I had wondered where they were.

'Nah. Naebody kens what's happened to them.'

It turned out quite a few of the lads from our unit were missing; losses at the battle of Loos had been heavy. We sat smoking together quietly until we fell asleep where we sat.

I woke up with the sun searing my face. I screamed and pulled the blanket over my head. When Hootie saw the blisters on my face he helped me to the field hospital and told the doctor I couldn't tolerate light and that the sun was burning me. The doctor frowned and asked if I'd taken my gas mask off during the attack.

As he was talking to me I felt my blisters starting to heal just as my wounds had done and realised something had changed in me and that the stranger was responsible. His words kept coming into my head... *Take heed. The Germans are no longer your enemy. The sun and the whole of humanity is.* Something told me it would soon be hard, and perhaps risky, trying to explain things.

The ominous words forced themselves repeatedly into my mind *kill or be killed.* I didn't feel like killing anybody, I just wanted time to find out what was going on with me. I was scared and knew there was no one I could turn to. I'd read a few penny dreadfuls and whilst the conclusion seemed far-fetched, the symptoms were eerily familiar. The doctor had left me in a windowless room and gone to attend to the many wounded – apart from the horrendous blisters I must have seemed fine and happy just to be left in the dark, but I began to feel like a trapped animal.

As night fell, and my uneasiness grew, I panicked. I understood that my old life, my friends, the army and my family all had to be left behind. I became a deserter.

Chapter 2: Brit

1977 and the Côte d'Azur lay before me. The world was my oyster, or as Wee Tam once said, the world was my lobster – seafood and sayings weren't exactly his strengths. He wasn't the brightest, but he fair made us laugh. I was a very long way from Edinburgh and my childhood friends now though and even further away from the sweet and innocent boy that had gone off to war in 1914.

I had driven my car up the windy roads to a hill overlooking Nice Airport where they were reclaiming land for a second runway. A human would have seen just the lights in the distance, but I could see the second runway actually taking shape. I felt like Tony Curtis standing there, looking over Nice in my smart leather sports jacket and driving gloves. Only the Ford Granada let me down on the glamour side. I'd desperately wanted a Ferrari Dino like Curtis had in *The Persuaders*, but it simply didn't look big enough to hold an adult sized male in the boot. I had bought the Granada in England as it was spacious and I could hide in it during the day whilst on the road. It got hot and uncomfortable, but it saved me from burning to a crisp in the sun.

Most people came to Provence for the hours of sunshine, the sea and maybe even the smell of its lavender fields. I was attracted by the smell of money – it was almost as intoxicating as the smell of blood. It might have seemed a strange choice for a Scottish vampire; I had expected to be like a midge, that wee bloodsucking beastie that likes it up north, but I turned out to be more like a mosquito or even a cold-blooded reptile that thrives in a warm climate. Somehow, I really hate the cold!

I liked Nice and thought it very pretty lying there squeezed between the sea and the hills. I loved its Italian-style plazas and its wide boulevards with their palm trees. I've always liked palm trees and Fiona and I had often taken a walk to the botanical gardens to look at the one Edinburgh had in its glasshouse. They were just so wonderfully exotic. The Brits had messed about a bit with Nice but the end result was rather charming: its wide promenade stretching 7km from the port almost to the airfield, providing a space between beach and town for people to see and be seen. Promenade des Anglais they called it.

I hadn't been back to Scotland, and even England was too cold for my liking, so I had decided to go south and the Côte d'Azur seemed like a great place to be. I had bought a small apartment off the Rue Gambetta in Nice. It was close to both the town and the beach and there were shops and businesses in the area that stayed open late. I had never before lived in a city without an underground and I was under no illusions that living on the Côte d'Azur would bring its challenges.

I didn't know anyone yet but I'd always managed to find my feet in a new town, and I was sure Nice too would have a seedy underbelly where I could fence my stolen goods and nurture my criminal contacts. I would need a new identity and the papers to back it up.

Food wasn't a problem – in those days a cheap bottle of wine and some sleeping tablets were doing the trick. At night there'd be small groups of young people on the beach, sitting around barbecues or campfires. They'd lean against their backpacks and discuss their InterRail travels. I was young, or at least looked it, and had travelled a little so I fitted right in. They'd play their guitars and cook their cheap sausages while I provided them with drugged wine. Eventually they'd all be sound asleep and I would take my pick. The next morning there'd be no more damage than a few marks that looked like mosquito bites and a cheap wine headache. They'd be left wondering only where that nice chap Cameron was off to next.

Sometimes the French police would crack down on people sleeping on the beach and I had to put in a bit more work. One trick was to hang around Nice station with a map and ask some fellow travellers for help. I would be trying to find an apartment that a friend had lent me on the Rue Gambetta. Of course I would ask them if they had a place to stay and offer them the floor of my mate's apartment if they didn't. I met some lovely, but frankly very naïve, people in those days. Today we would have become Facebook friends, but in those days we exchanged addresses. I always gave my name as Alistair Henderson from Edinburgh and put Hootie's address. I hoped he was still living and at the same address – the thought of the 82-year-old getting strange cards from backpackers from all over Europe amused me no end!

One night I got talking to a Swedish girl. She was sitting in front of Nice station with her head in her hands and tears streaming down her face.

'What's the matter?' I asked, while my stomach rumbled.

'Someone stole my money,' she sobbed.

'Have you been to the police?' I asked with mock concern.

'What's the point? I know it was Anders.'

'Anders?' I asked and sat down next to her.

'My boyfriend who left me here. He asked me to get him some cigarettes while he watched the rucksacks and the money. Thank Christ he left me the rucksack. My InterRail card and my passport I carry with me but the money he had on him,' she explained, while she dried her tears. She was very pretty with a golden tan and almost white blonde hair.

'And where is the bastard now?' I enquired.

'Probably on his way to Greece. He told me the wrong departure time and now he is long gone.'

She told me they'd had an argument the day before. He had proposed to her on the beach and she thought that before she said yes she should be perfectly honest with him. She confessed that a few months before, in a moment of weakness, she had slept with his best friend Torsten. She'd asked Anders if he still wanted to marry her and they'd argued deep into the night. She thought they had finally kissed and made up. Obviously not!

'You poor thing! I'll tell you what. A friend lent me his apartment and you're welcome to stay.'

She looked at me suspiciously for a moment, but then her face broke into a smile. I looked so young and innocent, what harm could I possibly do?

'That would be fantastic,' she said.

'I can lend you enough money to get back to Sweden too,' I said, getting up and offering her my hand to help her to her feet.

'Thank you so much! That's very generous of you. I promise to pay you back.' Then, taking my hand, she said 'I am Brit Gustafson.'

'Hi. I am George Baxter from London.'

I knew a nine year old George Baxter in London. If this nice Swedish girl were to send back the money, it would no doubt make him very happy.

I took Brit to my apartment and suggested we have a bottle of wine and a pizza. I had placed a bin next to my chair and hoped she wouldn't notice me disposing of some of my food and drink. I decided to wait before dosing her with a sleeping pill as I had the idea that she liked me and would probably be grateful. I wasn't disappointed. Brit was not a shy girl and angry revenge sex makes for a great night. Getting intimate with a woman and smelling the blood rushing under the skin had become both an exciting and confusing experience for me. At first I'd tried to ignore it – the thought of feeding is exciting in itself – but then I explored a bit more and found that in the grip of passion I could get away with cutting a lip or scratching a neck. Once I tried to bite a girl in the heat of the moment, but she yelped and pushed me out of the bed. She screamed when she felt the blood running down her neck. I had to do a lot to calm her down and even convinced her she must have had an insect bite that I opened up again by being a bit too rough. I had become more careful over the years and Brit's blood would have to come later.

After we had made love for most of the night, I gave her a glass of water with the tablet saying it was aspirin and would stop her from having a hangover. She took it without question and went to brush her teeth. It was risky leaving it so late as she'd be asleep until about eleven o'clock, well after it had become daylight. I took the risk as, after all the exertions of the night, I was quite hungry. I could taste the sun and the sea in her and even the mild aroma of patchouli and sun cream in her blood was not unpleasant.

Afterwards, I put some insect bite ointment on her as it seemed to treat vampire bites too. Then I lay next to her and thought of the best way to get her out of the apartment. I couldn't let her stay. She'd want to open the curtains and go to the beach. She'd probably want to make me breakfast and suggest other things that a vampire just can't do. Best to deal with it swiftly.

By around ten o'clock I had a plan. I looked over at Brit lying naked on top of the covers, her long limbs stretched out and her blonde hair draped over her face and arms. I felt myself getting aroused again. Delicious Brit! How I wanted her to stay for another night, but it was daylight already and I had to get her to leave. I took a few deep breaths and gently shook her shoulder.

'Brit. Sorry love. You've got to wake up.'

She turned round and stretched her arms above her head. *Christ she was beautiful!* 'What time is it, George?'

I was incredibly turned on at the sight of her perfect little breasts. As I said, she wasn't shy and made no effort to cover up. *NO! She had to go.*

'Time to get up and get dressed,' I told her.

'Shall I get some croissants?' she offered as she slid out of bed.

'No, you have to go.' I handed her her clothes and got some money out of my wallet. It was a lot, easily enough to get her back to Sweden. She disappeared into the bathroom and I heard her showering and brushing her teeth. She came out dressed in a sleeveless summer dress and looking a bit sad. She went to open the curtains, but I grabbed her arms and told her again that she had to leave.

'Jeez George! Why the sudden rush?' She looked at me suspiciously for a moment, then started packing her rucksack.

'Erm... the friend that lend me the apartment is a bit more than a friend. She's my girlfriend and she'll be arriving from Nice airport at noon if her flight is on time.'

She whirled around. 'Fuck! FUCK! You bastard! We did it in your girlfriend's bed?'

'Come on Brit. We're both adults and you're obviously no angel. You needed a place to stay, we had fun and no harm was done. At least, not if you leave now,' I said cheerfully.

She angrily grabbed the pile of banknotes and I helped her put the rucksack on. Then she left.

'Bon voyage, Brit,' I said as the door slammed.

So like I said: not sweet, not innocent and always on the lookout for my next meal – preferably in attractive packaging.

Chapter 3: Andrei

We were the last two guests on the yacht. Andrei had really outdone himself. His parties usually had the best of everything, but the appearance of two Hollywood stars had made this night special. I saw my tender approaching, so I turned to Andrei and thanked him for a great night. I pointed to a girl that had fallen asleep on the sofa and asked if he knew her.

'That's Daphne,' he said. 'She is very annoying and drinks too much. She stays with some people on the *Coral Reef.*'

'Well I don't mind dropping her off on the *Coral Reef* if you give me a hand getting her in my launch.' I said.

Daphne moaned as we both grabbed an arm. She was very thin, probably surviving on a champagne diet. It didn't take us long to get her in the back of the tender which my crew member Roberto had brought round to collect me. Of course, I could easily have picked her up by myself, but I find it best to be as human as possible. We set off towards Juan les Pins where the *Coral Reef* was moored. As I was holding Daphne up with one arm firmly around her shoulders, I used the other to wave Andrei goodbye. I do love girls that get wasted on champagne; it gives their blood just a hint of a fizz. I pulled away from her neck after about two glasses. She would have an almighty hangover the next day but nothing more.

'Oh darn. Roberto, did you remember to bring the plasters?' I shouted over the noise of the tender as I held my fingers over the two bleeding punctures on her neck. Roberto cut the engine and started looking in one of the hatches. Soon he came over with a large plaster and I covered the two small holes. By the late morning they would look like two scratched open mosquito bites.

We carried on until we reached the *Coral Reef*. She was an attractive modern yacht of about 70 meters and quite a bit larger than my own. One of the crew helped us carry Daphne up on deck and down to her cabin. She moaned again as I laid her out on her bed and tore off the plaster. The puncture marks had stopped bleeding and didn't look too bad. I got back in the tender and headed back in the direction of Cannes.

'A most excellent start to the 2011 film festival Roberto,' I said as we sailed towards *The Count Dracula*, my pride and joy. Not the biggest or the most modern yacht in the bay of Juan, but she was mine. I had bought the 2003 Azimut Carat 80 foot yacht about four years before for about 1.5 million euros after we'd rescued Roberto and his father paid the reward. It was expensive to run, but I was doing ok with my hostage rescue business and the odd burglary. I climbed on board and went below decks to settle in for the day.

George, my captain, came and saw me in my office, I had blocked up the windows so I could spend the day there in complete comfort and safety. He handed me some DVDs of *The Twilight Saga*. I hadn't seen the movies yet as I found cinemas just too dangerous to be in – all those warm bodies packed together... *just too tempting!* The only cinema visits I could be bothered to muster up enough self-restraint for were at the Cannes film festival with its added glitz and glamour.

'Why can't you just jump up into trees too?' he asked me, leaning nonchalantly against the wall and sipping his coffee.

'I must have missed that bit in vampire school.'

'You never have any fights with werewolves either,' George went on.

'Get me a werewolf and I'll give it a try. Mind you I don't think I fancy my chances. They have teeth, claws and everything.'

'Sometimes I think you're just a freakishly strong weirdo

with pointy teeth,' he said, laughing.

'Pointy teeth that go in and out... and I have a daylight allergy... and don't forget I don't eat or drink.'

'I bet you stuff your face with doughnuts as soon as my back's turned,' he mocked.

'Right, George. Fuck off, then and let me get to my doughnuts.'

I was eager to watch the DVDs, as the chatrooms had been buzzing with the whole *Twilight* thing for a while and it was the bible for many a teenage vampire wannabe. I curled up on the sofa and put the first disk in, but I got bored and couldn't bring myself to watch the other disk. Maybe I was getting too old, but I just didn't get what all the fuss was all about. I had a few things in common with the main character, but I was much more fun.

***

I had met Andrei Klimov a few years earlier at an art gallery during an opening of an exhibition. We were standing next to each other admiring a local artist from the 1930s. Andrei was suitably impressed with my in-depth knowledge of the artist and my flair for telling amusing anecdotes about the painter's life. Andrei was one of these new money Russians that were simply invading the Côte d'Azur in those years. He usually had a very thin, bored Russian girl on one arm and a glass of something in the other hand. Andrei was an avid collector of early twentieth century art and even though he was fabulously wealthy, his dream of owning a Picasso remained a dream.

He soon invited me over to view his collection, which was not very well chosen but large. He had bought himself a villa near St Paul to house his collection and divided his time between St Paul, his yacht in Cannes and his apartment in St Petersburg.

'What business are you in Andrei?' I'd asked him.

'This and that Cameron. I have business in Russia.' I could tell he didn't want to give me more information, but I liked dealing with people who had secrets too.

'Good, much like me. But the this and the that shouldn't interfere too much with life,' I said.

He laughed and poured me a large vodka and we wandered out on to his terrace which offered an amazing view down the hill to the Marina Baie des Anges at Villeneuve-Loubet. It was a development of three large apartment blocks constructed mostly in the 1970s and visible for miles around.

'Do you like those buildings,' he asked me as I tipped my drink over the balustrade.

'I rather do. The architecture is bold and daring.'

'It is different, but they are just so white and visible,' he said, looking into the distance.

'No, I like them. And when you actually walk around the buildings they are very futuristic, very *Return to the Planet of the Apes.*'

We gazed in silence for a while, and then Andrei topped up our glasses.

'I love St Paul,' he said. 'Some of the best artists lived and worked here. It is the light that is just so fantastic here in the Provence.'

'Hmm, yes. The light. I try to avoid it. I swear staying out of the sun is the secret to my youthful complexion,' I said with a smile.

'Youthful, but very pale,' he said, eyeing me with concern.

'I'm Scottish. We only come in pale,' I explained.

Andrei shrugged his shoulders. He had a dark brown tan

and loved to spend time on the deck of his yacht, having girls over to sunbathe and drink champagne in his outdoor jacuzzi.

'I do believe Marc Chagal is buried here in the local cemetery,' I diverted the conversation.

'Really? I must go and find the grave. His work is superb and of course he was Russian,' Andrei said enthusiastically.

'It's a very unassuming grave, but he is buried here with his wife Vava and her brother. They were Russian too.'

As we were chatting, Tatiana, his latest thin and bored girl, had come out to join us.

'Andrei, can we go to Nice? I want to dance,' she whined, in Russian.

'No darling. I have this man over to look at my art,' he replied, still in Russian.

'Stupid pictures can wait,' she said, pulling a moody face.

'I invited him especially to look at the paintings,' Andrei said as he went over and stroked her arm.

One of the perks of my existence was that I acquired the linguistic skills of my victims when I drank their blood. When champagne-guzzling Russian girls started to appear all over the Côte d'Azur it wasn't long before I was able to add Russian to my skills. I just thought it was better not to let anyone know. I admitted to speaking French and English – the rest I kept to myself, which made for some fascinating listening in.

'You are sooo boring... I'll go anyway with Olga. Can I get some money?' Tatiana asked

Andrei gave her a few hundred euro bills and told her to enjoy herself. 'Let Sergei drive you. He will make sure you girls are safe,' he instructed.

'Sergei is a big gorilla. No one will ask us to dance,' she whined again.

'You can dance with Olga or Sergei if he is in a good mood,' he said and then looked bothered, 'Sergei better not be in a good mood, because that will mean he had too much vodka.'

Andrei made his excuses and the two of them left to find Sergei, a mountain of a man and Andrei's so-called driver. I knew that the next week there would probably be a new very thin girl on Andrei's arm.

Andrei came back a few moments later and topped us up again – a waste of good vodka. I hoped the plants below were enjoying the rain of strong Russian alcohol.

'Sorry Cameron. These girls! All they want to do is party, and party every night,' he said apologetically.

'Well most of them are only young once. They should enjoy themselves.'

'I know, but I'm getting too old to go to nightclubs every night, and they are so boring. Music so loud you can't have a conversation. Now come, I show you my art,' and he led me to his living room to show me his collection.

A few weeks later Andrei gave me a call sounding very excited. He had bought a picture at an auction in Paris. 'You have to come over to St Paul. I've bought this wonderful painting, Cameron. I'm sure you will love it.'

I agreed to come and see it that night as he sounded very enthusiastic. He greeted me at the door of his villa and introduced me to Svetlana, another of the thin young things that seemed to be his type. Tatiana wasn't the first or the last of his girlfriends that got replaced when they proved too demanding. Andrei led me into his living room and showed me his latest purchase.

I stopped in my tracks. 'Where did you get that?' I asked. 'That's a Hélène Bruchard.'

'I am impressed. Not much of her work is known,' he replied, surprised.

'All the better. It's not very good,' I said abruptly.

Andrei looked hurt. He obviously liked the painting a lot and wanted my approval.

'This one's ok, though' I offered. 'I know you like early Picasso and this is very much in the same style. Just never show it to me again.'

He gave me a quizzical look, but put the canvas in his bedroom. He had often wondered why I knew so much about art. I joked that I had known Matisse and Chagall in a previous life.

'I didn't think you believed in all that reincarnation nonsense, Cameron'

'I just feel that I've had many lives before,' I'd answered philosophically.

***

Andrei was older than me (as we appeared to the world) and shorter. He was blond, tanned and not unattractive. He liked to work out and was in pretty good shape for a man in his early 40s. He had done very well for himself in whatever sort of business he was doing, and we had a lot of similar interests. We both liked the champagne lifestyle, women, yachts and art. He came to rely on me to weed out the poor pieces and find what his collection needed. We didn't always agree on art but he started to trust my judgement more and more, once other experts had told him he had made a smart purchase.

The friendship had gained me entrance to all the best places and invitations to the most glamorous parties and I came to know Andrei very well over the next few years. We enjoyed each other's company and I believed we had become such good friends because he didn't perceive me as competition. I looked younger, but wasn't as rich as he was – and I didn't chase after the same women. I really didn't like those thin, sullen girls. We met often for parties and events, so I wasn't surprised to receive another one of his invitations for the 2011 Film Festival.

Andrei had come by some invitations to one of the midnight screenings and I was looking forward to rubbing shoulders with the glitterati, but I was not pleased when he told me he had rekindled his romance with his former girlfriend, Tatiana. I had first met her a few years previously when I came to look at Andrei's art collection in his house in St Paul and she'd struck me as being spoilt and moody. She had been absent for the past season and I couldn't understand why, of all of the 15 or so girlfriends that had come and gone since I'd known him, she would be worth a second chance.

Now, Andrei had set up a double date with Tatiana and one of her friends. I had met this girl, Olga, briefly two seasons before on Andrei's yacht. She wasn't a great beauty, but she was pretty enough and she enjoyed drinking champagne. The only thing about her that bothered me was that her English was very limited and conversation would be difficult.

Andrei wanted us to meet at the Majestic Hotel for a meal before the screening, a total waste of his money as both the girls and I pushed our food around our plates and barely ate a thing. I was happy that we had a table on the terrace built out over the sea, so I could jettison chunks of the swordfish back to his fish brethren and casually pour some wine down between the wooden boards. Tatiana was in a very good mood as Andrei had bought her a fantastic emerald cut diamond ring that I estimated to be about five carats. I'd raised my eyebrows at Andrei when she showed it off.

'The two of you got engaged?' I asked him and he didn't look too happy. Later he told me it was his mother's incessant nagging that had forced his hand.

'"Andrei, you are 42. When am I going to have some grandchildren?"' he mimicked.

'Tatiana wants children?' I asked, surprised. I didn't think she'd be the type to let anything spoil her figure.

'Part of the pre-nup. If we get divorced without children she gets nothing. So I think there will be children.'

'And do you want them?' I asked.

'Yes, I think so. It's time for me to settle down and think about my legacy.' He didn't sound convinced.

'Do you love her?' I asked him.

'She's a nice girl, a good Russian girl and I think she will be a good mother. She likes children,' he explained. I didn't like Tatiana, but I suddenly felt very jealous of Andrei.

When it was time for the premiere we made the short walk to the theatre on foot. Olga was already quite drunk and had to steady herself on my arm; the ridiculous heels she was wearing didn't make things any better. I was happy to use tall Olga as a shield for photographers. They wouldn't want photographs of us, specifically, but with digital cameras and previews there was always a risk of someone noticing me, or rather not noticing me, in the background of their photos. A celebrity had just turned up so the lenses where pointed elsewhere and we went in unnoticed.

Twenty minutes into the film, Olga fell asleep. With the film being in English she would have problems following the plot. I could always slip her a sleeping tablet later, as I was sure she would want to come back and stay the night with me. I had asked George to stock up on Cristal in anticipation.

After the film, I invited everyone to my yacht. I knew Andrei and Tatiana would make their excuses after a while and leave me alone with Olga. I preferred my women to have a bit more meat on them but she was blonde and had a nice face so she would do for adult entertainment and food.

Roberto was there to pick us up in the tender.

'Roberto. You work for Cameron?' asked Olga, surprised.

'Yes.' Roberto shot me an apologetic look. 'Erm, Olga and I were at French classes together.'

Roberto was clumsy and awkward for the rest of the night. I knew he wasn't comfortable with what was going to happen to Olga. He might even have fancied her, but I wasn't going to let the little brat spoil my dinner. He should have known by now that cinemas make me beyond hungry.

Soon Andrei and Tatiana left and I sent Roberto to bed.

'Does it have to be her?' he asked me, looking distressed

I rattled the tube of sleeping tablets in his face. 'She's here now and, trust me, she won't feel a thing. But first I'll give her a tour of the yacht, ending in my bedroom,' I said with a wink.

Roberto gave me a last pleading look and then slunk below decks.

In spite of its difficult start, my life had become pretty sweet and comfortable.

Chapter 4: Lily

I walked away from the front and the trenches, going south towards Paris, walking by night and hiding in dark places during the day. I wasn't yet sure what had happened to me and I was worried about being seen and arrested for desertion. I should never have gone back to my unit. Now I risked being shot. Dead Cameron should have stayed dead Cameron to be cried over by his loving fiancée and proud parents. But like my mum always said, no use crying over spilt milk.

I spent the first few days just getting away from the front but then hunger started to slow me down. I tried to eat a carrot that I found growing on the land, but my body rejected it, vomiting it out as soon as I had swallowed it. *Really? I can only drink blood now?* I said to the half-eaten carrot. It was the same with liquids; my body violently ejected anything I tried to drink. After three days without food, my stomach was hurting badly – and not just my stomach; all my internal organs screamed in pain. I needed to feed.

On day four, I found a farm with a few cows in a shed. My fangs immediately pushed themselves out at the smell of the warm bodies. I touched them and found that they were very sharp. Well here goes! I said to myself as I moved closer to one of the cows. I felt disgusted, but my stomach was hurting so badly I was willing to give it a try.

The cow let out an alarmed moo as I sank my fangs into its shoulder and the blood came running into my mouth. Oh, but it was good! I felt all the pain just ebbing away. I had a few pints from all four cows and felt sharp and alert. No sleeping today! I could have run for miles, but I knew instead that I had to hide from the daylight again. The hayloft seemed as good a hiding place as any and I reckoned I'd be able to stay there for a while.

Later that morning, I felt someone coming up the hayloft stairs, someone small, female and very quiet. I scented her as she crawled into the hay. She smelled lovely and I realised it was her blood I could detect. I kept very quiet. I certainly wasn't going to bite a wee girl!

'Lily!' I suddenly heard a man shout. 'Lily, where are you?'

I felt her stiffening and smelled fear. I could literally hear her heart speeding up at the sound of the man's voice.

'Get down here, Lily. I know you are up there,' he shouted impatiently.

'Oh God, no!' I heard her whimper. Lily was crying quietly.

I felt a heavy man come up the stairs to our loft and start to root around in the hay to find the girl. She was soon pulled out, screaming. I wondered what to do; it didn't look like it was going to end well for Lily.

I heard a blow and crawling forwards saw a young woman of about 18 on the ground with blood running from her nose. She was unconscious. A farmer of about 50 was crouched over her, pulling up her skirts. I dashed over and grabbed the farmer's leg, dragging him with ease under the hay with me. I sank my fangs into his fat neck and felt the warm blood gushing out. He struggled and kicked but it only made the blood run faster and soon he went limp. I drank for a long time. He was a big fellow and I wanted to drain him of every drop.

When I'd finished, the enormity of what I'd done washed over me. *I just killed a man!* But I felt good... I looked on the farmer's body and felt nothing for him. Inside, I had a wonderful glow, yet it frightened me that it was so much better than the cow's blood. Human blood was something else and it tasted great. My senses were sharpened and my strength and energy were much greater. I could imagine it becoming quite addictive, but instinct told me that I'd have to be careful – I could feel its corrupting influence too.

I heard the girl stirring and I went quiet again.

'Uncle Frédérick?' she called out softly. Then I heard her going downstairs. Once it was dark, I buried Uncle Frédérick behind the cowshed. Lily seemed to live alone on the farm and I didn't hear anyone else over the next few days.

Four nights later, I knocked on the farm door. Lily opened it but only a few inches. She looked at me with fear, but when she saw the British uniform she started to relax.

'Can I help you?' she asked.

'I'm afraid I have some bad news for you. Can I come in?'

I was amazed at my sudden ability to speak French. *How had that happened?*

'Yes, come in. Is it my uncle?' She opened the door wider and I went inside.

'Yes I'm afraid so,' I said, taking a seat by the small kitchen table. The farm really only consisted of a kitchen and a bedroom. There were few possessions.

'They told me in the village that a man named Frédérick lived here,' I explained.

'Yes Frédérick Lafontaine, he is my uncle – he is my only family now my father has gone to the front.'

'I'm so sorry. He got drunk a few nights ago and fell in the Seine. I saw him going in but he got swept away very quickly. We have been looking along the banks for many days but we can't find him. I'm afraid he must be dead,' I told her. I thought it a credible lie. Lily sat very still for a while, and then she got up to make some coffee.

'Will you be ok here by yourself, Mademoiselle?' I asked her

'I think so. I have been helping my uncle for a year now

and I think I can take care of the farm until my father comes back from the war.'

She put the coffee pot on the table and sat down again. She had started to cry now and I grabbed her hand to comfort her. She looked at me startled.

'Your hands are freezing. Here, have some hot coffee.'

'No, that's ok,' I told her, hastening to get away. 'I should really get back to my unit. I don't want to be shot for desertion now.' I left and walked on to find another farm where I could feed and hide.

One Sunday not long after, I was hiding in another hayloft and when it got dark I came out to look for some livestock. I watched the farmhouse and spotted the farmer and his wife coming out of the front door all dressed up in their finest clothes. They must have been on their way to a party or suchlike. I saw my opportunity to go in and steal some clothes. I'd noticed that I had become rather wild and unkempt and I was sure the farmer would have a razor and some scissors. I went in and got some water to shave, but then I got quite a fright. I was prepared for not having any reflection at all – I was not prepared to see my dead, decaying self staring back at me. I sat on the bed for a while, shaking, and then I reached over carefully to put the bedspread over the mirror. *Christ, I never wanted to look at that again!*

I had to re-learn shaving by touch and at first I had a few mishaps with the sharp razor. But we vampires heal and learn quickly. My haircut must have been bizarre though, as I could only blindly snip away at my black locks.

***

Sitting still and not doing anything for many hours at a time had never been one of my strong points and now the daytime boredom became my biggest challenge. At first, I amused myself with trying to control my fangs, concentrating hard on making them go in and out, but that soon stopped being fun. Often, the only place I had to hide was under a lot of hay, and there was nothing to do except lie still and think. It was hard, as I was missing my family and friends a lot.

The nights were spent looking for food. I found I didn't need much to keep the hunger at bay and the countryside provided enough animals for food and unattended washing lines for clothes. But my craving for human companionship grew stronger. I missed all the people I had known in Edinburgh; my friends, my family and Fiona. I knew I would never see them again, so I tried to push them out of my mind. I looked less and less at the picture of Fiona – that world now seemed unreal and very far away.

I wandered on, staying in the countryside around Paris until one cold November day the bells rang out for Armistice Day. I heard the parties and the cheering and I realised that war was finally over. Then I saw the soldiers marching home and men coming back to work the land and tend their farms. Normality was returning for most, but for me life was anything but normal.

At least, with the threat of being caught for desertion gone, I didn't need to hide at night anymore. I'd never been on my own for any length of time growing up, and I didn't want to be alone any longer. Gradually I started to come out of hiding and go into a village café now and then. I found the villagers friendly and warm and it did me a lot of good being amongst people again.

I survived on farm animals, but I craved something more. One night, I discovered I wasn't alone in the shed I had chosen as my daytime hideout. A man had decided to make his bed there too, but he was hiding there for the night. My stomach rumbled at the smell of his human blood. No one would miss this tramp, an unfortunate that needed to spend the night in a shed. It had been four years since I'd last tasted human blood – and Lily's uncle had deserved to die. I didn't want to kill, but my body gradually started to dictate otherwise and the urge became just too strong. The smell of the blood was almost hypnotic and it took over. I had to kill again.

Afterwards I felt nothing – no guilt, no shame, just a warm feeling of having quenched a thirst. I felt full of life, strong and more confident, yet I knew that too much would be bad for me. I found a shovel and buried the body. *Why should I hide, surviving on animals like another animal?* War was over and I wanted to live again.

Chapter 5: Fifi

Winter on the Côte d'Azur was always a quiet time and the winter of 2010 was no exception. Andrei had sailed off to Thailand at the beginning of October and my other acquaintances were starting to move on to warmer climes one by one. Roberto jetted off to Bogota for a family visit and George and I did what we had done the previous two winters and sailed *The Count Dracula* into Nice port where I had rented a mooring for the winter.

Every ten years or so I had to move on and create a new identity; not ageing does raise questions eventually. George had some interesting contacts who had constructed my latest identity for me. These days, officially, I went by the name of Cameron MacAdam, who would have been 22 by now if he had lived. Whilst my paperwork was fine for keeping the French authorities happy, I wasn't sure if it would stand up to the scrutiny that traveling requires, and there was always the risk of customs visiting *The Count Dracula* during daylight and wanting to see all passengers on deck. That year, I was happy to stay in Nice as George and I had a project to get on with.

We set to work on our latest venture following a call from the family of a hostage victim in Nigeria. The Nigerian contract looked to be quite complicated; George would have to travel there alone at some point to do some reconnaissance on the ground. Going on a plane was impossible for me, too many mirrors and machines that didn't detect me, but I always tried to help with the preparations. He joined me in my office to work out the mission details.

'Do you miss the army, George?' I asked him as he sipped his coffee.

'I do miss some things about the army,' he answered, unfolding some maps and papers.

'I have the feeling that even after the eight years you've been here, you've not quite settled in. I never see you mixing with the locals,' I continued.

'It's the language. Unlike you, I can't just suck it up,' he said ruefully.

'But it's been five years. Even Roberto's French is getting good, and he's met some interesting people at his French course.'

'I get by in French and I do have friends here.' He was getting defensive now.

'You mean Roger, your mate in Antibes?' I mocked.

'Roger's a great guy!' said George, looking at me surprised.

Roger was even worse than George at integrating into French life. He had got himself a job with an American family in Cap d'Antibes, a peninsula that stretched out into the Mediterranean, overlooking either Nice or Cannes and affordable only to the super wealthy. His job consisted of walking the dog, driving the family around and maintaining the grounds. He lived in a cottage in the grounds and had the use of a small Renault. In his five years in Antibes Roger hadn't learned a word of French. He had lunch at the same café every day because the waiter spoke excellent English and one lunchtime had got talking to George. Now, he too knew all the expat hangouts in Antibes. He and Roger and another few Englishmen played poker every week, no doubt bitching all the time about how much better England was.

'I know you can get by perfectly well on the Côte d'Azur without speaking much French, but I feel you are missing out on something,' I went on.

'Don't worry about me, Cameron. I'm happy enough,' he said, continuing to rummage through some papers.

'Really? I never hear you speak about women,' I pried further.

'I do alright, Cameron, but I'm hardly going to introduce you to any of my female companions. I don't want you mistaking my friends for food. Now, can we get some work done?' He was beginning to sound annoyed.

'Work? Never cared for it much. Would you believe I started out as a cooper's apprentice?'

George coughed up his last sip of coffee at that remark. '*You* were making barrels? That must have played havoc with your manicure.'

'I wasn't always this well looked after vision you see before you. My girlfriend at the time rather liked it. She said I was getting arms like a blacksmith. I worked for a number of years in a brewery, making barrels, before I joined the army. Here George, feel my biceps. Even after years of doing nothing they are still there.' I rolled up my sleeve to let him have a squeeze.

'Fuck off! And that is a lie. I see you at night powering through the water, no wonder you still have arms like a blacksmith,' George said jerking back in his chair and away from my impressive bicep.

'Anyway. As I said, I never cared much for work, especially manual labour. Now, what do you want me to do George?'

***

It hardly ever got really cold in Nice in the winter, but sometimes it rained for days. Snow was very rare but, when it came, traffic ground to a halt. The Côte d'Azurians didn't know how to drive in snow and with the roads being quite hilly it could be complete chaos when a few snowflakes did fall.

The city was never dull, even in winter. The old town

adjacent to the port had a lively nightlife and the casinos on the Promenade des Anglais kept me entertained at night. I often played poker online but it didn't beat the thrill of a live game. It was a good place in summer too, as the shops in the centre stayed open till midnight, so even I was able to indulge in some shopping.

Nice was also a good hunting ground for the likes of me. For the previous few nights I had been staking out a residence on the Promenade des Anglais, a building with a sea view popular with investors who wanted to run holiday lets and with wealthy retired people. Half of the apartments would be empty over winter, but others might have rich pickings. Often, the presence of a small dog gave away that an old lady lived there on her own.

As I walked through the hallway of the building, I heard high-pitched barking behind one of the doors. *What are you?* I wondered, stopping in front of the door and rummaging through my pockets for some dog biscuits. I quickly opened the lock with my tools and was confronted by a yapping Chihuahua. She calmed down as soon as I gave her the biscuit.

'What are you barking at, Fifi?' shouted a voice and a light came on under the bedroom door before the handle moved and the door began to open. As soon as the old dear saw me she tried to shut the door again, but I was too quick and pinned her against the wall with my hand over her mouth. I looked into her eyes which bulged with terror and lack of air. When I hissed and showed her my fangs she started to convulse. Soon she lost consciousness and went limp. She was dead, which was very convenient. It often works, the frightening an old dear to death routine.

Fifi had started barking again so I fed her another biscuit. I laid the old lady on her bed and then picked up Fifi. While stroking the little dog I walked through the apartment, it was a large three-bedroom apartment, but had not been decorated or modernised in a while. The sofa and chairs were covered in horrible fabric with big printed roses and there were lace doilies scattered about. She also collected ornaments of cats and dogs. I picked up a statuette of a kitten and let it smash on the floor.

'We don't like cats, do we Fifi? Ghastly creatures.' Fifi looked up at me with her big brown eyes and I gave her another biscuit and scratched her behind the ears.

'Well, I hope her taste in jewellery is better,' I said to the Chihuahua and she licked my hand.

I started going through all the drawers and cupboards systematically, making sure not to disturb things too much. The absence of a dog and some jewellery might not be noticed if the woman wasn't too close to anyone. Even if they were, I didn't think the police would organise a major manhunt to find Fifi and some baubles.

I found the jewellery box in her bedroom and tipped the contents out next to her body on the bed. I was pleased that most of jewellery was gold and was careful not to touch the silver pieces. *Oh, you do have good taste after all! I do like van Cleef and Arpels.* The piece was a magnificent sapphire and diamond brooch with their trademark invisible settings. It was even in its original box.

'Rashid will like this. These are always easy to sell,' I told Fifi, feeding her another biscuit. 'This should keep *The Count Dracula* afloat for a wee while.'

I also found about 200 euros in her purse and some other items that might be worth something.

'Right Fifi. Let's go. Nothing more to do here,' and I put the Chihuahua under my coat without resistance and left the apartment.

I always chose a residence with CCTV, as it often indicated

richer residents who felt safer with a camera at the entrance. It gave me immense pleasure to think of all the head scratching by anyone who bothered to monitor or watch the tape when the front door opened by itself.

Roberto always told me off for playing with my food, but I couldn't help it. Chihuahuas were just so much fun.

***

Before the invention of the internet, daytime was often long and tedious for me. After eating, I was so full of energy that it could be hard to sit still and read books for several hours. I had never been a big reader and if I had been a kid today they'd probably have told me I had attention deficit disorder. My ADD only got worse once I became a vampire.

As a child, I'd had trouble concentrating at school – there was always something more interesting going on outside. My equally restless friends and classmates didn't make things any better. The Tams, Malckie and I were each put in one of the corners of the classroom. I often got a fright when the teacher's belt thwacked down on the desk behind me as I sat backwards in my chair pulling faces at Big Tam. The only teacher I got on with was Mr Menzies who took us running and put us through our paces outside, where for once I was top of my class.

Once I became a vampire it was hard to get rid of all the energy. You couldn't just go running about the streets at night, especially when I'd lived in London; running along the road in the dark would have looked very suspicious. Then, during the day, I had to stay hidden and books were not a good way to get rid of pent up energy.

The internet opened a whole new and exciting world for me. Chatrooms, poker sites and all the news and information I could possibly want was suddenly at my fingertips, exactly what my restless soul needed. I didn't even need to sit still to use it, as I could play interactive games on the Wii. My internet use was really not that different from any other hyperactive teenager. I even had my own Facebook page: Cruftslover. I loved playing poker online and talking nonsense with all sorts of people from around the world, but sometimes online chat could get surreal:

YorkieLover: NH
Crufts56: THX
Crufts56: So are Yorkies your favourite?
Yorkielover: Oh yes, I could eat them all day.
Crufts56: Ok, you eat them too? Here in France they can be hard to get and so expensive.
YorkieLover: No problems here, corner shop sells them.
Aces4: NOM NOM Yorkie, they are chunky!
RacingMika: We do not have this Yorkie in Finland, what is it?
Crufts56: it's a dog.
YorkieLover: it's a chocolate bar.
Aces4: Crufts yr so funny LOL!
YorkieLover: Sick ILMFAO.
RacingMika: LOL NH.
Crufts56: THX.

Having the yacht in the Mediterranean opened up another outlet for my hyperactivity; nobody minded, or even saw, me going for long swims at night, often taking morsels of bread with me to attract fish in their hundreds. It was in the summer of 2010 that I broke into a shop selling fishing supplies as I wanted a spear gun and snorkel so I could hunt for fish and octopus. There wasn't any tasty blood in a fish, but Roberto loved seafood and George didn't mind the odd sea bass. I had gone to the shop all five previous nights and given the door a good kick so it set off the alarm. By night six the owners must've been tearing their hair out at their alarm going off for no reason and had left it unset. I smiled as I opened the shop door with my tools and went in without being spotted. Then, suddenly, I saw a shape coming towards me and before I knew it two paws were on my shoulders and a wet tongue was in my face.

'Oh hello, fun added bonus! Are you going to help me find a good snorkel?' The most useless guard dog in history brought me his green squeaky toy instead. From the disc on his collar I spotted he was called Rataplan, the name of an inept comic book dog that suited him well. I threw the toy and Rataplan bounced after it. I quickly found all the supplies I needed.

'Are you coming with me?' I asked Rataplan, and he pushed his toy towards me with his nose expectantly. I found a leash behind the counter and we made our way to the beach. I threw his toy for him to retrieve until I finally got bored. *Good grief! This dog was even more hyper than me!* I got into the tender and had to lift Rataplan in as he didn't fancy the jump from the quay. I had a late night meal under a full moon and decided to try out my new spear gun. I used the descending body for target practice, but then got out a slice of bread to attract some fish. I managed to spear about four good-sized specimens before I had to head back to the yacht. I gutted and descaled the fish and left them in the fridge for the boys to find.

It was the same summer that I told George I wanted a new tender. The one we had was ok to get us between shore and yacht, but it was too slow for my liking and I had seen an online video of people playing around in a Williams turbo jet yacht tender and now I wanted one badly. I had found someone that was selling his second hand in St Tropez and I asked George to go and check it out and arrange an evening visit for me if it was any good.

'It's a good tender that one, I think you will like it,' reported George, when he got back.

'Good. Can I see it one night?' I asked him.

'I got you a viewing next Monday.'

We drove out to St Tropez the following Monday, as soon as the sun set and arrived at about half nine.

'So who did you rob to pay for this latest toy?' said George as we walked along the quayside.

'If you're going to be like that I should have cracked a window and left you in the car,' I snapped.

'I'm sorry. It's none of my business how you acquire your toys.'

I knew he disapproved of my constant quest for the latest luxury or plaything. He put up with me as you do with a spoilt teenager. I was about 116 now but the world only saw a young man. My skin fitted me well and inside too I was still a 20 year old. I had the libido of a 20 year old who liked nothing better than to chase lassies and have a laugh with some mates, but I had also become spoilt, cruel, selfish and lacking in compassion. Plus I had learned a few tricks along the way.

It was indeed a very nice, fast little tender and I decided to buy it in cash on the spot. It was about 30,000 euros but it had been a good couple of weeks. I heard the turbo jet racing around *The Count Dracula* over the following days – George and Roberto where having a lot of fun with the new tender too. I was jealous of them frolicking up there in the daylight and swore I would drain them of every drop if they broke my new toy.

Chapter 6: Hélène

It was probably about 1921 and I had started to drift ever closer towards Paris. The countryside was safe but very boring for a young chap like me. I had always thought of myself as a city boy and the bright lights of Paris became too big an attraction for me to resist. The city of Edinburgh that I had left behind in 1915 was very different from the Paris of the 1920s. Most nights, I just walked around various parts of town in absolute amazement. The women! Wow! Their skirts were a lot shorter now and I couldn't imagine my wee timid Fiona dressing like that. It was even more eye-popping at night when they went out in their high heels, make-up and low-cut flapper dresses. Women were everywhere, trying to hold on to the new-found independence World War I had given them. They were confident and independent; they had thrown off their stiff corsets and were ready to have fun.

Even though Paris was starting to become the centre of the world again, there was a seedy underbelly of tramps and prostitutes and I blended right in with them without attracting attention. No one cared about the dirty, pale veteran who roamed the streets at night and slept in underground tunnels during the day, and no one missed the occasional down-on-his-luck tramp. I killed a man for his wallet, as I had cravings for something else too, and I went to see a prostitute. I was a young male with very strong urges after all. This time, I didn't need to be shown what to do!

I couldn't yet imagine killing a woman. We men had been shooting at each other over the trenches for the past four years, but women were different in my eyes. To me, they were creatures that should not be hurt. I did acquire a taste for dogs though, as there were many surviving on garbage and rats and, of course, for rat itself; horrid things that didn't taste too great, but they kept the hunger and bloodlust at bay.

I often found myself in the Montparnasse district as it had the most bars and cafés and was attracting a young and artsy crowd. Painters and writers came to discuss their work deep into the night. There were also many young, damaged men like myself who wanted a better and different world to the one they'd had before the Great War, and there was always someone willing to talk to a scruffy man in an old army coat. I soon found myself becoming part of society again, rather than feeling like an animal hiding in the countryside.

Late one night, I spotted a redhead arguing with a bar owner. She was clutching a bottle of Cognac to her chest and was fighting the man off with her free arm.

'Can I help?' I asked, intrigued by this unusual redhead.

'You can if you have two francs. Madame here is refusing to pay,' the barman told me.

The girl was unsteady on her feet. I moved closer to her, worried that she was about to fall. I had about three francs in my pocket, the previous night's added benefit. I paid the man his two francs and suddenly the girl flung an arm around my neck and kissed me full on the lips. 'Thank you. You're a real gentleman,' she slurred. I was a bit shocked, as I wasn't used to a woman being so forward.

'Good luck with that mate. Hélène is your problem now,' the barman laughed and went back inside, shaking his head.

'François, you are an arse!' she shouted after him. Then she took my arm and started dragging me up a small alleyway.

'You must have a drink with me, you paid for the bottle after all,' she said, holding on to my arm tightly.

'It's rather late,' I said loosening myself from her grip, but she got even closer and tried to kiss me again. Then she drew back and looked at me. She had very bright green eyes. She looked like one of these Celtic heroines you sometimes see in illustrations, with flowing red locks and fiery green eyes.

'You are quite handsome, you know. I could do something with you,' she said. I looked at her too and decided that she was very pretty.

'Do what with me?' I asked, innocently.

'Tidy you up; you need a good wash and a haircut. Then you could sit for me. What's your name?'

'Cameron. Cameron Blair,' I told her.

'Cameron? That's not a French name,' she said, surprised.

'I'm Scottish, but I have lived here for a while now.'

'Your French is amazing!' She looked at me with admiration.

'I pick languages up easily,' I said. I still didn't understand exactly how, but I knew it must come with the blood.

She grabbed my chin and turned my face to view it from all angles in the streetlight.

'You have the most unusual eyes. They are very blue,' she said, studying my features.

'Like a field of Scottish bluebells my mother used to say.'

'Well, come with me Cameron. I want to immortalise you,' and she dragged me along until we came to a green door much in need of some paint. She opened it with a key that she had on a cord around her neck. 'My coat has so many holes in it, this seems the best way not to lose it,' she explained.

Her apartment was rather shabby and she had no furniture apart from a bed, a chair and a chest of drawers. The apartment was at the top of the building and was mostly glass. I could see why she had chosen it, as it made a perfect artist's studio, but it wouldn't be a good place for me to be after sunrise. She did have a bath tub and I was grateful for the chance to get cleaned up. Meanwhile she washed my clothes and hung them up to dry by her coal fire stove.

I sat on her bed, in her dressing gown, while she poured Cognac.

'Gosh Cameron. How long have you been living on the street?' she asked, as she looked over my clothes. They'd become quite ragged and had holes everywhere. In Paris, it hadn't been that easy finding washing lines at night, and people locked their doors.

She had taken out some thread and was trying to patch my trousers up as best she could. They looked a little better, but not much. She explained that she only had green and red thread in her sewing box, and she was also quite drunk.

'I didn't want to go back to my old life after the war, so I've been sleeping rough for a while now,' I answered.

'I know. It is hard to make it here. I don't want to go back home either and my parents are just so bourgeois. They had my life all planned out: marry my father's junior partner, a frightfully dull lawyer, and then have lots of children. I think I would have died if I'd married that dullard and stayed in Rouen.' She went on to tell me how one day she had just decided to take the train to Paris. She had got herself an apartment and started to paint. She said she funded her new passion by working as an artist's model now and then. She had written to her parents telling them she was fine, but she didn't tell them where she was. She was determined to make it as an artist in Paris.

'Now I spend all my money on paint and canvas,' she said as she got up to pour another drink before going to look for something amongst the canvases leaning against the wall.

'Do you like my work?' she asked, holding up one of her paintings.

'I don't know much about art, but I'm sure they are very good,' I said, not sure if I liked what I saw. I had never seen painting like it before; it was all just shapes.

'It's cubism,' she said. 'It and Mr Picasso are taking the art world by storm.'

'OK. As I said, I know nothing about art,' I told her. I didn't want to upset the girl, but I didn't understand what she was on about.

'It's all about going back to the shapes in their purest, simplest forms. You know, I sat for Picasso once and I was just amazed with what he was doing. I think he is rather brilliant,' she told me excitedly.

'But didn't you want to paint me?' I asked. 'I mean, for those paintings you don't need anyone.'

'I do portraits as well, but they're probably a little different to what you are used to.'

She showed me a canvas of a woman, painted entirely in blue with rough brush strokes. She laughed at my confused look and came over to the bed, took my head in her hands and kissed me. 'You have much to learn, Cameron, but let me teach you,' she said with a wicked twinkle in her eyes.

I had known prostitutes and was not a complete innocent, but this was different. Hélène was beautiful and full of life and I was very attracted to her. Our lovemaking was passionate. I found her interesting and exciting and she had such fire in her eyes when she talked about art. She would never be food. She quenched my other urges – lust and the need for companionship – and she very briefly made me forget what I was.

Hélène made me feel human again and it felt wonderful. Fiona had only ever let me kiss her, so this was the first time I'd made love to a woman I actually cared about. She was so soft and beautiful and I didn't want to leave her, but as daybreak came I had to go.

'Will you come back tomorrow?' she asked and I kissed her and promised I would.

How was this going to work? We could never have a normal life together, but I refused to think about that as I left her apartment and descended into the metro, mingling with the working masses going off to their jobs. For once, I was just like any other young man, sitting smiling on the metro, thinking of his girl on the way to work. Fiona had become a fond but distant memory over the years and though I still had her picture and looked at it from time to time, I knew I would never see her again. Gradually I had begun to forget her, and now there was a new lassie in my life.

I couldn't wait to see her again and as soon as she opened the door that night I swept her up and kissed her. I could feel she felt the same and we didn't do much that night other than make mad, passionate love on her narrow bed. When I wanted to leave, she held on to me and asked me to stay. I told her I couldn't, but that I would love to see her again. She told me her door would always be open to me.

The night after, she cut my hair and gave me some clothes. She wanted me to sit for a portrait, so I agreed to pose for her but only at night. As she sketched, we talked about our time growing up. I don't think she had been very happy and had always felt rather out of place growing up in Normandy. We both thought Paris was wonderful. She told me she was enjoying life here, but I could see she struggled to make ends meet and it was obvious she had been on her own for too long. She needed me as much as I needed her, I had not realised until then how much I craved human, and especially female, attention.

'I want you to stay with me Cameron,' she said after a few weeks. 'You don't have to leave every morning, I really like having you around.'

I sat back down on the bed and stared at the wall not quite knowing what to tell her. Then I turned to her and said softly,

'I'm a much damaged man Hélène. I don't think I can be the man you want in your life.' It made me sad to say it. I wanted to be with her all the time too.

'We're all damaged,' she said, and started to cry. She told me she'd only been with one other man. She'd met him when she first came to Paris and had moved in with him, but he'd turned violent and been cruel to her. I asked her who he was, but she told me she wanted to forget the whole episode and he wasn't worth getting worked up about. I wondered if she'd seen the flicker in my eye and realised what I was capable of.

'It has taken me a long time to let someone into my life again, but I would like to try, Cameron,' she insisted as she held my hand. I told her that I had enlisted and lied about my age, that I had gone to war when I was still a child and it had affected me greatly. I couldn't eat if anyone watched me, I couldn't stand my own reflection anymore and, I told her, I was afraid of daylight and needed to spend my daytimes underground and by myself.

It must have seemed very strange to her, but I looked so young and so pale that she accepted my story. She wanted to help and change me, but I played the part of the damaged young veteran well. I decided to risk it and brought the few possessions I owned along the next night. Hélène was delighted and freed up some space in her chest of drawers.

The first few weeks were heavenly, just staying in her apartment and being unable to keep our hands off each other. We'd talk for hours while she sketched me. Hélène taught me about art and gradually I started to see the world differently; she made me see and appreciate beauty. Sometimes, we'd take a walk and she'd point out interesting architecture and decorative features on buildings. For the first two months, we wanted only each other for company, but then one night she sat me down for a talk.

'I think we should go out more, Cameron. My friends have been asking to meet the mysterious man I've been seeing,' she started off cheerfully. I wholeheartedly agreed with her as I loved meeting new people.

'To go out, we need money and we also need to pay the rent,' she continued more seriously.

'I'll try and find some work,' I assured her.

'You do have to start getting back to normality somehow,' she told me.

'I can't do that, but I will try for the money,' I said quietly. Hélène gave me a hug and a kiss and went back to her painting. I was relieved the conversation had ended there.

Making a living during the hours of darkness was a challenge, but I found that in the early morning I could make some money at Les Halles helping the traders set up. I was young and strong and they found me to be a good worker. I also resorted to pick-pocketing on the metro, but I had mixed success with that. I even got caught once trying to get a wallet out of a pocket. The victim grabbed me and I allowed him to restrain me until the metro stopped. I had become fiendishly strong so when the doors opened I tore myself easily from his grasp, jumped out the carriage and off the platform and ran down a tunnel. It was dangerous, but what the hell. I was already dead and I needed to get away.

I stole a pocket watch once and told Hélène I had found it. I'm not sure she believed me, but we needed the money and she sold it straight away the next day. I was surprised that she had managed to sell it so easily and asked her where she had gone. In wintertime it was easy to find shops still open when it was dark, and I went to find where she'd taken it. I watched the shop for a number of days and observed that the clientele was dodgy-looking at best. The wee jeweller was friendly and didn't ask too many questions. I gained his trust and he proved to be a good introductory contact for the identity papers I'd need next.

Going out with Hélène's friends was mostly great fun and I got along with most of them – except when Hélène drank too much. She got jealous and paranoid when she'd had too much. One night, we had drifted to different parts of the room and when we left she was not in a good mood. I asked her if I'd done something wrong.

'What were you saying to Chagall,' she hissed on the way back to the apartment. 'The two of you were laughing at me. Was it about my painting?'

'No! Of course not! He told me about this American who wants to buy his painting, but absolutely insists on him painting her poodle into said picture. Some people are cretins! Of course he refused and told her to put her dollars where the sun doesn't shine.'

'Him and his rich clients! I bet he does laugh at my work and tells you I will never sell anything,' she said angrily.

'He likes your painting. He thinks you're very talented,' I told her and put my arm around her shoulders as we reached our apartment building.

'He does? Really?' and she turned to me and smiled shyly. 'Do you think I'm talented?' she asked, looking up at me with her beautiful, green eyes.

'Abso-bloody-lutely!' I said enthusiastically, and picked her up and carried her up the stairs, delighted she was happy again.

It was exhausting trying to feed during the day, spend all my night time with Hélène and get some money to help her with the rent. I survived mostly on rats and dogs, as I was concerned about taking human blood. I suggested we set up shop on the banks of the Seine in the evenings, so that people on a night out or returning from dinner could stop and look at her paintings. Slowly the money started trickling in.

Hélène liked to go dancing, so often, after a successful night by the river, we would go out the following night and spend the proceeds in one of the dance halls. She had bought an emerald green dress with fringes that moved when she danced, and she looked amazing in it with her red hair. I had bought her one of the new fashionable bandeaus. It was imitation diamond and emerald but it was a nice piece and she loved it. We were trying to learn a new dance – the Charleston – and we were having a lot of fun trying out the steps.

Hélène was a lot of fun and I was happiest when we lay on her bed, looking at the stars and talking. We both loved going dancing and having a good time, but we also enjoyed, on a winter's night, looking at Cartier's shop window and picking out the pieces we liked best. We both agreed on emeralds for Hélène and we lusted after a diamond tiara with Indian-cut emerald drops on its tips.

'When would I ever wear a grand tiara like that, Cameron?' she asked, as we stood in front of the window.

'I think it would look spectacular with your apron, doing the dishes. I mean, when you have something that beautiful you'd want to wear it all the time.' I kissed her neck.

'Think if we go in they will let me try it on?' she asked.

I looked at our scruffy coats and doubted they'd even let us in.

'Sure! Let's try. The worst they can do is say no.'

Of course they said no, but as we were discussing the unfairness, a wealthy-looking customer overheard us.

'He is right, you know. A beautiful redhead like you should have an emerald tiara. Wait here. I'll see if they'll let you try it on for me,' and he went inside to talk to the shop assistant.

He must have been a good customer, as they agreed. I had

to stay outside. They didn't trust the both of us to be near something so valuable, but I was glad; the place had way too many mirrors. I could see her through the door, looking like a princess with the fabulous tiara on her head. Her face lit up with excitement and happiness. Hélène asked for the man's name and address so she could give him a painting as a thank you, which turned out quite well. He liked her work and it led to a few commissions.

As Hélène's work began to be recognised, she started to get invitations to glitzy parties. Through her and her new friends I was developing an eye for jewellery and a liking for the finer things of life. Paris in the 1920s attracted rich Americans and I found I mingled well with the new and affluent crowd. I was popular as I spoke perfect English and French and the Americans adored my Scottish accent. We were at one of these parties when Hélène got angry with me again.

'What do you say to these Americans about me? You're always talking to them.' She didn't like it when she couldn't understand what I was saying. I had tried to teach her a few words, but English isn't an easy language for French people and she struggled with it.

'You should be glad I'm talking to them. They could become very good customers,' I replied calmly, trying to sound upbeat. I didn't want us to have a fight at such an important party.

'It's all about the money with you, isn't it Cameron?' she jibed angrily.

'Stop it, Hélène. It was you that was always complaining you never had any, and now we are a good team. You paint and I sell.'

I could see she was in a fighting mood. Cognac always made her aggressive. I tried to get her to leave the party – I didn't want a scene.

She snarled at me when she felt me leading her out to the door, 'So now you are embarrassed by me! Silly drunk Hélène, always causing a scene!'

'You said it, not me,' I snapped back. People's heads were starting to turn and I felt very uncomfortable.

'How dare you criticise *my* behaviour,' she hissed.

'Can we please go?' I begged her. Thankfully, she realised that having public rows was bad for business and she let me take her home. If we had problems, it was mostly on account of drink. More often, fun, sparkling, witty Hélène would come out, the Hélène that loved to go dancing and could party all night and still have the energy to make passionate love to me. Angry Hélène I liked less, as I hated fighting with her, but she forgave quickly and the make-up sex was pretty good too.

Mostly, I hated sombre Hélène – she frightened me. Sometimes, the lights just went out in her eyes. She would stare, unseeing, into the distance and nothing I could say or do then would cheer her up. One cold night, we were walking back from a party and I saw her mood changing. We stopped on a bridge and she stared out over the water.

'If you were married, you could tell me,' she said quietly. 'I'd rather be the mistress than not have you.'

I grabbed her arms to make her face me. 'Where is this coming from? I lived on the streets before I met you and you must know I love only you,'

'You have so many secrets. Sometimes I think I don't know you at all.' She turned to face me, but it was as though she was looking through me.

'Hélène, trust me, you are the only one and you know how much you mean to me,' I said pulling her close.

'Then stop leaving me every morning before the sun even comes up!' she said, and I could hear desperation in her voice.

'I have to,' I said quietly. It was already very late and I

would have to hide soon. 'Let's talk tonight. I just can't be here.' I started breathing heavily, pretending to be in a panic, and turned to walk away.

'Don't you dare leave, Cameron!' she shouted after me with the threat of tears in her voice and I felt something hit my back. Then her other shoe whizzed past me. This was bad, but I kept on walking. I couldn't stay and reveal to her the monster that I was.

I hoped she'd be in a better mood when I went to the apartment that night, but she wasn't and I considered leaving straight away as I didn't fancy another fight. I decided to have a bath instead, she always thought I looked adorable with wet messed up hair and I hoped it would win her over. When I came out of the bathroom, dressed only in a towel, I was shocked to see her standing in the middle of the room holding a knife.

'Who the fuck is this?' she screamed, holding up the photo of Fiona which I still carried in my wallet. She must have gone through my pockets.

'That is Fiona. I told you about her,' I said standing stock-still.

'Why are you still carrying her picture? Do you still think about her?' she yelled.

'Burn the picture. I don't care anymore,' I said and she immediately grabbed a box of matches and set fire to the old photo, all the while looking at me, studying my face for a reaction. I was sad to see the picture burn, but it had to be done. There was now only one woman in my life and she was my life. I gently took the knife out of her hand and she let me kiss her. Slowly, I felt her relax and respond to my kisses. We made love slowly and tenderly that night and then just lay in each other's arms without speaking a word, but I could feel the sombre mood hadn't let go yet.

A few days later, when I left the apartment, she followed me. It was winter so, luckily, I had gone to Les Halles to help the market traders set up in the dark. I was furious when I spotted her.

'Don't you dare follow me!' I shouted grabbing her arms and shaking her violently. 'Hélène, I swear it is over if you do that again!' I was so angry. What if she had seen me sink my teeth into a rat?

'I'm sorry! Please, please don't leave!' she cried, clinging to me tightly. I noticed we had drawn quite a crowd and became embarrassed, so I just stood there cuddling her until the men drifted off and went about their business again.

'Christ, I am sorry,' I murmured, 'but please don't follow me. You saw a side of me you didn't like just now, but you could see much worse,' I said, lifting her head up to make her look into my eyes. She stopped crying, tidied herself up and went home without saying a word. It was awkward for a few days after. I thought I had frightened her with my violent outburst as she didn't question my whereabouts again. She loved me and seemed not to want to know if there was a dark secret. The fact was that we were daft about each other and wanted to be together, no matter what.

Then, in 1925, we met Charley Webber. He had bought one of Hélène's paintings, so when he spotted her at a party later the same week he came over to talk to her. I could tell that she liked him as he was one of the few Americans that spoke excellent French. I eyed him up suspiciously. He was tall and athletic like me, but he had blond, unruly curls that flopped over his forehead. He was handsome in a healthy country boy sort of way, but Charley was anything but a country boy. He was dressed in the latest fashion and I could tell his suit was expensive. Hélène introduced me as her boyfriend, but he didn't seem to mind and included me in the conversation. He was a lively and animated character and I found him easy to talk to.

'So what brings you to Paris, Charley?' I asked him.

'Firstly, you can't get a drink in the States and secondly, I like a bit of distance between me and mummy,' he told us.

'What? You can't get alcohol in America?' asked Hélène, her eyes widening in amazement. I smiled wryly at that remark, I couldn't imagine Hélène surviving one week without a drink.

'Well, I suppose you can – there are these illegal bars called speakeasies but, as I said, they are illegal. Yep! Prohibition is a bitch!' he said, raising his glass of champagne.

He invited us to his house for dinner and handed us his card from a beautiful diamond encrusted Fabergé card case. When he saw my eyes widening he let me have a look at it.

'Mummy got it for my 21st. It's nice, but a bit old-fashioned now, and Cartier is doing rather exciting things in the new art deco style,' said Charley.

'I think it's one of the most beautiful things – apart, of course, from Hélène – that I have ever seen,' I said, looking the card case over before handing it back to him.

'Well then, remind me to show you some of my other trinkets when you come round,' he said, as he put the case back in his pocket.

'You'll have to forgive Cameron when we come for dinner, he doesn't eat at night.' Hélène smiled and stuck her tongue out at me as I shot her a dirty look.

'Really Cameron? Why not?' Charley asked me, surprised.

'War hangover,' I mumbled. 'Evening bombardments put me off my food.'

'And you'll have to remove the mirrors!' Hélène went on, playfully. She thought this quirk was just hilarious, but she did always go in first to check if a place was free of them. I knew I would have to come up with something better at some point, but in 1925 the war was still a good excuse for most odd behaviour. We agreed to come for dinner the following week and Charley went off after a waiter with a tray of full champagne glasses.

Charley had a large apartment on the Rue de Rivoli overlooking the Tuileries gardens. When we went in, Hélène held my hand and pulled me close. Neither of us had ever been in such a magnificent place and I think she felt quite overwhelmed. Charley and Hélène had a sumptuous dinner while I was given what he called a box of trinkets to look at. I appreciated that he avoided the embarrassment of me having to sit through dinner with an empty plate.

The box was full of some of the best pieces the famous jewellery houses were producing at the time. There was a pink and yellow gold cigarette case by Cartier and a rather striking Tiffany green and black enamel pill box in the Japanese style. Charley also had a bewildering collection of cufflinks and tie-pins, many of which were diamond-set.

Hélène was walking on air on our way back home and couldn't stop talking about all the divine dishes she had tasted. I felt a wee bit down, as I knew I could never provide her with such luxury. I didn't know if she felt my mood but she turned to me and said, 'I don't think I'd like to be Charley, always wondering if people liked me only for my money.'

'True, but I would still like you to become rich and famous. I think I would like to be rich,' I said, smiling dreamily.

'Yes Cameron, you are becoming quite a magpie. You do like shiny, pretty things,' she said, cuddling into me.

'Yes I do like pretty things,' I said, and put my arm around her.

We stopped on one of the bridges and kissed for a long time. For us Paris was one of the most romantic places in the world, and at times I almost forgot that I had died – until the rising sun reminded me.

Charley often came to our apartment. I think he liked our Bohemian lifestyle and enjoyed sitting on our floor drinking cheap wine and discussing art. Sometimes, he took us around Paris in his enormous Packard roadster. Hélène would scream and hold her arms up in the air as he drove at high speed along the Champs-Elysées. I was very excited when he offered to teach me how to drive. The power and the speed of this enormous car were unbelievable. I only wished my Edinburgh friends could see me driving along the streets of Paris. Hootie would have been green with envy, as he always told us he would love to have a car. Charley gave us a taste of how the other half lived and we were glad to have him as a friend.

One night, Charley suggested we take a trip to Deauville. We would go to the races and visit Honfleur where there were a few artists Charley was interested in. I could see Hélène was desperate to go, but I of course couldn't. I had got to know Charley quite well and he was always the perfect gentleman, but to let him take my girlfriend alone on a trip would be a step too far.

'Why can't you come, Cameron?' Charley asked me, surprised.

'Don't even bother. The wife won't let him.' Hélène snapped. I sat in a corner and brooded. *This was just getting impossible.* There was a long awkward silence, and Charley looked from one to the other trying to figure out what was going on between us.

'We could always take one of Hélène's friends if you can't go and you are worried I won't behave myself,' Charley said, after a while.

Hélène grew very excited at this and went off to ask her friend Véronique straight away. When she was out of the apartment, Charley asked me if I was indeed married.

'No I am not! It's another war hangover that I have to be underground during the day. Somehow, at night, I feel safe as long as I don't have my dinner, but during the day I think the bombs will rain down on me and I need to be underground,' I explained trying to sound scared and damaged.

'Why don't you take her below grounds then?' he asked. 'She wants to know where you go.'

'I can't have her there when I am cowering in the metro and I can't eat if I'm with someone,' I said, not even having to pretend to be in great pain. Charley put his arm around my shoulder and gave me a hug.

'Boy, oh boy, do you need a good psychiatrist!'

Charley did take the girls on his trip and by all accounts they had an excellent time. Hélène came back sunburned, but she didn't care and couldn't stop talking about all the things they had seen and done.

'The sea and the light Cameron, it was so... just so... inspirational!' She gushed. 'I would love to live there and just sit by the seaside and paint. The cloud formations and the sea – it was beautiful!'

I sat there in silence and listened. I was worried that in time I would lose her to Charley and there was nothing I could do to stop it from happening. After the trip, Hélène sometimes met him during the day and I think the two of them were becoming good friends. I didn't like it, but I had to resign myself to the fact that in the daytime she would live her life without me. She was an artist and loved the light – it was her inspiration and her reason for living and I could not share it.

Then one day Charlie came by and told us he had to go back to America for a few months. His dad wanted him to meet an heiress and was hoping he would marry and settle down. 'I'll take her to a few balls, play their game for a while, then tell them she isn't the one and come back,' he told us, light-heartedly.

'Think they'll let you off the hook?' I asked.

'I'm terribly good at throwing tantrums. Mummy doesn't dare say no to me and Daddy doesn't dare to say no to her,' he said with a smile.

'Don't you want to get married?' asked Hélène. I was immediately uneasy. I knew such a life could never be ours, but I also knew she would want to get married eventually.

'I don't think I could stand to have a woman around the place all the time,' he said emphatically.

'I think Cameron is like that. Even before daybreak he just has to get out of the place,' and she started to cry. 'Why do you both leave me? I can't stand it,' she sobbed. I put my arms around her, but she pushed me away and flung herself on the bed.

'I will come back, dear girl, don't worry. And I will write to you too,' said Charley and he shot me a worried look. I sat on the bed to console her. Charley stood around looking awkward for a few seconds then left with a quick goodbye.

Hélène didn't paint for the next two weeks and I was worried about how much Charley's absence was affecting her. I was jealous of him being so important in her life, but I also hoped he would come back so she could be happy again. It took a lot to shake her out of her mood again. Eventually I got her to go out, but things weren't the same.

'I think you have a wife somewhere' she snapped at me again one night, as I came in. I spotted a half empty wine bottle on the table and got annoyed.

'Not this again! Why do I have to keep telling you I am not married' I shot back.

'You said it yourself. We make good money together. You don't need to work, so where the fuck are you all day?'

She was starting to cry and I put my arms around her. 'You *know* I love you. I *promise* there is nobody else,' I said wearily. My anger came and went as quickly as hers. We both hated fighting, but I was tiring of having the same argument again and fearful of what would happen if she ever found out the truth.

She began to calm down but looked very tired. I undressed her and put her into bed, then got in beside her hoping she would go to sleep. She was working a lot again, but drinking a lot too. Her paintings had become very popular and she had an important commission to paint a large mural in a church. I thought she was struggling with the scale of the work and it caused her great anxiety – she still wasn't at all convinced of her own abilities. We were also invited to a lot of parties after which she wanted to stay up and make love to me or talk until I couldn't stay any longer.

'You need to sleep,' I told her the next day, when I noticed it was getting very late.

'How can I when I know you're going to be gone when I wake up?' she said, eyes heavy with tiredness.

'I always come back don't I?'

'With Charley gone too, I feel so lost during the day,' she said, pouring herself another glass. I wanted to pick up the bottle and smash it against the wall. *Why did she have to drink so much?* It wasn't doing her any good. But I wasn't there during the day; I couldn't stop her.

'Doesn't your painting fulfil you?' I asked her, but she just shrugged her shoulders and stared out of the window. The poor girl was exhausted. I may never have broken her skin, but I still found myself draining her of life and slowly killing her.

I began to realise that I could never give Hélène a normal life and to believe that she would be better off without me. She needed rest and I hoped that some time away from me would do her good. I knew that eventually I would have to break our relationship off and, much as I hated the idea of her being with another man, I wanted to wait until Charley was back before I left for good. He was rich and a nice fellow and could give her all she needed. I hoped that she would seek solace in his arms.

I wrote her a note swearing that I would be back in two weeks, but that I had a job up north in a coal mine and she should rest while I was away. Then I left.

I got myself an apartment and worked at becoming a cat burglar. There was a lot of wealth in the city and I found that I was quite skilled at getting into places and it was less risky than pick-pocketing. After two weeks I missed Hélène dreadfully and was desperate to see how she was. I wasn't sure how she'd have taken my sudden departure, but hoped she had rested and that her mural was progressing well. I went back to her apartment with mixed feelings of excitement and dread.

'Cameron!' she sobbed, throwing herself into my arms as I came in. She clung to me as she cried on my chest. After a while, she let me go and wiped her eyes.

'Don't ever do that again, you bastard! I swear I'll kill myself if you ever leave me again!' Her face was red and puffy, she had already drunk a lot and the crying wasn't making things better. From the looks of the apartment she hadn't done anything but drown her sorrows in alcohol since I'd left; there were bottles everywhere and the same canvas she had started two weeks before sat unfinished on the easel.

I sat her down and made her a cup of tea. She watched me in silence as I tidied the place up. I found she had burned all the sketches she'd made of me and it sent a shiver down my spine. *What was I doing? I didn't want her out of my life!* I ran her a bath and washed her hair for her. Then we just lay on her bed in each other's arms. Soon she fell asleep and I was happy just to be near to her and hold her. As dawn approached, I got up carefully so as not to wake her, but she woke anyway and grabbed my wrist.

'Stay the whole day with me! Please! I don't want you to leave me again,' she pleaded. 'I want you to see the mural I'm doing, I want you to tell me if it's any good.'

'I *can't*,' I said loosening her fingers from my wrist. There was simply nowhere to hide in her apartment and I certainly couldn't walk to a church in broad daylight. *Should I tell her the truth? Did she love me enough to accept me?* 'Can you not just love me and trust me to come back to you? I will *always* be faithful to you and I *swear* there is no one else!' There was desperation in my voice. 'And Hélène, you have to trust in yourself. You are extremely talented,' I said. And I meant it.

'I just die when you're not with me,' she said quietly and turned away from me. I knew she was crying now, but above me, through that cursed glass roof, I saw the night sky brightening. I had to go.

'I have to go *now*, but I promise to be back tonight. Please go to work, and when you come back put a nice dress on for me and we'll spend the night here – just the two of us.' I kissed her cheek. She promised, but I could feel it was tearing her apart.

***

I found her that evening, lying in the bath tub. She had cut deep into her arms with a razor and the water was red with her blood. She was already dead and there was nothing I could do. There was no more I wanted to do... I had drained her of life after all.

I could have brought her back – we could have been together for all eternity – but denying Hélène her treasured light would have been a fate so much worse than death for her. I took the portrait she had painted of me and left.

Chapter 7: Fergus

In 2007, curiosity got the better of me. Ninety-two years after I'd left, nobody would be alive to recognise me, so I made arrangements to visit Edinburgh. Sailing my yacht into Ocean Terminal and mooring next to the royal yacht *Britannia* would cause quite a stir, so I had George rent an apartment for me in the New Town. In my parents' day it had been an ordinary area, but George assured me it was very posh now. He rented a flat on Great King Street not far from where I had grown up in Clarence Street.

I couldn't just get on a plane though. Someone like me would cause all sorts problems at security. There were just too many questions and machines that didn't detect and mirrors that didn't reflect me. The trip overland and by boat took three days, despite me driving by night and Roberto taking over by day. When we arrived, I was feeling stiff, cold and hungry, but George had arranged a fantastic dinner courtesy of the Seafield Edinburgh Cat and Dog Home. I opened the door to our flat and a most adorable Scotty dog came running towards us. I turned to George and smiled.

'You really shouldn't have, George!'

'I know what a cranky bastard you can be after you've been restrained for a while,' George said as Roberto fled to his room, *the wee wuss!*

As George cleaned away the rest of dinner I sat down to read the *Edinburgh Evening News*. George informed me that this was the paper for finding all the best spots for the impending Hogmanay party. Edinburgh on 30 December was the ideal place for me. No daylight til nine o'clock and sunset at four. Edinburgh; a city rife with junkies, dossers and other elements the police wouldn't investigate for too long. Truth was, though, I hated the cold. It made my bones ache and it made me hungry. I resorted to putting a hot water bottle under my jumper to keep me warm and the hunger at bay. Hunger was a problem, as satisfying it often led to questions and a hasty departure. But I was here for a reason.

'So, George, did you find her?' I asked

'Eventually. But, she is dead,' he replied drily.

'Well I expected that. She'd be a 112 if she was still alive!' I said getting up to boil another kettle for my hot water bottle. I was surprised I'd ever managed to live here in this cold, damp climate.

'I found her grave. Her married name was Henderson and she left three children and eight grandchildren.'

Good for her! I was genuinely pleased Fiona had moved on with her life, but something bothered me.

'Hang on. Henderson, you said?'

'Yes, Cameron. She married an Alistair Henderson,' George said handing me the digital camera so I could look at a picture of the gravestone.

'Fucking Hootie! She married fucking Hootie!' I cried in disgust.

'Her husband died in 1960,' George told me.

'Just as well, the treacherous bastard,' I said outraged.

'Do you want to know about your parents?' he asked.

'Don't tell me they are still alive...' I gave George a look that told him not to answer that. 'No I don't want to know. I just wanted to know about Fiona,' I told him.

I'd never wanted to go back home before as the shame of my 'desertion' would have been hard for my family to bear. I should have staged my own death back at the beginning, but I was young and scared and by the time I realised what I had done, it was too late. I'd never looked my family up, scared I might discover something that would upset me, but later that night I went out alone to have a look around the old neighbourhood.

Edinburgh had changed; my old family home was still there, but now there where BMWs and ugly black wheelie bins in front of it. I watched the large sash and case windows for a long time until the current inhabitants switched off their lights, then I let myself in and climbed to the second floor. 'Hodge' the shiny brass plate said.

I'm not proud of what I did next. Whether it was the nostalgia or the cold and the hunger a crime took place that kept the Lothian and Borders police busy for many months and I know that they still haven't solved the case. No one could fathom why a nice middle class couple should be found in their bed with their throats cut. I knew – they'd had the misfortune of being in *my house*. I was glad the couple wasn't discovered for a few days and that in the end it didn't make the French news. I knew George and Roberto would have disapproved.

As I wiped the blood from my mouth, I looked around. The flat was very different now with its new IKEA kitchen and plush furnishings. My brothers and I used to share the room that had now become a dining room. Our coal fire in the living room had been replaced with a fake gas fireplace. I needed to get out of there! After a quick search I found a few interesting pieces of jewellery and left. I walked briskly uphill to George Street, as I knew some of the bars and clubs there would still be open. I stopped in the middle of the street and screamed at the top of my lungs in frustration, swore, then screamed again. I would have loved nothing more than to have come home in my uniform, taken Fiona in my arms and gone back to my old life, but the war and a stupid vampire had robbed me of the chance. It still made me angry.

Two lads came up to me and put their arms around me. By

the looks of it they had been drinking for a while. 'Let it all out, pal! You'll feel better afters.'

Things hadn't changed that much then. The human warmth and the abuse of alcohol were still there. Ian and Stewart, as I later discovered they were called, guided me towards The Dome, which was – according to them – the best place to be. I laughed when they dragged me up to the commercial bank in George Street.

'Aye right, the commercial bank will be serving the likes of me a drink now,' I said, smiling, thinking they wouldn't be opening their doors at this time of night. But the former bank had been transformed into a swanky bar. I bought the lads drinks for the rest of the night. Compared with the Côte d'Azur it was a cheap night and I felt at home talking to some Edinburgh lads like me.

The next day, George woke me with a Westie. It was a sweet little thing that followed George around like, erm, well like a puppy dog.

'Do you like dogs, George? 'I asked.

'Not really. I'm not an animal person and dogs? Well, I think the little critters smell!' At that point I had my breakfast.

'Hogmanay, George! What's happening tonight then?' I asked him merrily. Food always put me in a good mood.

'I think you are best to just go up to Princes Street and mingle with the crowds'

'Anybody we know in town?'

'I don't think so, Cameron, but Kasabian is playing.'

'I like them. Can anyone go and see them?' I asked.

'No, unfortunately not and I didn't manage to get you tickets to the concert in the gardens, but I heard the street party is pretty good and you'll probably hear the bands playing in the gardens from there.'

'We'll make do, dear George. Just make sure you get me a

few hot water bottles otherwise I'll eat the lot of them.' Being warm made me less hungry and therefore less dangerous.

At about ten o'clock I made my way towards Princes Street where there were already crowds of people. George had decided to stay home; the thought of being surrounded by heavily drinking Scots put him off. Roberto had decided to meet up with a girl he had met in French class during the summer. She lived in Edinburgh and he'd arranged to meet her and her friends in a pub. Roberto was staying out of my way in Edinburgh. He felt I was dangerous and on edge, despite my upbeat banter.

I didn't mind going out by myself, as socialising with the two of them was often difficult and I felt like behaving badly that night, throwing myself into the party and seeing what happened. I pushed my way through to Princes Street until I was standing right behind the Ross bandstand. Fiona and I had gone there a few times to listen to the music on a Sunday afternoon, but the crowd tonight was quite different.

The mix of alcohol and warm, dancing bodies made me feel rather light-headed. I had tasted sweet innocent Fiona's lips, but I found myself wondering how her blood would have tasted. And what would the vodka-infused blood of a modern, not-so-innocent Edinburgh woman taste like? The crowd was getting more and more dense and a girl with a scarf and a woolly hat bounced against me. She looked up and smiled.

'You're gorgeous!' she yelled above the noise.

'Erm, I like your hat!' I said surprised.

'You got any booze?' she asked me. *My oh my, Edinburgh lasses were very different these days!*

'Just a wee dram of whisky.' I didn't drink the stuff, but I thought I'd look the part carrying a hipflask, and now it had the desired effect of attracting some prey.

'Let's drink that and then find some more. I don't like whisky but I'll have it. Then let's see if we can get some port. I love port!' she yelled. She took a large swig from my hipflask, put her arm around my waist and gazed up drunkenly. I bent down and kissed her hard. She didn't feel the cut I made in her lip with my fang. Just as well I'd had breakfast or the mix of blood and alcohol might have made me do something really stupid.

Fucking vodka! Fucking cheap vodka at that. 'Why do you want port if you have been drinking vodka all night?' I asked her as I pulled away.

'You can taste that?' she asked, bemused.

'Yes. That and something vile and chemical,' I said with distaste.

'That'll be the Red Bull. It keeps you awake, man!' she yelled excitedly.

'Have you ever considered champagne?' I asked.

'Yeah, I have champagne all the time, you Tory twat!' she said, giving me a disgusted look. Then she kissed me again and I snacked until the bells went off.

'Happy bloody 2008,' she slurred.

'Happy 2008, Fiona,' I murmured.

'I'm *Cathy* by the way,' she said, punching me in the ribs. And then she smeared her bloodied lips all over my mouth again. Soon after, we walked down to her place on Leith Walk.

'We need some fucking port,' shouted Cathy, as we reached the top of the road. 'Now! Port! You promised, you bastard!' she yelled.

'I'm not sure there's anywhere still open,' I told her looking around. I was getting a wee bit bored of this girl; she was just so loud and drunk and vodka was not my favourite flavouring.

I was about to call it a night when she said 'Alright, let's go back to mine. Fergus will be clawing at the door by now anyway. I bet my da' fell asleep and didn't pay him any attention.'

'Who's Fergus?' I asked, trying not to sound too interested.

'He's ma dug.'

'Oh, well! Let's go and meet Fergus then,' I said cheerfully, putting my arm around her shoulders again.

We came to one of the Georgian tenements and she told me to keep quiet as we went in. When we reached her front door, I heard the dog scratching at the other side and, when he heard Cathy putting her key in the lock, start to bark excitedly.

'Shut the fuck up, Fergus. You'll wake my da',' she hissed.

We shouldn't have worried, her dad had passed out on the couch surrounded by beer cans, and the telly was still on.

'Fucking brilliant, man. Port!' she said, lifting a bottle off the table and putting it to her mouth. She offered me the bottle, but I declined.

'I think I've had enough, ta.'

'Suit yersel. Let's go to my room; I don't want to wake ma da',' she said, grabbing my hand and leading me to her room. Then the hat, scarf and coat came off and I discovered she had pink stringy hair and about five earrings in each ear. She had that pale skin colour you only get by living in Scotland for many years and avoiding vegetables. She had a pretty enough face though, and if I closed my eyes I could just about forget the pink hair.

I sat on the bed and pulled her on to my lap. Just as I was undoing her bra, Fergus managed to get into the room, leaped on to the bed and tried to lick my face.

'Get off,' Cathy shouted. But she didn't look too hot at this point and suddenly made a bee line to the bathroom, where I heard her throw up.

'I'll take Fergus for a walk...' I shouted through the bathroom door. 'I'll be back soon.'

'Breughhhh' came the answer, so I put the leash on Fergus and we disappeared into the Edinburgh night.

Fergus loved being in the car and just wouldn't settle down. He tried to jump on to the front seat and George swore he was going to kill him before we even reached Haddington. I managed to convince him not to, as I do like my food fresh and this bouncy Alsatian would keep me satisfied until Dover.

Chapter 8: Charley

In the days that followed Hélène's death, I didn't feel much like going out or doing anything, I just lay on the bed in my apartment torturing myself with could haves and should haves. After 14 days, the pain in my stomach became unbearable and snapped me out of my thoughts. I went looking for some easy food, the kind you find under many a bridge in Paris.

I was soon unable to pay my rent and so I moved my few possessions back into the catacombs. I wasn't upset about leaving my apartment, I had got the place to leave Hélène and now I hated it. Exploring the miles of catacomb tunnels kept my mind occupied and I was able to avoid meeting anyone I knew. I ventured out only to feed on the banks of the Seine – the murder rate must have gone up in 1926.

Before, and during, my time with Hélène I hadn't taken a lot of human blood. It was seriously tasty, but it also changed me somehow. I was afraid that it was addictive and that after a while I wouldn't be able to control myself. Now, though, I didn't care and I felt the blood affecting me even more than I'd feared. It altered me physically; I could now see as well in the dark as in the light, my hearing had improved tremendously and my sense of smell was different. I could now smell only the blood or, more accurately, emotion and the state of the blood. I could detect fear, excitement and illness, but the usual human smells were gone. I could no longer smell a woman's perfume or the stench of a tramp.

The worst thing about human blood, I was to find out much later. It was a change of character. Maybe I was the devil's creation, as the seven sins became more alluring and my virtues diminished. I began to see the world through different eyes. I killed my first woman, an unfortunate prostitute in the wrong place at the wrong time. I thought I would feel different, but the killing left me emotionless. To feed, to kill – it felt good – and it healed the pain. Afterwards, there was a lifeless body, but it meant nothing to me.

One night, I was walking along the Seine when I heard my name shouted from above.

'Cameron! Is that you?'

To my great surprise, I spotted my friend Charley leaning over the wall. I must have been a shocking sight, as I'd lived on the streets for a while and my clothes were torn and dirty.

'Cameron! Wait up, I'll come down,' he shouted as he ran along to the bridge and the stairs.

'Charley. How are you?' I said, reluctantly, when he joined me on the riverbank. I was embarrassed about my clothes and didn't want to speak to him.

'Good golly! Look at you! Have you been living on the streets?' he asked, looking me up and down.

'Yes. For a while now. It really isn't that bad,' I said, wanting to go. I was feeling very uncomfortable.

'I am so sorry, Cameron. I tried to find you when I came back to Paris and heard about Hélène.'

I didn't like the look of pity in his eyes so I replied angrily. 'I'm fine Charley. Apartments are overrated. Money, possessions – it's all very bourgeois.'

'Let me help you. Please...' Charley pleaded, and he moved closer to me.

'I have to go. I'll see you around.' I turned round abruptly and started to walk away.

Charley shouted after me: 'I still live at the same place. Please come and visit, if only to have a bath. Jesus Christ man, I could smell you from half a mile away!'

I had to walk away quickly. All I could see were the veins

in Charley's neck. The smell of his healthy, well-nourished blood was making me quite dizzy. *Bloody hell! What am I becoming?* How deep had I descended that I wanted to sink my teeth into my best friend? That was the problem with human blood; it healed and made you feel better, but it also washed the humanity and moral sense right out of you. I went on a crash diet of rat and dog, avoiding humans even more than usual, but it wasn't easy – human blood was addictive and my body screamed out for it.

When I felt I could mingle with people again without wanting to sink my fangs into them, I went and visited Charley. His apartment was much the same, but I noticed a few new objects. My eye was immediately drawn to a Fabergé easter egg sitting on the mantelpiece.

'I thought you'd like that,' he said gaily, 'but come let's get you cleaned up. You smell like you've been living in a sewer.'

I put the egg down reluctantly, the workmanship and the luminous pink, guilloché enamel were dazzling. The urge to keep it was very strong. I looked around me. I'd been in this house several times before, but I had never felt such a strong feeling of envy. I wanted *this* and I wanted it badly!

'So Charley. Still happy surrounded by all your meaningless treasures?' I asked, as I looked around, my eyes picking out the items of value. Charley gently pushed me upstairs to the bathroom and gave me some of his clothes.

'Leave yours in this bag. I'll get the maid to burn them,' he told me.

Later, when I was clean and dressed, we sat down in the study, Charley with a cigar and a Cognac.

'Are you still sponging off your parents and shirking your responsibilities while supporting a struggling painter that really should give up and find something better to do?' I asked, as I sat moping in my chair.

'Miaow, Cameron!' Then, in a soft voice, 'I suppose I can't blame you for being bitter.'

'How was America?' I asked, trying to sound friendlier.

'Mummy wouldn't cave. She rather likes this drab girl, as she's the daughter of her friend Rosemary Watson – of the Pennsylvania Watsons. So both Mummy and Dad wanted this marriage. It was that or no more money and Paris,' he told me.

'So you got married?' I asked, surprised.

'Yes. And it is *awful*. She hasn't stopped complaining since we got back here! The food is bad, the French are rude, the streets are dirty and so on and so on. Oh, Cameron! I am so glad you are back in the land of the living!'

'Well, I wouldn't go that far, Charley,' I murmured, fidgeting with the buttons on my suit jacket.

'We need to cheer you up. We need to have some serious fun!' he said happily.

'Will your new wife be joining us?' I asked him with a wink.

'God, I hope not! Now Cameron, I want to show you something.' We got up and made our way down to his garage. He switched on the light and there before me was a brand new beauty of a car. I was pleased to see he had the latest Packard model, the 343 Dietrich convertible in dark green, with white wheel trims and a white, soft-top roof. It was majestic. I thought again of sinking my teeth into Charley's neck and driving off with this beauty until the sun came up. Charley opened the garage door and we got into his car. We sped off around Paris, eventually stopping on a quiet street in the 6th arrondissement close, to the Jardin du Luxembourg, but also to the more lively Montparnasse area. We went into one of the buildings and walked up to the 3rd floor. Before we went in, I asked if there were any mirrors.

'Aha! No. I remembered that! Cameron, my friend, you are

really not doing well with getting over all your issues,' he said, shaking his head as he opened the door. He led me around a comfortable two-bedroom apartment and told me I could stay there. He had decorated it simply but tastefully. There was a sofa, two comfortable chairs and a coffee table, and he had invested in a rather nice art deco drinks cabinet and matching cupboard. The kitchen had space for a small dining table and some chairs. There were two bedrooms, each with a double bed, wardrobe and a couple of bedside cabinets. I liked the lamps on them and he told me he had bought them at Tiffany's in New York on his last trip home. I was also pleased to find that there was a large, windowless cloakroom just off the hallway. I would be able to spend the daytime there in comfort.

As he showed me around, Charley explained, 'I got this place to get away from Hope now and then. It's just so much easier to crash here after a night out than to go home and deal with the nagging.'

'Good grief, man! How long have you been married?' I asked him.

'Five weeks too long,' he said, sighing deeply.

'I'm getting rather curious to meet this woman now. No one can be that bad!'

'Yes, I know, I'm sure she *is* a sweet girl, I just…'

We went back into the study and Charley started rooting around in the drinks cabinet and pulled out a bottle of whisky. 'Listen Cameron. Stay here as long as you like, just put me up now and then.' He offered me a whisky, which I refused.

'Of course,' I said. 'It's your place.'

'Anyway, I hope to do most of my partying with you anyway, so you can carry me back. Or do you drink too these days?' he asked.

'Only in moderation and never in public.'

'Yes, you are rather an oddball with your food, drink and mirrors,' he said, laughing. He sat down with his whisky.

'Wait until I tell you my latest phobia, well it isn't so much a phobia as a skin condition. I can't tolerate sunlight at all,' I told him with a big smile. Maybe if I treated it all like a big joke, just some oddball things I did, Charley would let me be.

'Allergy? I thought it was due to the war,' he asked me, surprised.

'It started out that way, but now my skin actually blisters in sunlight. I think since I've spent so much time in the dark my skin can't handle the light anymore.'

'Why didn't you ever tell Hélène?' he asked me, looking troubled.

'I couldn't. She already found the not eating in public very hard to deal with so to add that I couldn't be out in daylight, I don't think she would have taken it well. In retrospect, she didn't take my not telling her well either,' I said wryly and I got up to look around the apartment again.

'Sorry I brought it up, Cameron. I suppose you have a right to be an oddball, you've been through a lot with the war and then Hélène. I imagine living on the streets can't be easy either,' he said, quietly.

'There is something else you need to know about me,' I said, pulling out some identity papers, 'I now go by the name of François Beaufort.'

Surprised, Charley looked at the fake identity papers. 'Why are you pretending to be French?'

'I lost my papers and frankly I don't want to be found. It was just easier to get some French papers.' It was no problem for me to pretend to be French; people were genuinely surprised when I told them I wasn't.

'Are you a wanted man?' Charley asked me, eyeing me suspiciously.

'Probably am now for having stolen papers,' I joked. I wanted the conversation to end there so I distracted Charley by asking him if I could have a shot of his car. We went downstairs and he let me take the wheel of a machine that must have cost more than my dad probably earned in several years. It was fast and powerful and for the first time in a long while I felt some happiness again.

Charley pulled me back into the light again, metaphorically, and we immersed ourselves in the luxurious and debauched party scene of 1920's Paris. With his wealth and connections, Charley got invited to the most extravagant gatherings and I loved it. He was the life and soul of most of these parties and I thrived in the presence of his sparkling personality. But I was also viewing the world with different eyes now; lust, envy and greed had become my driving forces and I knew I would kill to get what I wanted.

I met Hope a few weeks after I moved into Charley's apartment. As it was a balmy summer's night, Charley and I had chosen a table outside a café and he had ordered a large bottle of champagne, which was like flypaper to the girls in the late 1920s (and I'm sure it still is). There was something irresistible about the stuff and I was soon to find out that it attracted me too.

We asked two comely secretaries, who worked in the city and were enjoying an after work drink, if they wanted to join us and they readily agreed. Suddenly Hope appeared, standing next to our table and crying. She was small, with doll-like but not unattractive features and with lustrous, wavy, auburn hair. If she hadn't been crying, I'd have thought her actually quite pretty.

'Hope! What the hell?' Charley sounded annoyed.

'Oh Charles. I'm so sorry to come out here, but I just received the telegram. I am so, so sorry but your father has died,' Hope sobbed as she handed him the telegram.

Charley read the telegram, then got up and hugged her, but only briefly. He turned to us and said, 'You'll have to excuse me. It appears that I have a funeral to go to.'

'I am so sorry,' we said, almost in chorus.

'Now Cameron, buy the ladies another round and make sure they get home safe.'

He handed me a large wad of cash and told me he'd probably be in America for a few weeks and to take care of myself. Then he and Hope got in a taxi and left for home.

The girls were quite happy to stay and drink another bottle of champagne with me and they got rather drunk. When I suggested going back to my place for a nightcap they readily agreed. With an arm around each girl's waist to hold them up, I walked them to the apartment. Mrs Maréchal, came out into the hallway as we were making so much noise going up the stairs.

'Monsieur Beaufort! Can you please ask your lady guests to be a little quieter. It is two o'clock in the morning!' she said, in a hushed but very angry voice, as she glared up the stairwell at us.

'Sorry, Madame Maréchal,' I said, leaning over the bannister and giving her an apologetic smile.

'And you girls – you should be ashamed of yourselves. Young ladies should not get drunk and visit a gentleman's apartment,' she added which only made the girls giggle louder. Madame Maréchal shook her head and went back to her apartment.

I managed to drag the giggling girls inside and opened another bottle of champagne. It wasn't long before the two of them were sound asleep on the sofa. *Would they feel it if I just had a wee nibble? Where would be the best place to bite and not leave a suspicious mark?* I decided to go for the wrist first on

Sandrine. I punctured the vein with one fang and started drinking, she moaned and tried to move her arm, but was soon sound asleep again.

This was the first time I had drunk champagne-infused blood. It was light and slightly fizzy on the tongue. Really very, very good! I didn't drink too much; about half a litre which any average sized human could spare without any problems. I selected a vein on Séverine's leg and had another fabulous drink. I struggled to pull my fangs out of her shapely leg as she tasted just too good, but I knew I had to show restraint. There had been witnesses, so killing them would certainly get me in trouble. I didn't find it hard to kill humans any more, but I had a strong survival instinct. Killing humans just leads to trouble.

I tried to wake Séverine, as I was feeling very much awake, but she pushed me away drowsily. I felt so alive and awake that I just had to get out of the apartment and walk off some of my energy. I returned to the apartment a few hours later, still buzzing on their blood. I woke the girls an hour before sunrise.

'Now. You girls were a bit accident prone last night,' I told them. 'You Sandrine, were running your arm over a railing and pricked yourself on a nail that was sticking out, and you Séverine stabbed yourself with a corkscrew trying to open a bottle of wine.'

'I did?' asked Séverine, frowning and rubbing her leg.

'Yes. You did. Now, you'd better go home and put some iodine on those cuts. I don't have any in the house, but you shouldn't take risks – that nail was quite rusty.' I kissed them both on the cheek and ushered them out of the apartment. I was pleased with myself. Champagne-flavoured blood without any killing! I had the idea that with small doses like that I might be able to keep my urges in check.

***

Charley stayed in America for two months. When he came back, he looked older and tired.

'Did you get me anything?' I asked, cheerfully.

'Screw you! Did you get *me* anything more like?' he asked, smiling.

'I could make Hope disappear in return for that Fabergé egg if you asked me nicely.'

Charley gave me a quizzical look. Perhaps I had spoken with too much gusto. I quickly went on. 'Anyway. How was America?'

'Of course Mummy wanted me to stay, help my older brother run the business. But Mummy knows I'm no good at running a business and my brother is a serious bore!' He headed straight for the drinks cabinet. Prohibition time America must have been hard for Champagne Charley.

'Did Hope come back with you?' I asked him.

'She insisted. I think the silly girl is actually in love with me,' he said, leaning back in his chair with a large whisky in his hand.

'She's not bad looking. Very dainty and sweet,' I commented.

'Dainty and sweet! A minute ago you were offering to kill her!' he cried in mock horror.

'I said *disappear* not kill. There is a difference,' I said defensively.

'Explain, Cameron. How were you going to make Hope disappear without killing her? I'd like to hear that option,' he said, raising his eyebrows questioningly.

'I could rent a basement and keep her locked up, using her for my own perverted pleasures,' I told him with great glee.

'Good God! The idea of you rogering my wife is almost as

revolting as *me* rogering my wife, so no, we can't do that, Cameron. As you said, she is rather sweet, but somehow I just can't stand being with her.' He helped himself to another glass of whisky.

'That's sad, Charley. Could you not get a divorce now your dad has kicked the bucket?'

'No. Not until Mummy dies too and I think the old dear has a few years left in her yet. Her mother lived till she was 98 and her father made it to a 100. Divorce is really not the done thing in our family. Mind you, neither is drinking, smoking or having fun.' He downed his drink and we got ready to go out.

We picked up where we had left off with our partying, but I soon became frustrated. Charley never wanted any of the girls to come back to our place. He was the heart and soul of a party, but always remained the perfect gentleman despite getting blind drunk at times. He was happy to go dancing with girls, and buy them champagne all night, but that was it. I was starting to resent him. He had everything – he was alive, married and rich – and he was stopping me getting what I needed.

'I'm a married man and have a reputation to uphold,' he explained one night. 'The American expats talk to each other! You know if my wife caught me sleeping with another woman she'd have grounds for divorce. That can be expensive, and my family would be mortified.'

'I think, if she wanted, she'd have grounds for divorce already,' I replied.

'Well I'm not taking any risks!'

I didn't appreciate until later that Charley desperately wanted just to be himself, but that even from across the Atlantic his powerful family had an iron grip on him. He knew exactly what he could get away with and what he couldn't.

For the moment, he chose to divert the conversation to a different subject: me. 'Tell me Cameron. How do you stay so young-looking?' He looked me over with great interest. 'I mean, I spotted my first grey hair this morning and I'm sure I'm younger than you. You fought in the Great War, that must make you at least 27, but you look about 20.'

'I lied about my age when I signed up, so I've just turned 26. But not going out in sunlight does keep your skin looking younger,' I quipped.

Soon my frustration boiled over and I started to take it out on Charley. I blamed him squarely for keeping me off my new favourite food and away from adult fun. Of course, there was always adult fun to be had out there, but I preferred not to pay for it. If Charley went to the bathroom while we were out, I would tell the girls that he was married and only after one thing. Mostly, this resulted in Charley getting slapped on his return, or in a glass being emptied over his head.

One night, astonished as he wiped the dripping champagne from his face, he asked 'What on earth did you tell them?'

'Charley, you frightful bore. You never have any fun with these girls, anyway. I might as well create a bit of entertainment for myself,' I grinned mischievously, but it grew nastier. On another night, while we were out in a bar, I went over to a big guy and told him that Charley had said some rude things about the shape of his girlfriend's bottom. The man was quite drunk and didn't need much of an excuse to start a fight. Foppish dandy that Charley was, the fight didn't last long and I soon carried him, his nose bleeding heavily, back to the apartment. I cleaned him up and couldn't help myself from licking my fingers.

'Cameron! Eew! Did you just lick my blood off your fingers?' he cried, in disgust.

'Eh? No! Em, I think it was mine,' I flustered, 'I've got a cut too.' I disappeared into the kitchen to wash my hands. His blood had tasted disturbingly good.

A few nights later, Charley invited me over to the house. I didn't often go there now he had a wife to avoid, but according to Charley there was a dinner party he couldn't get out of. Hope had invited some dull, important people and he'd decided he simply had to have his drinking buddy there to survive the evening. Hope opened the door. She was wearing a long evening dress of pink taffeta and I had to admit that she looked radiant. My eyes were drawn immediately to the small diamond and pearl tiara she wore with its matching necklace.

'Hope darling! You look wonderful,' I said as I stuck out my hand. 'It's so rare one has the occasion to wear a tiara these days, but you, dear, should wear one every day!'

'Cameron! So nice to finally get to know you a little better,' she said, politely but without a hint of a smile.

Frankly, I wasn't surprised at her frosty reception. She must've hated me for leading her husband astray and keeping him out partying all night. She was a very polite and well-mannered wee girl, though, so she wasn't going to create a scene or make me uncomfortable. Maybe if Charley had liked her more we could all have been friends. I didn't understand why he didn't try harder.

She held out her hand reluctantly and I took it. There was something different about her. She looked at me worriedly when I didn't let go of her hand. I could feel and smell her blood, but there was a faint hint of something else.

'Hope... there are two of you,' I said finally, letting go of her hand. Charley had now come into the hallway behind us and had heard the last words.

'What do you mean, there are two of you?' he asked, looking puzzled.

Hope turned her gaze downwards and softly said that she wasn't sure yet, but she thought that she was with child. She asked us not to tell anyone, as she hadn't been to see a doctor.

The dinner party was indeed full of terribly dull people and I couldn't wait to leave. Charley seemed unusually chipper and was very attentive to Hope. Later, in his study, he told me it was because he was relieved. Mummy was apparently still threatening to withhold the inheritance if there weren't any babies – he had done his duty and now he could concentrate on fully ignoring his wife.

'You never used to be so cruel,' I told him.

'Neither were you, but life and love do terrible things to a man,' he said quietly. I left him to his dull party and went out looking for some stray dogs, but my body was screaming out for champagne-infused human.

Charley really was spoiling my dinners. We didn't go out together all the time, but when we did he poured champagne into the girls, getting them ready for a perfect meal, and then deprived me of taking them home as he was too drunk to find his way back to the apartment alone. I often had to carry him up the stairs when we got there too.

I began to get more and more inventive in finding ways to hurt him and I think Charley was beginning to realise my mischief had become dark, but he pretended not to notice. I had recently broken into a pharmacy and had come across a large supply of sleeping pills. Crushing a tablet and mixing it in with the champagne helped things along nicely. The girls didn't feel a thing and it only made me a tad groggy.

Charley had drunk rather a lot one night and could barely stand. We had to say goodbye to two nice girls who looked particularly tasty and I was not best pleased. I led Charley to a park bench in the Jardin du Luxembourg and left him there to sleep it off. He came home the next morning missing his jacket, wallet and everything else of value he'd had on him. Someone had robbed him blind while he was sound asleep.

'Why did you leave me there, Cameron?' he asked, hurt. 'That was a horrible thing to do.'

'Maybe it'll teach you not to drink so much,' I snapped at him.

'What's going on with you? I thought we were friends?' He looked very down and I realised that I had to stop this behaviour and find a solution. As much as I lusted after women and craved blood, Charley was great company and a generous host. I wanted him around.

'I'm sorry Charley,' I sighed. 'It won't happen again.'

He looked at me, unconvinced. He didn't understood why I was being so horrible to him.

'It's just that sometimes I need to bring a girl back here and have my way with her. And you're always... such a gentleman.'

'There is nothing wrong with being a gentleman, Cameron.'

'You have a wife, but I am young and single and I have needs!' I finally burst out. 'I'm sorry I've taken my frustration out on you but things have to change!'

Charley remained in a terrible strop with me and didn't talk to me for a good few days, but then the tedium of his home life drove him back to my doorstep again.

On our next night out, he let me bring the car so I could drop him off at home and do as I pleased with the girls. Having that big car at my disposal would help things along nicely! Girls loved being in a flash car and would hardly refuse a lift and a nightcap at the apartment.

'Hope isn't happy about my coming home drunk, but she's happier with me home at night, no matter in what state, now she's pregnant. No, things are definitely better. She has even agreed to separate bedrooms,' Charley told me jovially one night. *Maybe the woman snores,* I thought innocently.

When it finally happened, Charley took well to fatherhood, spending a lot more time at home with Hope and little Joseph. Maybe there was hope for their marriage yet. I began to miss him. Chasing women is a lot less fun without a wingman, but I managed. Charley had taught me about fashion and how to dress and a new, more dashing and confident Cameron started to emerge. I became quite the debonair man about town and women fell for it. I thought I was becoming like Charley, but I totally lacked his compassion or generosity.

Then, in October 1929, everything changed. The roaring twenties ended with a big ugly crash. Charley had to sell up and get back to America; the family business was in serious trouble and his mother demanded he come home. Charley was inconsolable and cried uncontrollably when the new owner drove his prized Packard away.

Hope seemed to take it all quite well, busying herself with packing and keeping a lively toddler in check. She'd never really settled in Paris and was pleased to be going back to the States. I felt somewhat tearful too when I went over to their house about a week before they were due to leave, and saw her packing away the beautiful pink Fabergé egg. Charley took me into the study and sat me down.

'We do have to sell a lot of our things but I would like you to have this,' he said, handing me some documents.

'You don't have to give me anything, old boy. I'll take care of myself,' I said, surprised. He'd already given me so much.

'I don't want you to end up on the streets again,' he said and he looked concerned. He had given me the deeds to the apartment. His lawyer had signed it into my name. I was stunned. My own apartment! This was very generous indeed.

'Christ, Charley! I'll never be able to repay you,' I said, shaking his hand.

'I'll be happy just to think of you living the high life, while I'm stuck behind a desk,' he said, with a big sigh.

'Have they ended prohibition yet?' I asked.

'No, but with bootleggers running rampant they might change their minds soon.' He raised his glass. 'Here's hoping!'

Soon, all the crates where packed and ready to be shipped. Charley and Hope came to see me the night before their departure. Charley didn't say much and seemed depressed. Hope was excited and told me she was looking forward to seeing all her friends and family again. Later, I walked them down to their taxi. Charley couldn't bring himself to say goodbye to me and sat in the taxi sulking. Hope lingered on the pavement, and then suddenly she hugged me and whispered in my ear, 'You know he *loves* you.'

I pulled back surprised, but she quickly got in the taxi and then they were gone for good. Of course! *How could I have been so naïve?* Everything suddenly made sense and I felt desperately sad for him. We'd both been hiding a secret that we couldn't tell the world.

I never saw Charley again, but we wrote to each other occasionally. Reading between the lines I sensed he was very unhappy, but his family needed him so he took up the job in the family firm and worked there every day until his death. We lost touch during the Second World War and it wasn't until much later that I found out he had died of a heart attack in 1955, aged just 56. His son Joseph went on to run the family firm and became one of the richest men in New York state.

***

The 1930s arrived and Europe was getting darker. Charley had gone, the parties slowly fizzled out and times grew harder for everybody. People were leaving Germany and coming to Paris to get away from the new threat they called the Nazis. It was all anyone talked about in the cafés back then.

I'd never been interested in politics and I wasn't going to start now. Paris had lost its sparkle and I became bored. It had quite literally lost its sparkle; the riches were leaving the city and Europe. On my nightly burglary sessions, I found fewer pieces and those I did were of lesser quality. That meant that during the daytime there was less loot to assess and at times the days felt frustratingly long.

I decided to improve myself culturally, and started Homer's *Iliad* five times. Then I tore out the pages, stuck them together and folded myself a pirate's hat. Crime novels were more my thing as there was always something I could learn from them. The only good thing was the emergence of Swing and I had some good times going to the clubs and throwing girls around on the dance floor. I liked the music, but not the stupid Zazous that were into it. I mean, frankly, carrying a bloody umbrella everywhere even on a fair day is a dumb fashion statement.

When I went out I heard someone say that there might be another war, but at home it had already started. Madame Maréchal couldn't help but criticise my behaviour and had a snide remark ready every time she saw me. I had started to call her by her first name, Madeleine, and used the familiar 'tu' form instead of the customary and formal 'vous'. It infuriated her.

Sometimes when I was bored during the day I coaxed Lulu, Madame Maréchal's little poodle, into my apartment. The wee dog amused me. One of its hind legs was paralysed, I think, and when it walked it stumbled to the right at every other step. It looked so cute! Just like a newborn lamb learning how to walk. She was with me one day when I heard Madeleine calling out for her, but I was hungry and Madeleine's shrill voice annoyed me. Lulu became revenge and a quick meal, but then I was quickly bored again. Playing with your food was often short-lived entertainment at best.

I was fed up with my neighbours, the poverty and the depressing mood around me. When war loomed, I wasn't sorry to leave Paris.

Chapter 9: Rashid

'Nice! That's a great piece. I should get a buyer for that no problem. I know this guy that collects van Cleef and Arpels in Moscow,' said Rashid as he put his loupe back in his pocket and leaned back in his seat. Rashid was my jewellery dealer and had come to see me on my yacht where I was showing him the items I had stolen from Fifi's owner.

'Is it likely to be reported?' he asked me.

'Not sure. It is possible with it being such a valuable piece,' I said, pouring him a cup of coffee.

'I don't think my buyer would be too bothered. I'm certain that buying stolen goods isn't his only shady practice,' he said, looking through some of the other pieces.

We were discussing our transaction sitting in my windowless office, which allows me to work or surf the internet during the day. Next to it is a windowless bedroom. Hollywood films would have you believe we sleep in coffins during the day, but I liked to have my yacht as normal as possible. I can't speak for all vampires, but I couldn't imagine any of them going in for this coffin lark. Why on earth would anyone want to lie in a wooden box? It looks so comfortable.

'So, you're staying here for a while,' Rashid asked me.

'Certainly until the end of the season,' I replied.

Rashid was in his forties and a diet of curries and very little exercise had made him rather fat. 'I'll pay the money into your account when I've sold the pieces, which should be in a few weeks. I think I can get you about 250,000 euros.' He placed the brooch back in its box and put it with the other jewellery in his briefcase. 'I'll come to your yacht here next month then?' he asked me.

'Yes. I should have some more pieces for you by then. The

Cannes Film Festival is always a good time.'

Rashid got up and left with the briefcase. I had met him in Afghanistan where his family's wealth had made him an obvious kidnap target. Over the years, George had built up a reputation as the go-to guy for kidnapping cases when you didn't want to involve the authorities or had no faith in them. No one cared who or what we were as long as we got their loved one back. When it finally happened to Rashid, his father contacted us.

In 2007, there was still a lot of fighting between the Nato forces and the Taliban. We'd not only have to get in undetected by the kidnappers, we'd have to avoid both fighting parties too. But Rashid's family suspected it was the Taliban that had taken him anyway and that they wanted the ransom to fund their war effort. They didn't trust the Taliban to release him as he was a foreigner to their land and dressed in western clothes. His parents were afraid he would be killed.

Going into Afghanistan wasn't easy, especially as we couldn't operate in daylight. I relied on George to keep me hidden during the day; as an ex-SAS man, he was very useful to have along for the job.

We'd found out that Rashid was being held in a compound west of Kandahar. At night we were able to travel at great speed and unseen, as my vampire-improved vision meant I could drive fast without headlights. We drove our Land Rover into the compound before the kidnappers got off a single shot. In the confusion and the dark I managed to get to most of the captors quickly. George secured the hostage until I had dealt with the last of them. Whilst it hurt when I got shot, I'd be all right as long as my head didn't get separated from the rest of me. I healed quickly after a feeding frenzy too, so I enjoyed myself that night, as there was no need for restraint. We later covered up my work with some gunshots. I wondered if anyone had ever questioned why every single one of the guards was shot in the neck.

'You've been shot. Are you ok?' asked Rashid when he saw me with five chest wounds.

'It stings like a bitch, but I'll walk it off,' I said airily. I was well fed and in an excellent mood despite the pain. I felt the wounds healing as we got back in the Land Rover – Rashid would have to be told why the wounds were no longer there. When we did reveal my secret, he was surprised, but so relieved to be out of there, he didn't seem to care.

We met with Rashid and his family a few days later and I was in an extremely bad mood. George had been away all day at their compound concluding the money side of things with Rashid's father, so I had been left by myself in our small, windowless hotel room in downtown Karachi with no internet access. I had to amuse myself by catching cockroaches. Even though I was in a foul mood, I knew I had to bring my A game to the meeting and be as charming as I could. These were the clients after all.

The family's compound was large and well-secured with high walls, barbed wire and even an armed guard. Inside I was introduced to what must have been 20 or so aunties and uncles.

'Eat, eat,' they said, as a multitude of curried dishes were put before us.

'I'm ever so sorry, but I haven't been able to keep anything down today, that's why I stayed in a dark room all day,' I explained, as the aunties flocked around me and offered me all sorts of foods and potions that were sure to make me feel better. 'I'm ok, honestly. If I just don't eat or drink anything I'll be fine tomorrow,' I said pushing all offered foods away.

'You must drink. You must stay hydrated,' they insisted. At this point Rashid stepped in and told them to leave me be.

They looked hurt, but I soon distracted them with talk about gems and jewellery, which was the family business.

'You're not going to try anything are you,' whispered George in my ear as I admired a stunning ruby necklace that dated from the Mughal period.

'Course not!' I hissed back.

'So Rashid. How did you come to be in Afghanistan?' I asked him.

'I was sourcing some turquoise, Mr Blair,' he explained.

'Call me Cameron, please, and yes, Afghanistan does have some very fine turquoises, but I believe they're currently using dynamite to blast open whole hillsides to mine them.'

'Nobody is happy about that, or that the Taliban controls the mines, but I have demand, so I try and find supply,' he told me.

'Seems like you're willing to take a few risks. War-torn Afghanistan is a dangerous place to do business,' I said, picking up and admiring some more beads he had put in front of me.

'Sometimes big risks – but look at the quality of these turquoises and then this Badahkshan lapis lazuli!' he said enthusiastically, presenting another tray of beads. 'I had done business with the Taliban before, as they control some of the mines, but this time I found a different guy in charge who didn't like the look of me and thought he could make more money by taking me hostage,' he explained, handing me a string of very fine blue beads.

'That lapis is stunning! So, do you think you'll go back there?' I asked.

'Not for a while. I'll go and see if I can do some more trading in Europe.'

'Might be able to help there,' I said, handing him my card.

Rashid's family were grateful and generous, but only

Rashid knew what I was. I discovered he was a pragmatic fellow who operated on the grey side of legal. He was a shrewd businessman and an international jewellery dealer with useful contacts around the world and an instinct for who to trust. I had nurtured many contacts over the years in the criminal underworld, but I was now coming across some very fine pieces of jewellery that were too valuable for my local fence to shift; for such expensive pieces you needed to know serious collectors and shady gem dealers. Rashid knew just such people and he owed me his life.

I had amassed quite a collection of big diamond-set pieces by the time I met Rashid and our meeting turned out to be lucrative for us both. As he took my collection away, he asked me if I wanted to keep any of it, as I had talked about it with great passion and knowledge, but I told him no. I had learned to appreciate beauty but then to let it go; I had learned not to get attached to people or things – when you live for all eternity you can't afford to be sentimental.

Chapter 10: Ivana

I had been avoiding Hélène's friends as much as I could since I re-emerged and started living in Charley's apartment, but as Charley and I were often drinking in the Montparnasse district it was inevitable that I would bump into some of them eventually. I couldn't stand their looks of pity and their commiserations, but Charley was usually at hand to chase them away with a catty comment.

Ivana was harder to get rid of. She hadn't been a friend exactly, as she and Hélène both worked as artist's models and competition amongst the girls was fierce.

'Charley, Cameron! So nice to see you,' she said one night when she spotted us in a bar.

'Ivana, darling. You look fabulous,' said Charley, and he got up to kiss her on both cheeks. As she turned to me, he simulated vomiting. I smiled and kissed her too.

'So boys, what are we celebrating?' she asked, pointing at the bottle of champagne in front of us.

'*We* are celebrating a boy's night out,' said Charley pointedly.

'That's an awfully big bottle of champagne and I am one of the boys, aren't I?' she asked, smiling sweetly.

'I wish you were a boy, then you'd probably leave us alone,' said Charley, not looking happy.

'Don't be nasty Charley. We all know you and Cameron are sitting here waiting to pick up girls anyway, so why not pour little old me a glass,' she said with a forgiving smile.

Charley pulled up a chair reluctantly and asked the waiter for another glass.

Like a lot of Russians, Ivana had come to France when the Bolsheviks took power. She was the mistress of some baron or other and he took her with him to Paris. She had been a great beauty in her day with her long, jet-black hair and noble features, but she was no spring chicken by the time they arrived in Paris and the baron soon tired of her and kicked her and her fur coat out on to the street.

She'd managed to find work as a model, sometimes staying on as the artist's mistress and housekeeper too. When I met her again in 1928 she was in her early forties and her looks were fading. Her last boyfriend had kicked her out and I knew she'd be finding it hard to make ends meet. She'd be on the hunt for a new man to keep her and Charley would be a prime candidate. She might even have considered me, though she knew I wasn't rich. I felt sorry for the woman, but I wasn't going to let her into our life.

Charley made hints that he wanted to leave and I thought about it for a moment, but then remembered I had a sleeping tablet in my pocket and was feeling rather hungry. 'You go ahead. I'll just take Ivana home – you know how dangerous the streets of Paris can be,' I said, gleefully.

'Really Cameron? Her?' he hissed, in my ear as he left.

Ivana looked rather pleased with herself, walking on the arm of a chap that looked young enough to be her son. Charley would no doubt tell me I was a slapper and that this was a new low, but I didn't care. She had drunk champagne and I was hungry. She took me to a rundown old building and pushed the front door open. Behind it was a dark hallway with a staircase. I don't think anyone living there could afford to fix the light or give the place a coat of paint.

Ivana lived on the second floor in a small, one-room apartment with a tiny kitchen and bathroom. The place was a filthy mess; clothes and dirty dishes were scattered all over the floor and I don't think the windows had ever been cleaned. She picked up two glasses from the floor and took them into the kitchen to give them a wash. She didn't apologise for the mess and I was almost tempted to start tidying up. Instead I sat on her bed, as it was the only thing not covered in stuff. Under the covers something moved and I jumped up.

'That will be Monet,' she said, laughing at the fact that I was startled.

A large, white tomcat crawled from under the covers and stretched its body. I have never been a fan of cats; it's their expressions. They have a look on their faces as if to say *So, vampire boy! I know what you are and I don't give a shit*. They know they taste horrible and as a vampire you make that mistake only once, as it takes days to get the putrid taste out of your mouth. Monet looked at me mockingly and rubbed himself against my leg. Blasted cat was getting hair all over my nice black trousers.

'He likes you. He normally doesn't like anybody. You must be a good person – cats can feel that,' she said as she handed me a glass of wine and disappeared into the bathroom. Silly human thinking they understand their pet. Monet knows exactly what I am and takes great delight in letting me know how much he despises me. But two can play at that game!

'Excellent, Monet,' I said to him. 'We can send mummy to sleep now.' He gave me a look as if to say, *Yeah, whatever!*

When she emerged from the bathroom, Ivana had changed into a Japanese-style silk peignoir and had loosened her long black hair. In the semi-darkness of her room she still looked beautiful so I got up and walked over to her. I slipped my hand into her gown and discovered that her breasts were still round and firm. Her pink nipples hardened to my touch as I explored her body. I ran my hand between her legs and she bit my neck in pleasure. *You like to bite too!* I thought and it got me very excited. I picked her up and leaned her against the wall as I covered her neck and throat with kisses. She moaned and put her legs around me.

'Gosh, you are a strong boy,' she whispered, admiringly as I carried her to the bed and then took off my clothes. There was nowhere to put them so I had to drop them on the filthy floor. Monet came straight over and turned round a few times on top of them, then lay down, curled his paws under him and stared at me with narrowed eyes, which I thought gave him a smug expression. I'm sure he was trying to put me off doing unspeakable things to his mistress. I shot him a filthy look but not many things put me off doing unspeakable things and I soon had Ivana purring with delight. When we were finished, I was really hungry so I went to hand her the glass of wine with the sleeping tablet in, but she was already rummaging around in her handbag from which she pulled out a reefer.

'Have you ever smoked marijuana, Cameron?' she asked.

'Can't say I have.'

She lit the thing and took a deep breath full of smoke and exhaled slowly. She then handed it to me. I was pleased she had picked up her glass and was drinking the wine. I took a careful puff and waited. It wasn't very good and had quite a sharp taste. I had never been much of a smoker and I didn't like this stuff.

'Deep breath. It will be good, trust me,' she encouraged.

I took another puff, drawing the smoke deep into my lungs and it gave me a coughing fit. I handed her the reefer back hoping she wouldn't ask me to take another puff. She took another drag herself and then stubbed the thing out on a dirty plate.

'I can't afford to smoke it all at once.' She yawned and I could see the pill was starting to have an effect. A moment later she was sound asleep on her back, snoring loudly. I found a nice vein in her arm and finally had my dinner. I was suddenly feeling quite tired too, probably a combination of the sleeping pill-infused blood and the marijuana. So I lay on the bed next to her, just to have a rest for a moment.

I woke up suddenly, and felt my skin burning.

Shit! I'd fallen asleep and now it was daylight! I was trapped with this woman and her cat in a filthy room. I dashed to the window and pulled the curtains, then I cowered in the darkest corner with a blanket wrapped around me. I was feeling mighty strange and uneasy. Monet came over and sat in front of me.

'So there you are, vampire boy. Trapped until nightfall,' he said to me.

'Why can you talk?' I asked him, amazed at this suddenly speaking cat.

'Silence! I only have the strength to say a few words. At nightfall the vampire slayer will come for you and cut off your head with his sword,' he told me in a pompous and serious voice.

'What vampire slayer? How does he know I'm here?' I asked, alarmed.

'Big experienced slayer with a huge sword,' Monet giggled. 'He knows, because I told my mate Gaston, who told Minette, who told Belle. And Belle is the slayer's cat.'

'What does he look like? Can I escape?' I asked panicking.

'You must run as soon as it gets dark. Now I need my snooze,' and Monet strolled off and jumped up on the bed. He curled himself into a ball and closed his eyes.

Ivana woke up at eleven. She stretched, put on her peignoir then got a fright when she saw me sitting in the corner.

'Oh! Hi, Cameron. You're still here... do you want some coffee?' she asked.

'No. And please don't open the curtains,' I pleaded.

'Come on! Your hangover can't be that bad! I hardly saw you drink a drop.'

She started moving towards the window, so I jumped up and threw her towards the bed. She landed on top of Monet who hissed and jumped away.

'You spoiled my snooze, you bastard,' he growled in passing.

'Jeez Cameron! Are you alright?' she asked. I went back to my corner and pulled the blanket back over me.

'No I'm not. What sort of stuff was that you made me smoke last night? Now I'm trapped here and someone is coming to kill me tonight. Monet grassed me up,' I said, nervously rocking back and forth under my blanket.

'Who is coming to kill you? And what about Monet?' she asked raising her eyebrows.

'Never mind. What *was* that you gave me? I feel very strange.'

'It was only marijuana. I've never seen anyone reacting to it this badly. Are you sure you don't want a coffee,' she asked looking at me with concern.

'No. Just leave me here in the dark,' I said pulling the blanket further up to my chin.

Ivana showered and got dressed. She washed a cup and a plate and made herself breakfast then sat next to me on the floor and tried to feed me some toast.

'It will wear off soon, Cameron, don't worry,' she reassured me. 'Marijuana is normally pretty harmless. Did you take anything else?'

In the kitchen, I heard Monet eating his food. He had started to sing an annoying tune.

'Slayer's going to get you, oh, oh, slayer's going to get you!'

He had a terrible, screechy singing voice and he was trying to eat at the same time.

'No, I don't think so. And could you tell Monet to shut up, he's a terrible singer.' I pulled the blanket over my ears.

'Monet? You hear him singing?' she asked, looking alarmed.

'Yes. And not very well at that.' I was now rocking back and forwards holding my hands over my ears. 'Anyhow. I have a job for this afternoon so just let yourself out when you want to.' I knew it was a lie, but I didn't blame her for not wanting to be in the same room as this mad man.

As soon as darkness fell, I ran to our apartment, but because Charley wasn't there I ran to the station and got on the first train out of Paris, which was the sleeper to Marseilles. A couple of hours into the trip my head started to clear and I felt like myself again. I got off at the next station and found a place to hide for the day. Getting back to Paris took two days, as the return trains couldn't get me all the way in one night. When I reached the apartment, Charley was there waiting.

'What happened? Where have you been for the last four days?' he asked, worried.

'Ivana gave me marijuana. It didn't agree with me.'

'Really? It's mostly pretty harmless,' he said, amazed.

'Well not to me. It makes me paranoid in the extreme,' I said and disappeared into the bathroom.

The next time we saw Ivana she said hi and that she was in a terrible rush and she hastily went on her way.

'Good God, Cameron! I think you dodged a bullet there. I thought she'd be a real clinger. What did you do to the old girl?' he asked.

'I told her that her cat was a terrible singer,' I explained cheerfully, adding another amusing quirk to my already extensive repertoire.

'And was he?' asked Charley, bemused.

'Worst singer I ever heard,' I said, and I wasn't joking.

I had become very aware of my good looks and how they got me things. When I'd arrived in Paris I had lived like a down and out until Hélène had taken me under her wing. She had dressed me and styled me as she did herself, as an impoverished artist, and it had worked as we made our way into the art collectors' world.

Then Charley had taken me under his wing and I had grown to admire and resent him in equal measure. I wanted to be him. He'd taught me everything there was to know about fashion and how to be the well-dressed man about town, but I wasn't Charley and couldn't afford his tailor. I knew what to look out for though and if I spotted a snazzy suit in my size, I would follow it home and it would disappear into my closet the next night. I told Charley that I now worked as a metro driver. He had no clue about how much money metro drivers made and he didn't question the growing wardrobe or the fact that I suddenly seemed to have a lot more cash.

Older women, in particular, responded to the well-dressed, handsome young man I'd become. Through Charley's continued presence on the party circuit, I encountered many wealthy, older women who were pleasantly surprised at my new look. They occasionally asked me if I would accompany them to a party or an exhibition and I'd shamelessly admit to having nothing to wear. Then something would just turn up in a nice, expensive box.

I didn't mind older women; they had experience and I liked that. I had something to sell and they didn't mind paying for it. Charley didn't like it at all.

'First Ivana and now Mrs Taylor and Mrs Warner. You're turning into a right hussy!'

'They're nice women and they buy me stuff, look Mrs

Warner bought me these cufflinks,' I said showing off my latest gift.

'I could give you money if you're that hard up,' snapped Charley

'Now where would be the challenge in that?' I asked calmly. I liked beautiful things and I didn't care how I acquired them.

'I don't like what you are becoming. You're cold and calculating,' he told me with a disapproving look.

'Nonsense. Everyone's happy with the arrangement. Women use their looks to their advantage all the time. Why can't I?'

Charley leaned back, smoking, and gave me a long hard stare. 'You know your problem Cameron? You're just too handsome for your own darn good.'

I didn't care that he thought that was a bad thing. In my mind, you couldn't possibly be too rich or too handsome and I had no intention of letting anything get in the way of my gathering treasure or feeding.

Chapter 11: Yvette

In 2011 I staged a break-in to steal some mirrors. I'm sure the missing mirrors had the neighbours puzzled for days. Why would anyone have forced open a door to unscrew and steal some worthless mirrors from a lift?

I had met Yvette a few times at various parties and admired the large, emerald ring on her finger. Sometimes she wore the matching necklace and earrings. She also had a Yorkshire terrier, which I had to admit was my favourite doggy food. Yvette would be worth taking a few risks for. The last time we'd met, she had invited me back to her apartment. She'd drunk a lot of champagne and kept insisting.

'You have to meet Cleo.'

'Who is Cleo?' I asked.

'She is my adorable Yorkshire terrier, almost as adorable as you.'

'Yvette darling, I'm honoured to be more adorable than a little dog.'

'You are!' she purred drunkenly.

'I can't tonight, but I'm sure I'll pay the two of you a visit one day. I do have to meet the dog that is almost as cute as me.' I loosened her arms from my neck and promised I would go with her next time. Leaving a party with her would be far too risky. I found out which party she was attending next and since it was one I wasn't invited to, I waited for her outside and followed her home. When she reached her apartment she dropped her bag as she was looking for her keys and nearly fell over trying to pick it up.

Ah! Champagne! I smiled.

'Yvette! What are you doing here' I said, walking up to her and pretending to just be passing.

'Cameron, darling! Hi! I live here. What are you doing here?' She was surprised but she seemed pleased to see me.

'I just left a party and I'm trying to find my way back to the marina. I don't think I'm doing too well as I've been walking for an hour and I'm shattered,' I told her.

'Oh you poor thing! Well you must come up for a drink then.'

I agreed and followed her up to the front door. It opened on to a marble hallway with some post boxes and a lift.

'Can you believe that some guy broke into our building and stole the mirrors from our lift?' she said as we got in.

Her apartment was on the top floor, right on the Boulevard de la Croisette and had a stunning view over the Golfe du Juan.

'Well look at that. The marina is right there. I can even see my yacht from here,' I said with mock astonishment.

'And this is Cleo. She's a little shy,' Yvette said, picking up a small Yorkshire terrier.

I took the little Yorkie from her and walked around the apartment, asking her about the artwork on the walls. I felt the little dog quivering in my arms. I stroked her, trying to calm her down. *I think she is on to me!*

'Champagne, darling?' she offered, holding up a bottle of Veuve-Cliquot.

'Yes please, and could you do me an enormous favour and show me that emerald necklace of yours. I've been dying to have a closer look at it,' I said, trying to sound casual.

'I didn't know you were into jewellery,' she said, surprised.

'My mother used to take me jewellery shopping with her. She loved Cartier in Paris and we spent many an afternoon on the Place Vendôme,' I enthused.

As if! My mother only had her wedding band and a wee silver locket my dad had given her. I don't think she'd ever set foot in France let alone Paris. She'd probably never even left Edinburgh. I realised I didn't know when my mother had died.

'You'll like my safe, then, it's just full of Cartier.' Without any hesitation Yvette opened a wall safe behind a painting and started pulling out a multitude of boxes.

'My dad bought my mum lots of stuff, well, any time they had an argument, which was often,' she said, opening some boxes to let me have a look at their valuable contents.

'The emeralds were from the time my mum caught him with the au pair. He knew it had to be something extra special,' she said, holding up the necklace.

I checked my watch and noticed it was four in the morning already. I'd have to make my way back soon and Yvette wasn't just going to let me walk out with her jewellery. She was young and healthy and an apparently sudden death from natural causes was unlikely, but she did have to die; this was too good an opportunity.

I knew with this amount of jewellery there'd be an investigation, so a murder on top of a theft wasn't going to make much difference. I took a scalpel out of my pocket, positioned myself behind her, put my hand over her mouth and easily wrestled her to the ground. I sliced her throat open just wide enough to be able to put my mouth over the incision and drink some of the delicious champagne-flavoured blood.

After a few seconds I pulled away and cut her throat deeper and wider, being careful not to get too much blood on my clothes. I had dressed in black, but her arms and legs were flailing and I must have got quite a lot on me anyway. She soon went limp and I let go and got up. I looked at her body on the ground and saw, jealously, how the puddle of blood around her grew larger.

What a waste! But best not to complicate the crime scene. I washed my hands and face and quickly gathered up the jewellery and put it in a bag. Then I went looking for Cleo. I found her cowering in a corner. She whimpered as I bent down and picked her up.

'Not stupid are you Cleo? You know I'm no friend,' I said as I put the shivering dog in the bag with the jewellery. On the way out, I kicked in the front door so it wouldn't look like Yvette had just let her killer in, then I ran out of the building before anyone came out to investigate. I swam to the boat as I didn't want to get blood traces all over the tender. Cleo whimpered all the way even though I made sure the bag stayed above the water.

I contacted Rashid and asked him to meet me in Monaco. I thought it was best he didn't come to my yacht this time, so we met in a hotel. When he saw what I had brought for him, he looked horrified.

'That's from that murder in Cannes, isn't it,' he asked.

'Yes Rashid. Is it too hot for you?' I'd got away with an awful lot of things for a very long time but I began to realise I might have gone too far this time. The lifestyle was going to my head. 'I'm sorry Rashid. I'll be more careful in future. This will be the last job for a good wee while,' I said.

Rashid could barely bring himself to touch the pieces. He wiped his brow and took a sip of water then got up and paced around the room for a while, wringing his hands and thinking hard. He eventually sat down again and I could see that greed was overcoming his disgust. He had stronger morals than I, but not by much.

'I think I'll take it to Pakistan and break it all up. It'll just be the scrap value, but this is way too hot to go and sell.' He quickly put all the items back in the bag. He looked anxious and didn't want to stay for a moment longer than he had to. We shook hands as he left, but I knew our business relationship had probably come to an end.

Rashid was right to be cautious: the horrific murder and robbery of socialite Yvette Jaunet made international news for several days and was the talk of all the parties for the rest of the season. Many of my acquaintances had known Yvette and they were distraught and nervous. Her circle of friends was rich and influential, so I knew the investigation was going to be very thorough. I had reached for the stars and now I feared a rapid and painful fall.

Chapter 12: George the Elder

It was about two weeks after Yvette's murder that the French police came to see me on my yacht. George led them into my office below decks and offered them coffee. They asked me about Yvette and I confirmed that I had met her at various parties and that we had spoken to each other on a number of occasions. They didn't ask me about the night of the murder, so I knew they were early on in their investigation and were not yet following any firm leads. When they'd left, George came into my office and sat down.

'It was you that killed her, wasn't it?' he accused.

'Yes George. I couldn't see another way. She was young and fit and she knew me. You should have seen her jewellery collection, it was just too good,' I explained.

'There's always another way, Cameron. I wish you'd talked to me first.' He sounded very disappointed.

'I try not to get you involved in my robberies. I know you don't approve,' I said.

'But I *am* involved,' he said, angrily.

'Do you want to leave?' I asked him quietly.

'I don't know Cameron. I do owe you and we've done some great things together, and I'd be lying if I said I didn't enjoy the lifestyle, but you've gone too far this time!'

My meeting with George had been no accident – it was the result of a promise I had made many years before. World War Two was a dangerous time for everyone, me included. *Fucking Nazis!* I swear they had a bitter taste. Like a lot of people, I'd believed the Germans would respect Dutch neutrality so when war loomed I'd made my way north. I'd heard stories about the Nazis and I knew if they invaded Paris it would be a very tricky time to be in the city. I thought it'd be better to live in the countryside again and I knew Holland had a large population of cows and other livestock.

In August 1939, I arrived in Rotterdam, then the largest harbour in Europe. The outbreak of war in September was a disaster for the normally thriving port which relied on the free movement of ships, but I decided to stay anyway. I still believed Holland was the best place to be and I liked the town with its seedy nightlife that catered to the visiting sailors. The rural, cow-filled areas of Brabant to the south weren't too far away.

On the 10th of May, Germany invaded the Netherlands and Rotterdam was thrust into the thick of it. The German attack was unexpected and the city was ill-prepared. From my hiding place in the deep, damp and narrow cellar of an old house, I heard fierce fighting in the distance. I stayed there until I heard bombs rain down. The ground shook and I was thrown up and out into the air. The fires and the afternoon light burned my skin and I ran to find some cover. Many were killed and I was not proud of eating that night, but I was injured and had been stuck in a small, dank place for four days. I knew I would need strength to get out of the hell Rotterdam had become.

As I made my way south I came across some soldiers' bodies and decided to change into a Dutch uniform. A blood-stained uniform might be useful to get me out of a tricky situation and I was rather good at playing dead.

I followed the front into Belgium where the Allies were trying to hold on to the port cities. The German army was advancing fast, totally wrong-footing the Allies with their attack from the north and I followed the advance into northern France. I was back in war-torn France where I had first learned to survive nearly 30 years earlier. I rapidly came to realise that the German invasion was not being halted and that Paris would probably fall into German hands before too long.

Normandy seemed like a good place to ride out the storm; more livestock and fewer Nazis. I stayed there in relative calm and safety until the D-Day landings when my cowshed was suddenly caught up in the middle of a battle. It was bright daylight and I was terrified that the cows and I would be blown to high heavens with me then burning to a crisp out in the summer sunshine. However, miraculously, we all made it through and later that night calm returned to the countryside.

I ventured out and it was that night that I found George the Elder. He had been mortally wounded by German machine-gun fire and was lying in a ditch, bleeding heavily and close to death. He was a British soldier and I estimated that he was about 25. He had short, dark hair and was a good-looking man. I could imagine him making a good wingman. The solitude of being in hiding for so long and keeping out of everyone's way was starting to bother me and I had begun talking to myself and to the cows during my nightly snacks. I was desperate for some conversation and companionship so I drained George of his remaining blood and then brought him back with some drops of my own.

Unlike my maker, I stayed with my victim and told him what I was and who he now was. I had always been annoyed with my maker. Why on earth had he created another vampire and then left the poor bastard to his own devices? *Downright rude if you ask me!*

When I'd finished, George was very quiet and sat with his head in his hands for a long time.

'So how do you die?' he asked me.

'I don't know. Why would you though? I just brought you back!' I said, alarmed.

'Does the sunlight kill you?' he asked.

'I think so, and it hurts like hell.'

'Do you *have* to drink blood?' he asked, and I could see he was mortified by the prospect.

'Again, it hurts like hell if you don't. I've never gone more than 14 days without and frankly I wouldn't want to!' I said.

'It doesn't have to be human blood though?' he asked.

'No. Dog and cow are rather good too. Nazis not so much – they're a bit like cod liver oil. Nasty flavour, but they're meant to be very good for you,' I quipped.

George gave me a wry smile, but then he put his head in his hands again.

Daylight was just an hour away so I took George to my hiding place at the farm. He refused to drink cow, saying he wasn't quite believing it yet.

George wanted to follow the front as he felt it was his duty to continue the war. He didn't mind getting shot – I think he thrived on it – but he refused to use his fangs to kill, preferring a gun instead. After five days he was exhausted and in agony.

'You have to feed, George,' I pleaded.

'Let's just see what happens. It might get better, it might not all be true,' he said, lying down and looking in great discomfort.

But it didn't get better, it got worse and eventually George passed out. I was left with a choice. It looked as though he could die; *should I make him drink against his wishes?* I had been on my own for a long time, I craved companionship almost as much as blood. I had been obsessed with trying to survive and stopping the pain in my stomach at whatever cost. George, from day one, had not wanted to cross that line. I could have left him there and made a new companion, but I wanted to convince him. I was sure he would eventually become like me and kill if the craving became too bad. Vampires are selfish, *if*

I wanted a friend I would bloody well create and have one!

As the cow blood trickled into his mouth, he slowly started to come back. Suddenly, he grabbed the cup and drank till the last drop, then he lay flat on his back and stared at the sky for a long time.

It took George a while to get back to full strength, but when he did, he was still determined to follow the front. The fight had moved on and the Americans were advancing quickly, but while George wanted to go north-west and kick the Germans back over their border, I dreamed of Paris. But there was no stopping him; he was determined to go on fighting.

We thought it best to dress in civilian clothes as it was confusing at times to know which army we were close to and I don't think either side catching us would have been a good thing, though we could have pretended to be French resistance.

George was feeding reluctantly on cow and slowly we started to bond. During the long daylight hours he would tell me about his wife, Gail, and boy, Thomas. He had grown up in London and hoped to get back to his job as an engineer after the war. Even though I was 49 at the time, George seemed way older: a job, a wife and a son – it was all very alien to me.

We ended up in the Ardennes in Belgium after a few months when the advance ground to a halt. It had become bitterly cold which made us both hungry and moody. George and I were working well as a guerrilla army, picking off Germans where we could and avoiding the Allies. One night it was so cold it had perhaps dulled our normally very sharp senses and we ended up with six German guns pointing at us. We raised our hands and let the Germans disarm us. Being armed in civilian clothes was sure to get us shot. I looked over at George and asked him if he was willing to do what was necessary. He slowly nodded his head, knowing he would finally have to cross the line.

The German patrol didn't expect to be so suddenly and so savagely attacked by two unarmed men. If you bite a man's neck and let your fangs rip the flesh, the human is immediately immobilised as their reflex is to put their hands over the wound to stop the blood gushing out. It was very swift and very violent, but George knew instinctively what to do. After the massacre, we ran away through the dense forest and eventually collapsed panting in the snow. George's face was covered with blood and he looked shell-shocked.

We didn't have time to gather our thoughts or discuss what had just happened, as all hell broke loose an instant later. The Ardennes offensive had started, as we later found out. The night sky lit up with blasts of exploding ammunition and we scrambled for cover. There had been a stalemate between the two armies for sometime while we were picking off a few German soldiers here and there when we could, so neither of us had expected this sudden onslaught.

The cold and the anger made George hungry, vicious and reckless. He was upset about the sudden change in the way the war was going and that he had just made his first kills as a vampire. I often had to bury his shot-up body under the snow to protect it from the daylight, but he fed now so he healed quickly.

At times it was tricky to stay hidden during the day and avoid stumbling across allied forces at night, but our superior hearing and excellent night vision gave us an advantage in figuring out if we were near friend or foe. One night, when we were eyeing up a German position, George turned to me and said, 'Cameron, will you promise me something?'

'Depends, George. I'm not like you,' I said, counting the Germans who were just about a hundred meters away.

'You owe me. You brought me back twice,' he whispered.

'Some people would say you owe *me* for that,' I whispered back, assessing whether the position could be taken.

'Are you happy, Cameron?'

'Sometimes.'

'I don't think I can be, being what we are,' said George, wiping snowflakes from his face.

It was a very cold night and surrounded by all the misery and mayhem of war I saw his point.

'This war won't last for ever. We'll go to Paris and live a life you can only dream of. I tell you George, you haven't lived until you've had champagne-soaked floozy,' I said gleefully.

'You really should hear yourself sometimes, Cameron. Those are human beings you're talking about.'

'So are Germans, George, but you were happy enough to board the landing craft to go and kill them,' I snapped back.

'We're *not human* anymore!' George put his helmet on and got a grenade ready. We always picked up what we found and we had got to know the German weapons and ammunitions well by now.

'Wait a while. I still haven't sussed out how many there are,' I warned, but he didn't listen.

He moved forward and threw the grenade at the German position. I sighed and got ready to follow George as he made his frenzied attack, to ensure he'd be safe for daybreak. He was reckless and I was tired of it.

I wanted to head to Paris, which I'd heard had been liberated without much fighting from some local French people. That had been back in August and I was already upset to have missed the celebration parties, but I was sure that people would still be in a festive mood. I also thought that in the post-war chaos it would be easy to move about and establish a new identity.

'Come to Paris with me George. I think you've done quite enough for the war effort already,' I said to him the next night.

'What would I do in Paris? I don't speak French and I'm not ready to leave the boys yet,' he said, as he cleaned a gun.

'The boys would kill you in an instant if they knew what you were. Remember, the Germans are not your only enemy now! And one of the perks of this thing is that you do speak French now. Do you not remember understanding those Germans the other day?' I asked him.

'Yes! How did that happen?'

'You had their blood and you had mine and with it you acquired all our linguistic skills,' I explained.

'Will you do me that favour then, if I come with you to Paris?' he asked again.

'Depends what it is. I still feel you owe me more than I do you.'

'Don't you ever wonder what happened to your family, Cameron?'

'Yes, but I know I could never go back and see them,' I told him.

'No, I couldn't either, but you could, just to see if they were ok. I'm worried about my wife Gail and my boy Thomas. He was only two when I left.'

'Crossing the Channel would be difficult,' I said.

'I'll stay with you in Paris for a year, but you have to promise me you'll look after my boy. You know, help him when you can.'

'What, frighten the bejesus out of the school yard bully and any blokes that come sniffing round your Gail,' I said jokingly.

'Seriously, Cameron. Just make sure they're all right,' he begged.

'Two years in Paris, doing life my way, and I'll be that boy's fairy godmother!' I promised as I shook his hand.

I was convinced that after two years of living the high life, George would get a taste for it and stay.

Chapter 13: Gianluca

I didn't socialise much with George and Roberto. George avoided bars and nightclubs and frankly any place where liquor was involved. Roberto was about my age at that time, but apart from our love of Facebook and chat sites we had little else in common. He was rather scared of me, but he also found me utterly fascinating. That was the problem with all those vampire movies. Roberto was totally intrigued by the fact that I was a vampire, but found it hard to deal with the day-to-day business of my need to feed. He annoyed me at times and I think he would have left if he'd known how often I thought of killing him.

What others would call partying was more like hunting to me – finding the latest clever way of sneaking a few pints without being noticed. I had the impression that Roberto found it pretty distasteful at times. One vice we all three had in common was horse-racing or, more accurately, betting. Roberto's family kept horses and he was very knowledgeable on whether a horse looked good or not. I needed to get close enough to the horses to smell their blood, then I could tell which were ill or too nervous.

In summer, the racetrack at Cagnes sur Mer near Nice, l'Hippodrome de la Côte d'Azur, held evening race meetings and we would occasionally go for a boy's night out. George would always moan that it was trots. In his eyes, it was just unnatural not to let a horse gallop.

'Stupid buggies! And then the poor horse gets disqualified for what comes naturally to him,' he complained.

'The French seem to enjoy it, so come on now, George, let's go and smell the horses and make some money,' I said heading for the paddock.

'Some people speak English here, Cameron, so let's keep your weirdness under wraps,' said George.

Roberto and I soon sniffed out the winner – Goliath Dancer – and we were both confident enough to put a hundred euros each on the nose. George wasn't convinced. 'I've seen that jockey before and he's a right porker. I mean, they've got it all wrong here. Fat jockeys, trots, buggies. Grrr!'

'Let it go, George. Trust us. Goliath Dancer is a winner and the weight of the jockey isn't that important in trots,' I said.

Reluctantly, he put some money down on the horse too and we headed to the stands to watch the race. Goliath Dancer didn't disappoint and the starting price wasn't bad so we walked away with a 600 euro profit each.

We headed back to the paddock to assess the next lot of horses. Roberto fancied a fantastic looking bay colt called Nelson's Revenge, but I could smell that something wasn't right.

'What do you sense, Cameron? He looks in great form,' Roberto asked.

'It's his heart. It doesn't seem right,' I said, taking in another deep breath.

'Do you think it's serious?' asked Roberto.

'I don't know, I'm not a vet. He just smells like a sick animal,' I said.

'Do you think he could die if he runs?' Roberto asked.

'Dunno, but I'm certainly not betting on this one,' I said, concentrating on another horse.

'I think we should tell his trainer,' Roberto said with urgency in his voice – the race was due to start in a few minutes.

'And tell him what, Roberto? Your horse smells funny – he may or may not have a heart condition.' I looked him in the eye sternly to convince him to let it go.

'He's right, Roberto. We can't have Cameron becoming the fucking horse whisperer now. His veterinarian advice would probably be to bleed the horse,' quipped George

'But Monsieur Blair! The horse could die!' Roberto pleaded.

It annoyed me that Roberto always called me Monsieur Blair when he got upset or nervous. 'Let it go! The horse will probably be fine,' I said.

But Roberto cared way too much for horses to let it go. He ran up to the entrance of the paddock and started to make frantic enquiries about the trainer of Nelson's Revenge.

'Silly boy. He'll look like a right idiot in a moment,' said George watching the scene unfold.

Roberto managed to say a few words to the trainer, but was waved away impatiently, and soon the horses were on the track. Roberto walked back over to us.

'What did he say?' George asked, with mildly concealed boredom. He really wasn't an animal person.

'He said the vet checked him over before the race and said he was fine.'

'Well, there you have it. From the horse's mouth. The horse has been checked and it's fine,' I said walking away to the stands. We watched the race even though we hadn't had time with all Roberto's antics to put money on it. Nelson's Revenge came second and did seem to be fine.

'See Roberto? I'm not a vet. He was probably just nervous before the race,' I told him.

'Ok, Cameron. I don't know what you sensed but I got worried for the horse,' said Roberto, shrugging his shoulders.

We had a couple more successful bets and were in high spirits as we waited to cash them in when suddenly, a man grabbed Roberto from behind and spun him.

'How did you know my horse was ill?' he demanded and we could see he was upset.

'But he isn't! He was fine! He came second,' Roberto said, startled.

'He just collapsed in his horse box – massive heart attack, the vet said. How the hell did you know?' The man searched Roberto's face for an explanation.

'See, it's his friend here who's a bit psychic,' piped up George, drily, trying to defuse the situation.

'I can sense now and then if an animal is sick,' I explained to Nelson's trainer, taking George's cue before trouble flared. Intrigued, the trainer began to question me and we all talked for a while before the racecourse was due to close and we needed to leave.

'You must visit my stable and look at my horses,' the trainer said, as we were leaving.

'I'm sure it was just a lucky guess. I don't think you want Cameron near your horses,' said George trying to steer me away from the man.

'Come now, George. I'm sure Roberto would love to visit this man's stable and I may get another of my hunches,' I said pulling myself free from George's grip, well aware of why he thought I should stay away.

The trainer introduced himself as Gianluca Parnella and gave us directions to his stables near Draguinan about an hour's drive from Cannes. We agreed to visit him there one night.

'Whatever you do Roberto, don't leave him alone with this man's horses,' said George, with a grin on his face.

'You two are just horrid! I got myself a sweet little gig as a horse whisperer and you're already trying to spoil my fun. You know the guys in the middle ages might have had it right after all. Bleeding is a cure for all major ailments,' I mock-ranted, while we walked to the car.

'Hmmm, I think I'll stick with modern science,' said

George. We got in the car and drove back to Cannes.

The next night, when I came on deck, Roberto and George were standing talking together. I had an idea that they were up to something when George gave Roberto a little nudge. The next thing I knew, the idiot was waving a teabag in my face.

'What are you doing with that?' I asked.

'It's verveine, or verbena in English,' he said mischievously.

'And?' I asked even more confused.

'I don't think it's working, George,' said Roberto upset.

'What the fuck are you two on this evening?' I asked, looking from one to the other.

'Verbena is meant to be like vampire kryptonite,' explained George.

'According to whom?' I asked.

'*Vampire Diaries*,' said Roberto.

'Which is...?'

'Latest teen vampire series,' said George.

'Oh goody! One I haven't seen yet. Now, give me that teabag.' I tore it open and rubbed the herb between my fingers, but it did nothing to me.

'Sorry boys. You'll have to think of something else to keep me in check,' I said amused.

'There's always the mirror thing,' George told Roberto. 'Cameron is shit-scared of them!'

I wasn't best pleased that George had revealed this to Roberto; I didn't want him to know my weaknesses.

'Nah! Get a mirror, George,' I said nonchalantly. It had been nearly a hundred years since I'd looked in a mirror. I was anxious, but curious at the same time. Rather too keenly for my liking, Roberto ran below deck and reappeared shortly after with a mirror. He held it excitedly in front of him pointing it at me. There was nothing there. No body, no reflection. The Flanders mud obviously didn't preserve flesh all that well! I smiled and sprang my fangs at Roberto.

'I'm dangerous and totally invincible now!' I hissed, turning to do my best Count Dracula impersonation, simulating hiding my fangs behind a cape. Then I set off for a night on the town.

Roberto and I took a drive out to Gianluca's stables the following week. Before we left, Roberto pleaded with George to come with us, but he was going for his weekly poker game in Antibes. He couldn't miss the chance of sitting around with other expats complaining about the French and the impossibility of getting a decent cup of tea.

'But Mr Baxter! What do I do if Mr Blair gets alone with a horse,' pleaded Roberto.

'Roberto! Cut the Mr shit, it's very annoying. Fuck me, this boy would make a terrible poker player,' said George. Roberto's nervous tick annoyed him too.

'I promise I'll behave,' I assured them. *No way! Any chance of a meal and I will take it.*

'I'm sure Cameron here will show restraint and not hurt the horses. Besides, horses are big animals. They should be OK in any case,' said George, not sounding in the least bothered.

'These are thoroughbreds. The smallest thing can unsettle them,' Roberto insisted. 'It's been known for a horse to die just because they changed his feed!'

But George wouldn't budge. He really didn't care one way or the other, so Roberto and I set off, just the two of us.

Gianluca's stables and paddocks were in the middle of the lavender fields. Roberto kept telling me how delightful it was, but all I could sense was the smell of his blood and his calm heartbeat. *Never ask a vampire if he can smell that delightful smell!* I didn't think his heartbeat would've been quite so calm if he'd known what I was thinking. I pressed my foot down harder on the accelerator to distract myself and soon we were driving up a dusty driveway surrounded by cypress trees. It was about ten o'clock at night and Gianluca was surprised we had come so late.

'I always sense the horse better when it's calm in the stable and there's nothing to get the horse nervous or excited,' I explained, 'so night is better.'

He gave us a tour around the stables and Roberto let his knowledge of horses show. 'You should come and work for me,' Gianluca told him and I smiled. It was more likely that Gianluca would work for Roberto one day, given his father's wealth.

He led us up to the stable of his latest star, Northern Palladium; an exquisite grey filly with what he assured me was an impeccable pedigree. He opened the stable door and we had a good look at her.

'She was very promising as a three-year-old, but recently she just seems... I don't know, she just doesn't run right. The vet can't find anything wrong with her, but to me she seems a bit listless,' Gianluca said, stroking the filly's neck.

'She's a very healthy horse.' I stroked her neck too and whispered her sweet nothings. I didn't know what to say to the man. I could detect nothing wrong with the horse. Maybe she just didn't want to race. 'Can I have a moment alone with her?' I heard myself say.

'Monsieur Blair. Are you sure?' I heard Roberto say. His voice had risen high.

'Sure,' said Gianluca. 'We'll be just outside. Take your time,' and he led Roberto away.

I found a nice vein in the filly's neck and took a few pints. Northern Palladium moved about uneasily in her stable, trying to pull away from the creature that had latched on to her neck, but she didn't make enough noise to give me away.

'I'm not sure it helped, but I gave the girl a wee pep talk,' I said coming out of the stables. 'Now, let's see your other horses.'

Gianluca ran a good stable and the horses were all well kept and in excellent physical condition. Gianluca told Roberto he could visit any time if he fancied riding and Roberto said he'd certainly take him up on the offer as he'd missed riding since he'd come to France. We said our goodbyes and asked Gianluca to keep us informed about Northern Palladium.

Needless to say, she didn't do any better at her next outings, coming sixth at Vincennes and fifth in Evreux. We decided we'd watch her run at her next visit to the Hippodrome de la Côte d'Azur and went to see her and Gianluca in the stables before the race. When I started speaking, she became agitated and moved about restlessly in her enclosure. When she was led out to the paddock she was still being difficult and when they put the buggy behind her she tried to kick the groom.

Gianluca joined us in the stands to watch the race. 'I haven't seen her worked up like this since she was a three-year-old. Something must have spooked her,' he told us.

'Cameron probably told her she'd be dog food if she didn't get her ass in gear and start running,' George quipped.

'George! That's a horrible thing to say. I did nothing of the sort,' I said, in mock indignation.

Northern Palladium was like a different horse that splendid summer night, and as the outsider she made us a lot of money. After the race we spoke to her trainer again.

'My God, Gianluca! She was on fire,' I said to him.

'I know! I have no idea why.'

I saw my opportunity to add some more 'wisdom'. 'I think she needs a bit of a fright before the race. When she got startled I felt her adrenaline pumping and it was almost as though she woke up suddenly. I know it isn't normally a good thing to frighten a horse, but I think she needs it.'

'Well, I'll try it with the next race and we will see what happens,' said Gianluca.

Frightening one horse without spooking the others isn't easy, so at Northern Palladium's next outing at Vincennes, Gianluca parked the horse box a small distance away from the others and then hit the side of the box with an iron crowbar. Northern Palladium reared up in the box and she was ready for her race. She beat the others by a length.

We saw her again when Roberto and I paid Gianluca another visit at his ranch. I didn't know it at the time but Roberto had his eye on a filly of another kind, the daughter-of-the-boss kind. Northern Palladium had changed. She was much more nervous and became even more jittery when she spotted me.

'I think we've frightened her enough, Gianluca. Best to go back to normal,' I told him

'I agree. She's becoming a little too nervous,' he said, stroking her nose to calm her down.

Gianluca had mixed success with her after that, but he introduced me anyway to some of his fellow trainers and horse owners as a sort of horse psychic. It became known that I had done something to improve Northern Palladium and I became quite friendly with the trainers and jockeys at the course. After a while, I had no trouble gaining access to the stables and the horses. To my credit, I did pick up a few things the vets hadn't. I explained to Roberto that I was probably doing more good than harm to the racing community, but he remained unconvinced and became even more wary of me.

It entertained me to make him feel uncomfortable, but George warned me to go easy on the lad. After all, Roberto was one of the few people who knew I was a vampire and was still willing to work for me. He'd be hard to replace if he left.

Chapter 14: Madeleine

Going back to Paris after the Second World War was going to require a bit of work. Some of my neighbours had known me for close to 18 years and to them I would be in my late thirties at least. George the Elder agreed that I didn't look it, so I decided to grow a moustache and we put white paint on a few hairs to age me. Even with those, George thought I could only pass for a youthful 30 at a push.

Before we went back to my apartment, I sought contact with my pre-war criminal acquaintances. I wanted some French uniforms and papers to match. Some of my contacts had done very well with various racketeering scams and I did a few jobs for them in exchange for some new identity papers and the uniforms. George, of course, disapproved, but I made it very clear to him that it wasn't possible to live as a vampire by any legal means and I forced him to accompany me on a robbery. We were to break into a warehouse and I made George the lookout on the job.

'I can't believe you're making me do this. I've never done anything illegal in my life,' he complained.

'The food problem, you can solve as you like, but you need clothes and papers.' He hated me for what I had made him become.

After my six-year absence, I was amazed to find my Paris apartment intact and, apart from a thick layer of dust, unchanged. I'm not sure why the neighbours hadn't looted the place or why the Germans hadn't raided it, but suspected the neighbours were on to me and wouldn't have dared set foot in the vampire's lair, just in case I jumped out of my coffin and killed the lot of them. I knew Madame Maréchal was terrified of me and had once accused me of stealing her dog. I'd been dressed up ready to go out for a party when she'd confronted me.

'I'm sure you took my Lulu! You were always giving her treats, trying to lure her into your place,' she said to me about three days after the dog had gone missing.

'What! Lulu is gone? You know I'm fond of that dog, but I wouldn't steal her! Feel free to come up and have a look for yourself,' I'd offered innocently.

I knew dear old Madeleine Maréchal would love to come up and have a good old nose around. Lulu was obviously long gone and I always tried to make the place look as normal as possible. My windowless room was just a cloakroom, there was a mirror in Charley's old room and hell I even kept some garlic in the kitchen, vile stuff which I have to handle with gloves. The wartime blackout curtains were doing an excellent job and allowed me to use my actual bedroom.

Madame Maréchal had had a good look around, even looking under the bed, while calling out for her little poodle. 'I don't trust men that don't work and just party all night. It's just not right,' she told me.

'I'm sorry. My dad left me with loads of money and no ambition. But I didn't take your dog!'

I know the next thing I did that night was pretty stupid, but it was worth it to see her face. I hissed at her as she walked out of my place and showed her my fangs.

'I'm sorry, Madame Maréchal! Fancy dress party tonight. Aren't these just *too* realistic?' I'd called after her. She'd almost run down the stairs before slamming her apartment door shut.

She had the same look on her face six years later when she spotted me and George in French uniforms coming into the entrance. She and Madame Robert were gossiping on the stairs.

'Trust you to have survived the front! I'm very surprised a

dandy like you even enlisted,' said Madame Maréchal.

'Glad to see you are looking well, Madame Maréchal!' I said as I lifted my cap in greeting. 'This is my friend Monsieur Valbonne. I'm trying to turn him into a useless waste of space like myself.'

'Well, we are all glad the war is over,' said Madame Robert, 'you and Monsieur Valbonne should enjoy the parties. It's so nice to see French uniforms again!'

'War has agreed with you Monsieur Beaufort. You look almost younger than when you left.' Madeleine looked me up and down suspiciously.

'Avoid sunlight ladies. Sunlight is simply murder on your skin!' I said giving them my most charming smile. With that we went upstairs and settled in for the day.

I was so pleased all my things were still there. Everything was covered in a thick layer of dust but we could deal with that once we'd had a rest. After months of roaming the countryside it was heaven to have clean towels and a bath at last. We took the dusty bedspreads off the beds and lay there resting and reading until night fell again.

George and I quickly became very popular with the many American soldiers in the city. We were able to translate between them and the local demoiselles and I liked them as they had the best things to trade with: nylons, alcohol and cigarettes. The Nazis had robbed Paris pretty clean and I had to make my money via other means.

George hadn't been happy since I'd met him and nothing changed. Although we had bonded while we fought the Germans, he now started to disapprove more and more of the way I behaved and conducted business. With the war over, he wanted to do no more killing or drinking human blood. He disliked my criminal buddies and wanted nothing to do with my shady activities. He often did what I had done in the early days and made money helping the traders at Les Halles.

He did enjoy going to the many jazz clubs and mingling with the soldiers and the French Zazous they attracted. He even started to dress like the Zazous, with their big coats and woollen ties. I had hated them before the war, but I was pleased George was mingling with the locals and I hoped he would start to love life in Paris.

We agreed that we would have to move though. Madame Maréchal was becoming very suspicious of me and didn't like the fact that we dragged young girls back to the apartment at all hours. Well, *I* dragged girls back to the apartment. George wouldn't have anything to do with them. He still considered himself to be a married man.

We found another apartment closer to the clubs and I made a tidy profit on the sale as we were leaving a rather good part of town. I didn't think of my old neighbours again until 1949 when I found myself back in the neighbourhood. I was eyeing up the property of a rich businessman, when I spotted an old lady walking a small dog across the road from me. *Madame Maréchal! My God, the last three years have not been kind to you.*

She had aged a lot and was now shuffling along the road with the help of a stick. Should I? Could I? Who would believe an old bat like her if she told people she had been attacked by a vampire that used to live in her building? I intercepted her by a small patch of derelict land, the old garden walls were still up, but the villa had gone. I dragged the old woman and the dog behind the wall before she had a chance to scream.

'If you are quiet, I will let you live,' I whispered in her ear

'Take my watch! I don't have any money... Oh, please don't hurt me!' she pleaded.

I turned her around so she could see me and her eyes widened in terror.

'Monsieur Beaufort! Please! Don't hurt me!'

'It's Mr Blair now actually and I am a vampire.' I sprung my fangs and hissed at her. She started to cry, clutching the little Pomeranian to her chest. The poor thing was struggling to get out of her tightening embrace.

'You're an evil, evil man! I've always known there was something very wrong with you.' She backed away from me, so I jumped forward and snatched the little dog from her, breaking the leash as she tried to hold on to it.

'No… No! Not my little Bisou! She's all I have,' she begged.

'Kiss her goodbye. She's going to join Lulu!' I said with great glee.

Now, Pomeranians are a bit hairy, but utterly delightful once you've managed to sink your fangs into that little throat. Madeleine let out an almighty scream and fell to her knees. I quickly disappeared into the night – the scream was certain to wake up the whole neighbourhood. Bisou, drained and limp, I tossed into the Seine.

About two weeks later, I overheard the following conversation between two men in a local café.

'Did you hear about Madame Maréchal?'

'No, what happened?'

'She was walking her dog when the leash broke. It ran off never to be seen again.'

'And?'

'She was found screaming blue murder saying that a vampire took and sucked the dog dry right in front of her.'

'A vampire?'

'She really has gone quite mad and walks around holding a large cross, saying that the vampires are coming to eat our dogs.'

'No…! To eat our dogs?'

'I know! She's completely bananas.'

'Another drink, Jean-Claude?'

'Nah. Best go home now. I don't want to be out too late if there are vampires about!' And with that the two men left the café, laughing heartily.

Chapter 15: Pavel

'Did I ever tell you about the time I learned to speak Slovenian?' I asked George one night as we sat in the living room of *The Count Dracula* watching football.

'Let me guess. You got a Slovenian girl drunk, shagged her, drugged her and then acquired Slovenian. You're very predictable!' said George, getting up to pour himself another cola.

'It's an interesting story actually. And, for once, it isn't about a girl.'

It was a rare occasion that the three of us spent an evening together, but football managed to get us together in front of the widescreen TV. As a Scot, it was at times difficult to follow my national team. As a Scottish vampire, I would have to suffer the ups – and the many downs – for all eternity. Amongst the three of us, winding up the person who was watching their national team had become a game in itself. For me, it was enough to have Roberto and George in England tops, but the Scottish team itself did a pretty good job of winding me up and many a cushion was destroyed in the course of watching a match. When Colombia played, we got no more inventive than Carlos Valderrama wigs and maracas.

As England was playing in the 2010 World Cup, but neither Colombia nor Scotland were, Roberto and I decided to get a wee bit more creative. Usually, a Germany or Argentina top was enough to get George worked up, but for the first round Roberto thought it would be nice to get USA tops.

Anybody who didn't know me would have thought getting George a mascot for the world cup was a sweet gesture, but George did, and he wasn't best pleased. I had managed to procure an English bulldog and had named him Churchill. I had found a little doggy England top and now Churchill waddled around our living room drooling and generally making a nuisance of himself.

George was in a foul mood, as the USA had just managed to equalise before half time and Churchill was trying to get into the bowl of crisps.

'Can you not get rid of this fucking dog!' he shouted, as he took a swipe at Churchill.

'But George!' whined Roberto and I. Roberto, the little wuss, had quite warmed to the huffing, puffing, drooling bulldog. I was just hoping that such a big, sturdy dog would last me for most of the World Cup.

'Cameron, just put the thing out of its misery,' George told me, and I could see he was fuming.

'He seems very happy to me,' I said amused.

'He got into my sock drawer the other day and destroyed five pairs. You're paying for that by the way,' he went on.

'I'll take him for a walk on deck,' said Roberto, grabbing the dog's collar and he took him up the stairs. He didn't mind looking after the dog and cleaning up all his mess. I would have to make it clear to him that Churchill wasn't staying. The lad really should have learned by this time that there wasn't much that kept me off my dinners.

When the match had ended on a 1-1 draw with the USA, George was in an even worse mood and was gunning for Churchill again. Roberto thought it best to get the dog out of harm's way and give him a few biscuits in the kitchen.

'Oh, you'll like this story George,' I said to cheer him up. 'I once took my American friend Charley to a football game in 1927. England won rather comfortably on that occasion.'

'Tell me more,' he said, sitting back in his chair.

'We saw France versus England at the old Olympic stadium in Paris. Charley was very excited as he didn't think they played football in France,' I continued.

'Oh dear. He must have been disappointed to have ended up at a soccer match,' said George looking happier already.

'Absolutely! He wouldn't stop moaning about them not picking the ball up and all the other stupid stuff that goes on in American football. I must say that the French and I rather wanted to forget that game as well. England thrashed them 6-0.'

Suddenly I saw George thinking deeply, a thought was forming in his head. 'That's utter bullshit, Cameron! They didn't have floodlighting in 1927, so there's no way you could have gone to that game!' he cried, sitting up in his chair.

'You know my motto George – never let the truth get in the way of a good story! Anyway, it was mostly true. I was annoyed at Charley so I got him a ticket and assured him this was a football game. He went by himself and was not best pleased when he came back.' I thought back fondly to all the nasty tricks I had played on Charley when he'd annoyed me.

George was in a forgiving mood by now though, so he decided to humour me. 'So Cameron, how did you learn Slovenian? Was she a backpacker or an au pair?'

I had not thought about Pavel or my difficult first years in Paris for a long time and I was immediately sorry I had brought it up.

'He was a pick-pocket,' I said.

'Ok, go on.'

It had been in my early days in Paris, probably around 1923 or so that I'd started needing money. As I could not do a normal job, the only option was to steal. I was in love with Hélène and living with her necessitated getting my hands on some cash. One day, I was working the metro during rush hour and had spotted a well-dressed man. His side-pocket was bulging, so I went to explore said pocket to see if there was a wallet. I had my hand on the leather wallet when I suddenly felt a warm hand touching mine.

I pulled back startled. The victim didn't turn round, yet over his shoulder I met a dark pair of eyes.

'Oooh! Competition. Did you rip his throat out on the spot?' interrupted George.

'No, it was rush hour. You can't go about doing that on a crowded Metro, it's frowned upon! Anyway I thought he might get to be the Artful Dodger to my Oliver Twist.'

I had watched the man get off at the next stop, but then lost sight of him. I spotted him again about five days later and managed to watch him work for a while: he was skilful. I followed him off the metro where he collapsed in a coughing fit on one of the platform benches. I noticed there was some blood on his handkerchief. I sat next to him and started talking.

'You don't seem well, pal Do you need some help?' He looked at me suspiciously, and then his eyes widened.

'It's you! What do you want?' he asked, alarmed.

'Listen.' I said to him. 'You're obviously ill, but you're much more skilful than I am. Teach me and I will help you.'

Pavel didn't have much to lose by this point. Destitute and ill, he couldn't work many hours at a time. He told me he had wanted to emigrate to America. He had fought in the Austrian-Hungarian army in World War One and suddenly found himself part of the Serbian kingdom when the empire was divided up. He told me he'd had a few cousins in America already that could set him up with work. Pavel wanted to take the boat at Le Havre to make the Atlantic crossing, but when he reached Paris he fell ill with pneumonia. He'd had to stay in hospital for several weeks and watched as his ticket money dwindled. He'd left the hospital way too soon to save some of the money, but now he was very ill indeed. His French was poor, but we managed to communicate. I looked after him for a few weeks and in exchange he taught me a few tricks and introduced me to his fence.

'Show us then, Cameron. See if you can get my wallet,' George challenged me.

'It's a lot easier on a crowded metro. You see, it's all about diversion,' I told George

Roberto was coming back down the stairs with Churchill. I kicked the dog so that he turned right in front of Roberto and made him trip. As I grabbed him to stop him from falling over, my other hand retrieved his wallet. He hadn't noticed a thing.

'Bravo,' said George, clapping his hands as I handed the wallet back to a very surprised Roberto.

'So what happened to Pavel?' George asked.

'When I felt he only had a few more days to live I had him for dinner,' I said drily.

'You really have no heart,' said George in mock horror.

'Why? He was going to die anyway and I do so hate to waste food,' I said innocently.

The rest of the World Cup didn't go well either for George or Churchill, but Roberto and I enjoyed the matches until the final between Spain and Holland, which I thought was one of the worst in World Cup history: ill-tempered players and only one goal. I had my suspicions about Iniesta too. He was a bit too pale and skilful. *Perhaps I should I play for Scotland?* I was fiendishly fast and had the reflexes of a cat. *Would it work if they had me in the team for evening matches only?*

Chapter 16: Eugene

Bloody, fucking Eugene Banks! He was one of those serious types you'd find in the quieter jazz clubs in 1940's Paris, who always wanted to discuss weighty issues. Every time I saw him I wanted to sink my fangs into his pale, thin neck. He and George had become quite inseparable because of their shared love of jazz and literature.

I'd come to realise that George and I were very different. He was much more serious, liked to read books and had an interest in politics. I would never say he enjoyed himself, but he liked going to jazz clubs and talking to other young people about literature and music. Eugene worked at the American embassy in Paris and I tolerated him as he was a useful contact to have, but the feeling of loathing was mutual.

'Why do you hate Eugene so much?' George asked me once.

'He hates me too. I just find him very pale and uninteresting and his girlfriend Elaine is ugly.' I'd have loved to chat her up and break Eugene's heart by getting off with her, but frankly she was so mousy it would have been embarrassing. I did have a reputation to uphold.

'Are you jealous of him?' he asked me.

'Jealous? What! Of that ginger weed?' I said outraged. I had hoped George and I would have become better friends, after all he was *my* creation, but he preferred Eugene's company to mine.

'And what is Eugene's problem with me? I am always charming.'

George gave me a mocking smile. 'He thinks you have no morals.'

'Pfff,' I said shrugging my shoulders.

The next time I needed to talk to Eugene I found him in a café somewhere near Montmartre. It was a fine spring night and he, ugly Elaine and George were discussing French politics. Something about a fourth republic and a referendum and I didn't understand any of it.

'God, you lot are boring,' I whined in frustration. None of them was particularly interested in art, so conversations were always difficult.

'I don't understand why you and Cameron live together,' said Eugene to George.

'It's my flat and George, my old army buddy, needed a place to stay. By the way. Were you in the army, Eugene?' I said, leaning back in my chair and looking at him intently.

'No. I didn't pass the medical,' Eugene said, his pale little eyes shooting daggers.

'Bet the doctor couldn't locate your spine,' I said, throwing him my most charming smile.

'Very funny, Cameron. But no, I have asthma,' he snapped at me looking uncomfortable.

George wasn't pleased with that conversation and told me so on the way home.

'How dare *you* bring up *his* army record? You're wanted for desertion and you were hiding out in a cowshed until I dragged you along reluctantly!' he hissed at me.

'Unfair! I died for my country! Most soldiers stop fighting at that point and I didn't want to be the exception!' I was pleased by the fact I had managed to annoy them both.

By the summer of 1946, I hardly saw George. By night, he hung out with Eugene and some other drab jazz enthusiasts and by day he wandered through the sewers and underground tunnels, addressing Paris's rat problem. He would come home in the early evening looking filthy, but only to have a shower and a change of clothes.

'Rats? Really George!' I said to him, often.

'It's a lot better than taking people's dogs, or snacking on drunken girls!' he said, sounding annoyed.

'But rats, George! They're filthy, horrid creatures!'

'All the more reason to get rid of them.'

'You're young, you're in Paris, why don't you enjoy yourself,' I said despairingly.

'And should I be young and enjoy myself for ever and ever and never see daylight again?' he asked, looking weary.

'Daylight is overrated. You never see the positive in a situation,' I said, giving him a friendly punch to the shoulder.

'I'm dead and I should be in a grave,' replied George, morbidly.

'I do now wish I had left you where I found you!' I said, exasperated. 'Of all the dying soldiers I had to go and pick the most boring and miserable one to keep me company.'

George shrugged his shoulders and headed for the bathroom. 'Six more months, Cameron, only six more months,' he muttered as he walked away.

I didn't get this new crowd. In the 1920s jazz had been fun and upbeat. The girls wore short skirts and high heels and they loved to dance. I know the years after the war were tough and nice things were in short supply, but honestly, there was no excuse for ugly shoes! These women just annoyed me. They wore the same clunky shoes as the men and sat around bobbing along to the music. I also suspected some of cutting their own hair, at least I hoped they had otherwise there was a dangerously unskilled hairdresser on the loose.

The music wasn't much better. Bebop, they called it. *More like bum notes.* I did like swing and the girls in that crowd were a lot livelier than the ones George and Eugene hung out with. They wore nice, short skirts and were happy to have some fun after the horrible years of occupation.

For the most part, my path rarely crossed George's unless I needed something from Eugene. One night I found them together in one of the small clubs in the Rue de Lombards. I had 'found' some jazz records that I knew would interest Eugene and he had an unlimited supply of nylon stockings and American cigarettes, *the* currency of 1946.

'I found these for you, Eugene. What would you be willing to give me for them?' I asked, pulling up a chair to their table.

'*Found* them?' he asked, his pale blue eyes widening behind his tortoiseshell spectacles.

'Where do you *find* jazz records, Cameron?' George added. 'Same place you keep finding jewellery?'

'You have to know the right people – there are always trades to be had,' I said leaning back casually and lighting a cigarette. I didn't smoke much, but I loved to blow smoke at asthmatic Eugene. I was so bored with the two of them! *How could this little ginger weed be so pale and still be alive? God, it would be disappointing if I finally ripped open that neck and didn't find any juice.*

'Well? Do you want them or not?' I asked hardly bothering not to sound impatient. I had noticed a girl coming up next to me, and I recognised her as one I'd taken back to the apartment the previous week. I was ignoring her, as I never bite the same girl twice, but eventually I had to look up. I said 'hi' then turned back to George and asked him if he knew any of the records. I could feel the girl's embarrassment as she walked away.

'You know, George, I think if murder didn't cause so much inconvenience, Cameron would quite happily snap a girl's neck once he was done with her,' I heard Eugene say.

What had George told this ginger wet blanket? I shot daggers at George, then turned to Eugene and gave him one of my *I don't give a fuck* looks as I slowly blew smoke in his direction.

'Not just the girls' necks. I have a wee boy on my wish list too!' I told him. Eugene looked nervous and started polishing his glasses. George came to his buddy's aid as usual.

'Don't you think Cameron's looking a little pale tonight, Eugene? He should get out in the sun a bit more, don't you agree?'

Eugene looked in surprise from me to George, not understanding the put down. I stubbed out my cigarette and got ready to leave. 'Right. Now we've all agreed to hate Cameron,' I told the two of them 'I must love you and leave you. So. Do you want these or not?'

We agreed on six packets of Chesterfield cigarettes and a couple of nylons and I quickly left to trade with another contact. Getting girls drunk was an expensive habit, but at least it was more fun than hanging out with those two.

One night I took a rather buxom brunette back to the apartment and was dismayed to find George and Eugene there. The living room was blue with smoke, which was strange as Eugene with his asthma really shouldn't have been smoking. Then I smelled something more worrying.

'George. Tell me you haven't been smoking that stuff!'

George looked at me with a dazed look and I realised it was too late.

'Oh, can I try some?' said Paulette, my latest conquest, and took the joint from Eugene. *Fuck! There goes dinner!* I sat next to her and started kissing her neck. Hopefully the sight of us making out would drive Eugene away before she had too much. I was worried about George and wondered if he would go off the rails as I had on the stuff. Soon he sank to the side and went to sleep. I asked Eugene to help me put him to bed.

'Now fuck off, Eugene. I'm in there!' I hissed when we came out of George's room. He grabbed his coat and to my great delight fucked off.

'Oh and Eugene,' I called out after him, 'if you ever give George drugs again I'll kill you.' He looked back at me with those pale, blue eyes and only the fact that scrumptious Paulette was there stopped me from going up and punching him. I don't think he realised how dangerous I was. Being so harmless himself he just couldn't see it. I slammed the door behind him and turned to Paulette.

'Now Paulette. Would you like to see my bedroom?' She would and she was a lot of fun in bed. She chose to go on top which allowed me to play with her beautiful, large breasts. I didn't give a flying fuck about what the neighbours or George thought, so I was rather enjoying the fact that Paulette had grabbed the head board and was banging it against the wall. She started to moan louder and louder as she worked her way to a climax then she came just after I did with one enormous scream and collapsed on top of me. Content and exhausted she snuggled into my arms. She had just fallen asleep when a naked George burst into our room.

'Cameron! We've got to run! I've seen him outside on his horse with an enormous sword,' he cried, eyes wide in absolute terror.

'Well George. Should we get dressed first?' I asked calmly.

'No time! HE IS OUTSIDE!' he shouted, looking panicked. Paulette had woken and was clinging on to me, scared by this screaming, naked man.

'I was worried about this, dear girl. The man gets the most horrendous nightmares after smoking marijuana,' I reassured her.

'George. Get dressed. I'll deal with it,' and I flung on a dressing gown, pushed George towards his room and went outside. Maybe if I came back unharmed he would calm down a bit. I had a quick look along the street just to make sure there really wasn't a sword-wielding madman out there and then turned back inside. When I came upstairs, I found Paulette unconscious on the bed and George sitting next to her with blood smeared around his mouth.

'What the fuck did you do?' I cried alarmed. 'Christ! Is she dead?'

'Must drink the virgin's blood to protect myself,' he said rocking back and forwards, looking quite insane.

'Good God you idiot! She's certainly no virgin! How much did you drink?' I asked him and checked her wrist. I felt a pulse and was pleased the girl was still alive. A lot of people had seen us together so her sudden disappearance would have led to awkward questions.

George got up and started pacing up and down mumbling stuff about the sword of justice. I managed to get him in his room and locked the door, hoping he wouldn't jump out of the window. I made a cup of tea and tried to get Paulette to wake up.

'Sweetheart? You fainted.'

'I think your friend bit me, Cameron,' she said rubbing her neck. 'What is going on?'

'I am so sorry, love. He really is a frightful beast when he's on marijuana. It certainly isn't as harmless as they say.' I held her and kissed her hair, hoping she'd believe me. 'He thinks he's a werewolf and I've locked him in his room,' I said, as George started banging on the door and screaming my name. 'Right. Get dressed and I'll take you home.'

It was about three in the morning and as it was winter, I'd be able to get her home and get back to see if George was still locked in before daylight. She lived just a few blocks away and I squeezed her tightly against me all the way. Hopefully she'd remember the nice guy Cameron who had protected her from his insane friend, and not realise she'd been lucky enough to escape alive from a vampire lair. I kissed her long and passionately, but knew I'd probably not see her again.

I was pleased to find that George hadn't done anything stupid in my absence, so I stayed and talked to him until I saw normality return to his eyes. It took hours.

'Did I really bite that poor girl?' he asked when he came to his senses, looking concerned.

'She's ok. I told her you thought you were a werewolf,' I tried to reassure him.

'Did she believe you?'

'I think we might have got away with it. I did warn you about drugs,' I said.

'Eugene is always fine on it so I thought I'd give it a try. Jesus Christ, Cameron. We are seriously dangerous!' he said, looking mortified.

'Just don't do drugs!' I said, but George took the experience hard and remained very upset about the girl. It took him a while to start going out again, but eventually I managed to persuade him to go and see an American musician who was in town. I even tried to be nice to Eugene, as I wanted George to start enjoying himself again.

Towards the end of that year, George took me aside and told me he wanted to leave. 'You will keep your promise, won't you Cameron? You'll look after my family?'

'What will you do George? Where are you going?' I asked him quietly, but I knew and had felt it coming for a long time.

'I stayed and tried for two years, now tell me you'll keep your side of the bargain,' he insisted, avoiding my question.

I swore to him that I would, then he grabbed his coat and left, leaving all his other belongings.

I had become a spiteful creature. I was angry at George for abandoning me but I couldn't hurt him if he wasn't there, so Eugene had to do. On a cold January night I didn't feel my mood improving as I waited for him around the corner from the American embassy. I followed him to the banks of the Seine and there I quickly pulled him down some stairs, holding my hand over his mouth to stop him from screaming.

At last I got to plant my fangs into that pale, little neck and I was not disappointed. Eugene was very much alive after all. I slipped his limp, little body into the river, where the current quickly took it.

'Fuck you George!' I muttered, as I crushed the hated tortoiseshell-rimmed specs under my heel.

Chapter 17: George the Younger

I finally got to England in 1950. Crossing the channel was a challenge, but in those days security wasn't as tight and for the right price you could get a fisherman to take you over in a boat at night. Paris had become too complicated. I kept bumping into people I had known for many years and the baffled looks at my youthful appearance had become awkward to deal with. I sold my apartment and was suddenly wealthy. I found that where large sums of money are involved you can get people to work to your hours and so we had the deal signed and notarised at night.

I wasn't going to risk travelling with a suitcase full of francs, so I converted most of the money into gold and gemstones, sure that they would allow me to introduce myself nicely into the London underworld. Once in London, I got a room in Soho and told the landlady I worked nightshifts so she wouldn't disturb me during the day.

The London underworld after the war and during rationing was thriving. Walking at night in the East End I quickly found out who the big boys and the little guys were, I had come to recognise their type in Paris. I found out where one of the gangs hung out and walked into their pub one night, wearing my most flamboyant Parisian suit. I got some looks as I started to make enquiries, pretending to be a hard man from Scotland looking to be a hired hand.

I was soon confronted with an 'Oi! Outside you baby-faced Scottish wanker!' and found myself facing two heavies with flick knives. I jumped on the largest and twisted his arm behind his back. He cried out in pain and let go of the knife. I cut his face with it and slowly licked the blood off his cheek and the knife. I asked the other one if he wanted some too. He stared at me in absolute horror and told me he didn't.

The big boss quickly realised he could use someone like me and hired me for a few jobs. Robbing warehouses and trading in pubs got me a new wardrobe and the contacts I built up allowed me to convert some of the gold into cash and papers. I found the role of violent thug rather amusing. I wasn't afraid of any of these London wide boys with their little knives, and getting paid for being violent was hilarious.

I started carrying a razor, as that drew more blood. My party-piece was to lick the bloodied razor which got me a lot of respect as a complete psycho. I made contacts quickly and settled into life in a new town. I enjoyed the role of mad Scottish gangster, it even let me get away with biting someone once, but it was an act. I didn't like any of my new 'friends', most were absolute philistines who couldn't tell the difference between a Mondriaan and a van Gogh. I didn't like the women much either. I do like a platinum blonde in a fur coat, but I prefer the coat to be real and the collar to match the cuffs.

There was one girl I did like: a beautiful Jamaican who sang in one of the clubs. Shirley had gorgeous dark skin, sultry eyes and a voice that would melt even a vampire's heart. Unfortunately, she was the girl of fellow gang member, Jimmy, and hence very much off limits while he was around. So Jimmy Webster would have to go. By all accounts he was a nasty piece of work and not particularly kind to Shirley, so I had no hesitation whatsoever in following him home one night and stabbing him several times in a dark alley before feasting on him until he ceased to be.

The following night I waited for Shirley at the stage door and offered to walk her home. She looked terrified, but I assured her Jimmy had gone up north for a job and he wanted his girl to be safe. Jimmy was found and the story hit the newspapers. Everyone thought it had been the other gang and things escalated nicely over the following week. I think Shirley had her suspicions, but she let me into her bed one night anyway. I didn't want her to get the wrong idea – you only get Cameron for one night so I made sure she saw me getting very friendly with one of the platinum blondes the night after and after a slap and a drink in my face she was safely out of my life.

For the most part, I didn't enjoy hanging out with the gangsters and would often head to Soho for a more genuine woman and better conversation. It was on one of those nights in Soho that I had a rather unsettling experience. As I was entering a bar, a fat man in his late fifties was coming out. When he saw me, he went white as a sheet, grabbed me by the lapels and stared long and hard at me.

'No! It couldn't be... it couldn't...' he said, looking at me intently.

'Are you alright, sir?' I said in my best English accent. I was intrigued. Did this man know me?

'You're just the spitting image of I chap I once knew,' he said to me, slowly letting go of my coat.

'Let me buy you a drink,' I said 'you seem much shaken up.' He let me guide him back in and we got two halves of ale and took a seat.

'I knew a chap before the war who looked just like you... before the Great War,' he told me and I was pleased it wasn't one of my brothers. This must have been someone I'd known.

'Let me introduce myself. I'm Eugene Banks,' I said.

'Ian Malcolm. Pleasure to make your acquaintance.'

Fat Malckie! I screamed inside. He must have made it out of there alive after all! I wanted to ask him so many questions, but knew I couldn't. I think he'd have had a heart attack there and then if I told him I really was Blairy. *Fat Malckie! My word! He never did manage to shift those pounds.*

'So how did you end up in London, Mr Malcolm? You are Scottish are you not?' I asked him.

'Aye, now that was all because I was wounded in the Great War. I was shot in the shoulder during my first battle, Battle of the Loos. A lot of the boys didn't survive that day, but I was lucky and just ended up with a hole in my shoulder. I got sent to a hospital in London to recuperate and that's where I met this charming English nurse, Harriet. When I was well enough, I went back to Edinburgh until the doctors thought I was ready to go back to the front. Harriet and I had been writing to each other, but after April 1918 I never received another letter,' he told me.

'Oh dear. Not the influenza I hope?' I asked, concerned.

'I was daft about that lassie, so like a right twat I went down to London looking for her after the war.'

'Did you find her? I asked him.

'Yes. She'd married another soldier a few months earlier, so I was heartbroken and didn't fancy going back to Edinburgh with my tail between my legs.' He sighed heavily.

'Did you ever get married?' I enquired.

'Ach, yes. After the war there were more women than men, so even a fat bastard like me didn't have too much trouble finding a nice girl. June and I will have been married 30 years next year and we've four wonderful kids,' he told me happily.

It was good to see Malckie. I was happy he had survived and that he had a good life, but I started to get uneasy. Soon he might tell me something I didn't want to hear. He was looking at me very closely again.

'Cameron Blair. That was his name. It's spooky how much like him you look.'

'Well, I'd love to chat to you all night, Mr Malcolm, but I have to go and meet someone,' I said, putting on my coat.

'He deserted, that boy. Never thought Blairy would run

away from a fight,' Malkie said, mostly to himself, shaking his head.

'I'm sorry. I've got to dash,' and I almost ran from the pub.

I walked and walked that night, pacing along the embankment until Big Ben struck five o'clock. No. Cameron wouldn't ever have walked away from a fight. I don't think he'd have hurt anyone either, but he wasn't me anymore. A train would have taken me back to Edinburgh overnight, and it was tempting. Seeing Fat Malckie had been as pleasant as it had been disturbing, but he had got so old! I realised I couldn't go back to Edinburgh, not until everyone was dead and buried.

A few weeks later, I started to look for George's wife, but I didn't find Gail Edwards at the address he had given me. One of the neighbours told me that Gail had remarried in 1948 and moved with her new husband to Weybridge. Gail Edwards was now called Gail Baxter and I found her living in a semi-detached house with a nice shiny new Rover in the driveway. Gail was an attractive woman and obviously not the type to play the grieving widow for long. I didn't think she'd ever need my help; she had done quite alright for herself and young Thomas.

I met Thomas's new dad in the local pub, where he went every Friday for a couple of pints and straight home. He seemed the sensible, boring type who'd keep the same job for his entire working life. I struck up a conversation with him, pretending I was a family man too. He talked about Thomas as if he were his own son, proudly telling me about the boy's aptitude for maths and science. He had bought him a microscope for Christmas and was sure the boy was going to be a famous scientist.

I looked in on George's family from time to time, making enquiries in the pub or the local shop and trying not to draw attention to myself. Things seemed to be going well until about 1962. By that time, Gail was still living in Weybridge but Thomas had moved out. In the local pub I found out that he had gone to London to study physics. So I followed him back to London and hung around the university campus and student bars until I spotted him.

Thomas was now a tall, shy young man without much of a social life. He preferred staying in and studying rather than sampling the delights that London in the 1960s had to offer.

I, on the other hand, enjoyed the London party scene to the fullest, loving the new miniskirts and the fun-loving girls that came in them. I decided to stay in London for a while longer and got myself an apartment near the King's Road which seemed to be the place all the hip and groovy young things were flocking to.

Since my days with Charley in Paris, I had been a sharp dresser, following the latest trends. Now, in London, I knew I looked good in my tailored Italian suits. I even got myself a Vespa scooter to get around town on. One night, I got a rather sozzled lovely back to my place. She had shiny, black hair cut in a Mary Quant-style bob and had on a very short suede skirt and white go-go boots. I just loved the fashion in those days! I'd never seen that much leg on display in public before!

'Do you smoke, Cameron?' she asked me, pulling out a funny-looking wee pipe.

'I don't care much for marijuana,' I told her. When I had tried it in Paris it had left me paranoid for hours, thinking a vampire hunter was on my trail. I was halfway to Marseille before the fog in my head started to clear and I realised I was getting myself in a tizzy over nothing.

'Do you want to try something stronger?' she asked, rummaging around in her bag.

'No, not really. If a weed like marijuana leaves me paranoid for days I definitely shouldn't do stronger stuff,' I said.

'Do you mind if I do?' She had taken out a box and lit one of my candles. I told her I didn't. 'Heroin. Man it is good!' she said, preparing some drug paraphernalia. She started to cook up above the candle flame then prepared a syringe and tied off her arm to find a vein. I eyed up her pale arm jealously, all those little marks! *Had someone got there before me?*

'Sure you don't want a hit,' she asked, offering me the syringe.

'Quite sure,' I said, observing her with interest.

She injected herself and fell back on the sofa with a content smile on her lips. She was completely out of it in no time and didn't feel my fangs opening up the vein again.

Uh oh! Bad mistake I thought, as the heroin-infused blood went into my system. I felt the room turn and an amazing feeling of warmth and well-being came over me.

Then it went black.

***

When I came to, Jane had gone – and so had everything else of value. Luckily, she hadn't found my main stash under the floor boards. *Fucking bitch! I'm never bringing another fucking junky back to my pad again.*

Then I noticed the keys to my Vespa had gone too and I couldn't let that slide. It was my pride and joy and an essential accessory for looking cool. It took me two weeks to find her, but one night, I saw Jane and some of her mod friends sitting on their scooters in Carnaby Street. They were smoking and drinking beer, trying to look cool. She was sitting on *my* scooter and had made quite a mess of it. One of the mirrors was missing and the side of the white Vespa was all scratched. I ran up to them and pushed her off violently.

'Oi,' she screamed, picking herself up from the pavement.

'I'll have this back, thank you very much, you stealing bitch!' I yelled back.

Some of her friends had got off their scooters and were coming towards me, but I calmly started the Vespa and drove away. I think they knew I was in the right.

Of course, little Jane wasn't going to get off that lightly. I found out where she lived and broke into her apartment – well, it was really just a single room with a kitchenette and a small bathroom to the side. She didn't have much in the way of furniture but the place was scattered with colourful cushions and she had some pop art on the wall. I went round putting any valuables in my pocket but there wasn't much.

When I heard her keys in the lock, I hid in the bathroom. She came in and seemed to be in a rush, throwing off her coat and rushing to get all her heroin paraphernalia out on the coffee table. She was soon lying semi-comatose on her cushions. I went and stood over her wondering what to do. She lifted her head slightly and recognised me. As the haze in her mind started to clear a bit, she realised why I was there and struggled to get up.

'What...? I can pay you back,' she said, looking scared. Such a shame I couldn't bite her, but that hadn't worked out so well the last time. I thought about pouring some turpentine over her and setting the place on fire, but the other tenants didn't deserve to die or even lose their homes. Then I spotted a little frame with a photo of a middle-aged couple and a little beagle. I couldn't do anything worse to Jane than she was already doing to herself, but this might work out well for me.

'Those three all still alive?' I asked, pointing at the picture.

'Yes. Those are my parents and Sophie our dog.'

'Get your coat. We're going to pay them a visit,' I said, pulling her up from the floor.

'Why?' she asked, surprised.

'You're going to pay me back,' I said, helping her put on her coat.

I hoped she wouldn't fall off the back of the scooter as we made our way to her parents' house in Wimbledon, but she clung on for dear life and we got there quickly. 'Now, go in and get me the dog,' I told her.

'The dog? Don't you want money?' she asked, alarmed.

'Naw. I always wanted a beagle and since you have been such a bitch I thought a bitch would be a good settlement.'

'My mum loves that dog,' she pleaded, 'please pick something else! You can't do this!'

I grabbed her arm and pulled a razor out of my pocket.

'Dog or face. You choose,' I told her, looking menacing.

'Ok. I'll get her,' she said quickly.

She let herself in with a key hidden in one of the plant pots. Luckily, her parents weren't in, but wee Sophie was. Soon both Jane and the dog came walking down the garden path.

'Now. You can take the bus home and I hope we never see each other again!' I said, putting the beagle under my coat. And I drove off.

***

Thomas never got into that sort of trouble. He finished university and got a teaching job in one of London's suburbs. He was still awkward and shy, but eventually, in 1968, he managed to convince one of his fellow teachers to marry him. A year later their son George was born and in 1974 they added a daughter, Olivia. Thomas hadn't needed me to look after him either, but George Junior was a different story. I was living in the south of France by the 1980s, but I came back to look in on young George when he was about 17. I had fulfilled my promise to George Senior, but felt I should have a look in on his grandson to see if he had taken after his dad.

Not a bit of it. Young George was a very different character. He was restless and had a violent streak. He soon rebelled against his teachers and parents by donning a Mohican and Doc Martens and hanging out with a bad crowd that liked to terrorise the local shopkeepers.

Even at 17 George had a commanding presence. He wasn't very tall, but he had an impressive physique and, as I was often to tell him, a face only a mother could love. Things got really bad when George met alcohol – the two really never should be in the same place. After a few drinks George liked to pick a fight and wouldn't always come out on top. I started to follow him every night he went out drinking and sometimes stepped in when things got out of hand.

One night he got into a fight with two skinheads and ended up taking quite a beating. I thought it best to hand him into the local accident and emergency as he looked in a bad way. As I dragged him along the road, he started to sober up. Suddenly, he stopped and looked me up and down suspiciously with the eye that hadn't swollen shut.

'I've seen you a few times,' he slurred.

'Could be. We probably drink in the same places. Now come on. We'd best get you to the hospital,' I told him, flagging down a taxi. He let me put him into the taxi and I dropped him off at the hospital.

When I next saw George, the stitches in his face and hands were healing nicely, but they didn't stop him from going out on the town again. He'd managed to track down one of the guys responsible for the beating and one night I found the two of them alone in a side alley where George was laying into the guy with a bicycle chain. I swooped in and pinned George to the wall, pressing my hand against his throat. The guy ran away, bleeding heavily from his ear.

'Stop! You were going to kill that guy,' I said pushing him hard against the wall.

'Fuck you! Get off!' he shouted, trying with all his might to take swings at me.

'George! What the fuck are you doing?' I said placing my hand under his chin and lifting him up a bit against the wall.

'Who the fuck *are* you? Why do you know my name?' he said, feeling the pain now and calming down.

'I was a friend of your grandad,' I told him quietly.

George was starting to calm down and I took my hand off his throat. He looked at me suspiciously. 'I think you have the wrong guy, pal. My grandad died in World War II,' he said straightening his clothes and frowning.

'Did they ever find his body?' I asked and gave him a wink.

'What the fuck are you on about, you fucking weirdo!'

He launched at me again and I grabbed his fist in mid strike and pinned him back against the wall, my hand firmly back against his throat. He started gasping for air.

'Oh, you don't want to mess with me boy!' I said, giving him my most chilling stare.

I finally saw fear in his eyes. Maybe he could be helped. 'Go home George,' I told him, 'but meet me here tomorrow and for Christ's sake, be sober. Honestly, I will mess you up if I catch you drinking again,' I threatened.

He left with hanging shoulders. He had felt an unknown strength and rage in me that left him chastened.

We met the next day and talked for many hours. He was the first human I ever told about myself. At first, he laughed. Then he realised it explained why he'd felt something in me that wasn't quite natural. Later, out of sight in the alley, I showed him my fangs and let him touch them. He thought they were very cool.

I don't know why I was so honest with him, but I felt I

could trust him knowing I had seen his more beastly side too. I found George very easy to talk to and far from being the mindless thug that I'd initially thought he was. He was intelligent and inquisitive, but had become bored with his surroundings. I could understand that; I got very nasty too when I was bored.

He asked me many questions about his grandfather and our time together and after that we met up every night and became firm friends. He also knew never to touch alcohol in my presence.

One night I asked him if he'd ever got a letter from Sweden in the late 1970s.

'How do you know about that?' he asked, astonished.

'This girl owed me a sum of money, but I didn't want her to know my real name or address. When I met backpackers I didn't give my real name. I mostly gave my friend Hootie's address in Edinburgh and he must have had lots of postcards from all sorts of destinations, but in this case there was money involved. I had to be sure there was someone still at the address so I gave her yours,' I told him.

'It was ever so funny! One day this letter turned up and my Mum asked me if I had a pen pal in Sweden. I said no, so it was my mother that opened the letter. All these pound notes fell out and it was quite a bit of money. Then she read the letter and went bright red. "What's the meaning of this George!" she cried and I said, "well I don't know, do I? I haven't read the letter, have I?"' He grinned.

'Did you ever get to read it?' I asked.

'No. My mother paraphrased it. I'm sure the language must have been a little more choice to make my mother blush, but she told me that apparently I had cheated on this girl with another girl. I had also given her money and she was paying back the loan,' George told me.

'But you were only ten or so. Did your mother not find that a bit hard to believe?' I asked.

'Yeah, once she calmed down she said it was obviously a misunderstanding, but as there was no return address they decided to put the money in my bank account and see if anyone contacted us again,' he told me.

'And no one ever did?' I asked.

'Indeed. And then, from the age of 12, every Christmas they gave me 20 quid of it to spend on whatever the hell I wanted and the rest I got when I was 18. I thought Swedish people were angels with their blonde hair and unexpected generosity,' George told me with great glee.

'Sorry to burst your bubble, but it was me who gave her your name and address. But you're welcome!'

'I'm surprised she paid you back at all,' he said.

'She was a nice girl, but when you're me it's often kinder to piss a girl off straight away. Being my friend never ends well,' I told him.

'Should I worry?' he asked me.

'Are you a girl?' I quipped.

'Fuck off, you Scottish twat!' George said outraged, and he flicked a cigarette butt at me.

I was surprised when he told me one night that he had joined the army. We agreed though that he needed some discipline and it would probably be the best outlet for his fighting spirit and restlessness.

George did well in the army, eventually joining the SAS and learning all the skills that would be so useful in our future joint ventures. We stayed in touch over the years and met when we could.

Chapter 18: Ermintrude

By about 1976, I had got tired of the city. London had stopped swinging and maybe I had been watching too many episodes of *The Good Life*, but I decided the countryside and self-sufficiency would be ideal for me. I had to move on and reinvent myself every few years and it seemed like a fun idea at the time.

In the 1950s I had hung around the East End being a sharp dressed and dangerous gangster. In the sixties I'd set myself right in the heart of swinging London. In the seventies I experimented with a few things. I was like all the other idiots in the seventies; we all did things we shouldn't have and self-sufficiency was just another concept.

In the 1970s you could still conduct trading in cash and I had amassed a small fortune. I bought a farm far away from everything in deepest Devon. I bought five Red Ruby Devonshire cows – they were known for the quality of their beef, so I was sure their blood would be good too – and two pairs of Yorkshire terriers, which I hoped to breed if I could hold back my appetite for long enough.

The farmhouse was small and I furnished it with just a few mismatched second-hand pieces. I thought it very quaint and rustic. I told the farmer who sold me the cows that I still worked in the city, so he'd have to deliver them in the evening. He looked at me with disdain, and I could tell he was thinking that here was another one of these city folks coming to the country, thinking they could have an easier life growing their own food – and trying to do it part time!

'So have you got any experience running a farm?' he'd asked me, with barely concealed contempt.

'I've read a lot about animal husbandry and I lived on a

farm when I was younger,' I'd told him beaming with confidence and excited about my new plan.

'We'll see. There's a lot you can't learn from books. And are you ready to get up in the dark of night and look after your animals,' he'd asked as he unloaded the cows from his trailer.

'I don't think getting up in the dark will be a problem,' I'd replied, helping him lead the Devonshires to their new home.

I also got a few chickens and some pigs, no use to me, but they'd keep the Yorkies fed. It wasn't easy for me to go to the shops and buy dog food, as they were only open during daylight hours. The whole growing your own dog food idea fitted in nicely with my self-sufficiency ethics too. I arranged with the farmer to have weekly deliveries of chicken and pig feed and there I was, totally self-sufficient.

My tailor in London had assured me I looked the part in my tweed jackets and corduroy trousers and I was pleased that knitwear was making a comeback. I'd met my tailor, Tigran, late one night on a back street somewhere in the East End. The little, dark-haired man was being threatened by a rather scary looking and much larger dark-haired man. I'd not been afraid of anything apart from daylight for a long time, so I decided to get involved. I overheard something about fingers breaking and money, so I addressed them.

'What seems to be the problem here, friends?'

The two men looked at me, their mouths gaping at my audacity, but after a while the big one spoke.

'You're Armenian too?' *Ah! So that was what I had last week!* I'd wondered what her accent was.

'Scottish actually, but I had dinner with an Armenian girl last week,' I said to confuse them a bit more.

'We have business and it is no business of yours,' said the big one, after sizing me up.

'Ah. You see, though, I don't like wee guys being

threatened by big guys,' I told him. Frankly I didn't care a toss, I was just in one of those moods and wanted a bit of fun.

'It is ok, sir,' pleaded the wee guy. 'It is our business and Ali and I are sorting it out.'

'Listen Ali,' I said, 'you'd better run along now and leave the wee man in peace.'

Ali eyed me with total disbelief; this pale young dandy must have lost his mind! He took a swing at me and I ducked out of the way, but at the same time drove my fist into his abdomen. I had gone easy on him though and he was lucky just to be rolling on the floor gasping for air.

'Now friend. What business are you in, exactly?' I asked the little guy, leading him away from the scene. He kept looking worriedly back at Ali, but slowly started telling me his story. He told me he'd had a tailor shop and was struggling to pay off his loan to Ali. He agreed to come to my flat in the evening to make me some new clothes.

He didn't find it strange that I didn't want to look in the mirror and that I relied on him to tell me if it looked good or not. Luckily, he was skilful and had impeccable taste in clothes, so there I was in Devon dressed like – what seemed to an Armenian and a dead Scot – the perfect English country gentleman. Judging by the looks I got from the locals, I gathered we had probably got it wrong.

The first couple of months on the farm were great. Ermintrudes 1, 2, 3, 4 and 5 didn't mind being snacked on at night, and proved indeed to be a very tasty breed that kept me off the Yorkies. The dogs I had named Felicity and Kendall, and the other pair Penelope and Keith. I had definitely watched one too many episodes... I'd also developed a serious crush on Felicity Kendall – I'm sure she would have tasted delicious.

Soon I had my first litter of tiny little pups and they were totally adorable. I just had to find out what Yorkie pup tasted like. It was mouth-watering, but barely yielded more than a small teacupful. I decided to let the others grow a bit more.

I spent the days cuddled up in a comfy chair with a good crime thriller and a couple of dogs on my lap. The nights were spent getting down and dirty on the farm, mucking out the pigsty and the chicken enclosure. *Who would have thought that farming was such hard work!* There wasn't anything for miles around, so burgling places became trickier. I also had to drive all the way to London to fence the stuff.

And then there was the lack of women. I tried the local pub once, but as soon as I walked into the Sheep's Head Inn, a deadly silence fell and every head turned to look at the stranger. I turned and walked straight out again. This was the kind of crowd that would form an angry mob with their pitchforks and torches. I was sure that even the slightest suspicion of me being a vampire would have them marching on the farm and burning it to the ground with me locked in the building.

Then winter came and even though 1976/7 wasn't the worst on record, it was bad enough. Walking through snow and having to go out in all weathers to feed the animals wasn't for me. I had enough to eat, but the cold made my bones ache all the time. I decided this was going to be my last winter in England. I'd had enough.

The farmer smiled when I came to ask if he wanted to buy my livestock back.

'You city folk are all the same. You're always surprised when you find out that farming is bloody hard work,' he told me, smiling sarcastically.

It turned out he actually wanted to buy the whole farm. The land was adjacent to his and he wanted the extra grazing pastures for his cows, so he offered me a decent price.

'Good grief! What did you do to these cows? They're thinner than when I sold them to you,' he said aghast when he came to collect the cows.

'It was a long, hard winter,' I said apologetically.

'And what do you call those furry rats?' he asked, derisively, pointing at the group of Yorkshires that were running around our feet. 'Those aren't real dogs.'

'They're Yorkshire terriers and I think they are rather sweet,' I told him.

'Why do you need so many of them?'

'They're pedigrees. I breed them.' I had been wonderfully restrained and now had about ten of them. A few didn't want to stop barking at the farmer.

'God, you are the most unlikely farmer I ever had the misfortune to come across,' he said, pushing the Ermintrudes back into his trailer.

'I know. I don't always make the best decisions, but it seemed a good idea at the time. Well, thanks for taking the Ermintrudes. I will miss the girls, but I don't think you'll see me on a farm again,' I said while I loaded the Yorkies on to the back seat of my Ford Granada.

Then I set off for Dover. It was time to head south – it was time to go back to France!

Chapter 19: Nanette

I had seen her around a few times – a slim brunette, possibly of Arabic descent and with exquisite taste. She looked to be in her early forties and was still very beautiful. I often saw her talking to people and while her mouth would sometimes pull into a smile, her eyes never did. She seemed mysterious and distant to me. Three weeks after the murder of Yvette she approached me at a yacht party.

'So Cameron. what do you do for a living?' she asked, obviously trying to sound bored as she looked beyond me at the lights of Cannes.

'As little as possible, my dear,' I said airily. *What did she want with me?* The men she hung around with were usually much older and richer. 'And what do you do, Nanette?' I asked.

She took a drag of her cigarette and blew the smoke in my face. 'I marry,' she said.

'I didn't know marrying was a profession,' I replied, intrigued by this glamorous but frosty woman.

'Oh trust me, it's hard work,' she said, slowly walking towards the back of the deck. I followed her wondering why she had wanted to talk to me. I'd heard her husband was bedridden and had not been seen in public for many years. 'So, you like jewellery?' she continued.

She must have noticed me looking at the fabulous Bulgari necklace and bracelet she was wearing. The bracelet was one of their gold and enamel snake designs from the 1960s and it suited her perfectly. I felt her bite would be venomous too.

'I like all beautiful things,' I said moving closer and giving her my most charming smile. She raised her eyebrows and looked at me mockingly. She took another drag of her cigarette, but I turned away before she could exhale in my face again. *I'm not a candidate for husband number two then. So what does she want with me?*

'It's a shame they're so often the cause for such ugliness. Wasn't that ghastly murder and robbery in Cannes that I read about in the papers terrible – one feels quite scared these days wearing jewellery.'

She looked at me intently with her strange, almost golden, eyes. *Did she know something?*

'I'm sure they'll catch the killer soon. The police will pull in all their resources to solve a high profile case like that,' I said. I tried to sound calm, but there was something unsettling about her.

'Hmm. They say the killer was almost like a ghost,' she said, holding my gaze. 'The building has CCTV but the only people seen entering were the residents.' *Oh my god! I'd never had a woman look at me with such hatred in her eyes!*

'Maybe it was a resident then. That's why I live on a boat; never trusted neighbours,' I said, trying to sound cheerful.

'Yes. *The Count Dracula*, isn't it? Funny name to choose,' and she gave me another of her looks. *What does she want and why does she hate me?* 'I never see you in any of the papers. It's almost as though you don't like having your picture taken,' she went on.

'Come to think of it, I never see yours either, Nanette. I suppose we're just not rich or famous enough,' I joked.

We were now standing alone by the railing. Nanette quickly looked around us, then snarled, 'I know what you are! We both stand around with a glass but never drink! How long have you been dead?'

I grabbed her arm and pulled her close. She was as cold as I was and I felt no pulse. *How had I not guessed it?* 'I died in 1915. How long have you been...?'

'Only since 1998, but I feel I know more about behaving inconspicuously than you do! You've been rather an idiot with this Yvette business,' she hissed.

'I don't think you have anything to worry about,' I said, trying not to be alarmed. *Fuck! She hates me* and *she could kill me.*

'Don't be naïve! Any high profile murder case brings unwanted attention, and that's bad for us both. The slightest hint of vampire would initiate a witch hunt. You should leave and I'll keep a low profile for a while.'

I didn't agree with her, but I knew that Nanette could become a big problem; if she wanted me gone, she'd find a way to make it happen.

'Just sail that ridiculous boat of yours to the Caribbean. I want you gone!'

With that, she pushed me out of the way and walked back into the crowd. I called Roberto on my mobile and asked him to bring the tender round. The party had gone stale.

***

I was as intrigued as I was annoyed. A vampire shows up and tells me to leave and I know nothing about her. I called George into my office and told him what had happened the previous night.We set to researching Nanette, looking for unexplained disappearances in 1998, and found some newspaper clippings about the suspected murder of a prostitute in Marseille. While the article didn't give much away, there was a nice picture of Nanette, as the police wanted information. I now knew that Nanette had been born Wided Achenoui, the daughter of poor Algerian immigrants, and that her married name was Medjnoun.

George and I searched the internet extensively but didn't

find any more about either Wided or Nanette until we came across a very small article in a society magazine from a few years before that talked about how Harold Weisman III, an 80-year-old millionaire who had lost the use of one arm after a stroke, had found love again with a 42-year-old woman named Nanette Dubois. After this we were able to follow her life up to the moment I had met her, as the society papers now and then mentioned the couple, but of course there were never any photos.

Wided had obviously done an excellent job of reinventing herself and landing a big fish like Harold. I could well imagine how Nanette must have worked on Harold charming him into marrying her within only two weeks of meeting him and how not long after he'd suffered another stroke that left him bedridden and unable to speak. *How convenient!*

It wasn't hard to imagine that during the day, Nanette played the devoted wife and nurse, sitting next to Harold in his windowless room and slowly sucking him dry. The nights she would spend partying and hunting for her next husband. I could also well imagine that she would not be happy about another vampire showing up, one that could unmask her and destroy her life. She'd be furious that I could also now reveal her as a former prostitute with very lowly beginnings.

I was unsure just how far Nanette would be prepared to go to have me out of the way. A dead vampire might suit her better than one in custody and staking me would probably leave no more trace than a small pile of dust. I told George to get ready to sail to Monaco – best to put a bit of distance between me and this pissed off vampire.

Chapter 20: Klaus

In 2010 I decided to explore the darker side of the internet a bit more. I had found that it was the only place I could truly be myself. I was amazed to discover that there were chatrooms where vampires actually talked to each other about their experiences and dark fantasies. I suspected that most of these characters weren't actually vampires, but when Gothgirl-67 described experiences that were so close to my own, I wondered and tried to make contact with her. I had chosen the name MacFangs for the vampire chatrooms.

> MacFangs: So Gothgirl, what's your favourite human prey?
> Gothgirl-67: I like young women, their soft necks really turn me on.

Alarm bells started ringing. *Why was there always an unusual sexual undertone with these people?* I reckoned myself to be quite a broadminded, modern vampire at that point, but 95 years or so on I still wasn't bored of girls or willing to change my sexual orientation. I had tried a man once in the seventies when a wealthy art dealer in his forties had propositioned me at a party and asked me what it would take to make me come home with him. He was dressed in a safari suit – fashionable at the time – and with his black, thick-rimmed spectacles he did look a little like Yves Saint Laurent. I spotted a gold Rolex watch on his wrist and while I thought them ugly, I knew they were worth a lot. He saw me looking and raised his eyebrows.

'Expensive pretty thing, you are!' He took his watch off and took me home to have his way with me. It wasn't totally dreadful and I did repeat the experience a few times as it was so lucrative, but I just found the bits on a girl way more interesting. I had my suspicions about Gothgirl, but carried on the conversation anyway:

MacFangs: Do you like them flavoured?
Gothgirl-67: What do you mean? Like strawberry and stuff?
MacFangs: Not a big fan of strawberry myself, strawberries are over-rated.
Gothgirl-67: So, you rub them with something before you bite, like BBQ sauce?
MacFangs: No, that would be weird; anyway I think you're a fake otherwise you'd know what I meant!
Gothgirl-67: No, you are a fake and MacFangs is a dumb name!

I realised I was probably chatting to a 14-year-old girl who had read one too many vampire novels so I left the chatroom. QueenofFangs had also described the taste of blood and what it did to her rather accurately. It was a few years and chats after we first engaged that we had the following conversation:

QueenofFangs: Strange how garlic is so poisonous, yet when it has entered into the blood stream it does add a very nice hint of something.
MacFangs: It's like that Japanese fugu fish I've read about – you just leave a smidgen of poison in its liver to give it flavour but too much and it will kill you.
QueenofFangs: Oh God, do you think it could kill you if someone had eaten a lot of garlic.
MacFangs: I'm sure it would be ok, not even sure if garlic does actually kill you. I stick to a Mediterranean diet; how about you?
QueenofFangs: I agree, the Mediterranean is really the best place to feed.

QueenofFangs: Especially if you throw some Chateaux Margaux into the mix.

MacFangs: You have expensive taste, but I have to admit that I have a weakness for champagne.

QueenofFangs: I like to eat well LOL.

MacFangs: That is the wonderful thing about the Mediterranean; you can eat very well here ILMAO

QueenofFangs: Would you believe there are weird f**kers that feed on dog!

MacFangs: Nanette?

QueenofFangs: F**k I thought that might be you!

We both quickly left the chatroom and made sure we were never in the same one again.

It was in a chatroom in around 2010 that I came across Klaus or IMtasty45, as he was known online. He was in a chatroom where so called vampires chatted with people who wanted to get bitten. Klaus seemed to have a desperate need to have his blood sucked and I decided to explore this further; the idea that people would willingly let someone bite them and suck their blood seemed bizarre to me, but by now I had learned that there is no species stranger than man.

MacFangs: So IMtasty45, how old are you?

IMtasty45: Does it matter?

MacFangs: Not really, I'll bite anyone, just wondered.

I wouldn't bite just anyone, though. Wrinkly old men were really not my favourite.

IMtasty45: Where do you want to bite me MacFangs?

MacFangs: I think the wrist, I don't want to leave any tell-tale marks.

IMtasty45: If you wanted to I would let you.
MacFangs: My dear man do you think once you let me in you would have a choice?

I knew this would make him hot under the collar; he was the ultimate submissive victim. I had no illusions as to what Klaus was doing at the other end of the web, knowing it would probably involve a box of tissues.

IMtasty45: Would you hold me captive and feed on me?
MacFangs: Yes, I would tie you up and feed on you for weeks.
IMtasty45: Would you kill me?
MacFangs: No. I would just leave once I fancied a different flavour of human.

There was a pause in the typing. *Was he disappointed with this answer?*

MacFangs: I could kill you, I would quite happily kill you, but we vampires don't like to leave too many bodies behind.
IMtasty: Yes, very wise. I would like you to feed on me.

After chatting with Klaus for several weeks, I decided to make contact with him directly, I had the impression he was serious about his vampire fetish and was intrigued to see how far it would go. He'd told me he lived in Frankfurt, Germany, and had been trying to meet someone who was willing to play out his vampire fantasy with him for many years. I made arrangements to go to Germany and meet him.

'George! I'm going away for a few days,' I said, excitedly.
'Do you want me to go with you?' George asked, surprised
'No, I think this will fall under the "I do not approve,

Cameron" section,' I said smiling mischievously.

'What are you up to?' he asked, eyeing me suspiciously.

'I promise no one will get hurt,' I said smiling gleefully, 'well, not much and entirely voluntarily!'

'May I ask where you are going?' he asked, wondering what I was up to.

'Germany.'

'What the hell are you going to do in Germany? You've never needed to go there before?' George became quite agitated at the news. *What is his problem?*

'Listen George. I think it's about time you forgave the Germans too. They've given us rather wonderful cars and I'm sure it's a beautiful country full of fascinating people,' I went on cheerfully.

'Where exactly are you going?' he asked, still very suspicious.

'I'm going to Frankfurt to see a man I met on the internet.'

'Since when are you into blokes?' he asked, surprised.

'I'm not going for *that,*' I told him.

'And it is just Frankfurt?' he asked.

'Yes George, just Frankfurt,' I said, trying to sound weary now. George's reaction had been odd, but he seemed to calm down a bit at this and began helping me with the preparations.

***

Frankfurt am Main was a very large modern city, and as with many German towns we allies had made rather a mess of things. The place had been rebuilt in a grey and uninspired way, but the town centre had some impressive skyscrapers that housed Germany's financial heart. As it was nearly daybreak when I arrived, I decided to spend the day exploring the metro and meeting up with Klaus at nightfall.

Klaus had become more cautious when I announced I wanted to see him and we had agreed to meet in a public place first. I was looking for a man with a brown coat and purple scarf on the Römerberg Platz, a square the authorities had decided to restore to its former glory after we Allies had rearranged the bricks of the old buildings. I wasn't sure about it; it seemed wrong to me to totally rebuild something that had been destroyed. Some of the buildings looked too new, and gave the impression of being a theme park.

I spotted Klaus and was not surprised to see a slightly balding, blond man in his forties with glasses. He was wearing beige trousers and a brown sports jacket, and simply oozed dullness and poor taste. He was looking around nervously. I had imagined him as a not very attractive loner, who was socially awkward and spent most of his life on the internet, and it looked like I'd been right.

Well Klaus, let's make your day, I said to myself. A man like Klaus would not have expected a very attractive twenty-something like me to show up.

'Hello Klaus, I'm Cameron,' I said holding out my hand.

'Hello… Cameron… your German is very good,' he blurted and I could see he could scarcely believe his eyes. His warm, clammy hand grabbed my own.

'Yes. I've had a few run ins with your people over the years and picked the language up in "drips" and drabs,' I explained.

'And you are very young,' he said, looking pleased and excited.

'You know us vampires, we don't age,' I said, winking at him.

Klaus laughed nervously and suggested we should go for a beer. Beer is not my favourite flavouring, but I wanted to put him at ease.

'You have a beer. I'll watch,' I said and I led him to the nearest beer cellar.

After a few drinks, Klaus plucked up the courage to ask me back to his place. I said I needed a place to stay and he agreed to let me stay at his apartment. We drove my car out to a rather colourless suburb where he owned an apartment.

The apartment was large and, looking around it, I realised that home decor was bottom of Klaus' list of interests. Everything was brown or beige except for a rather odd-coloured greenish carpet on the floor. *Maybe he's colour-blind!* He led me to the bedroom, where Klaus had obviously tried to use his imagination – with disastrous results.

He had decorated it like a 1970's porn set, with a tiger-stripe bedspread and some lava lamps. I was not surprised that his computer was located in this room. I'd never seen anything that would turn me on less! I quickly walked back out trying not to laugh.

Then he showed me to his small spare bedroom which was as colourless and boring as Klaus himself. There was a dull orange, synthetic bedspread on the bed which I thought I might burn if I got bored, but I was pleased to see the room didn't have any windows. I put my bags resolutely on the bed. *Surely I can live with ghastly surroundings for a while if it involves easy food?*

Klaus offered me a drink, but I was feeling hungry by now.

'So Klaus, you want me to drink your blood?' I asked him when we sat down on his couch.

'I... er... I do,' he stuttered. 'How... how are you going to bite me?'

He looked distinctly nervous now that he was actually confronted with his fantasy. *Be careful what you wish for,* I thought to myself as I took out a small scalpel. 'Best not to make any bite marks,' I said, as I showed him the scalpel with a reassuring smile. I was worried Klaus might freak out if I let my fangs protrude and revealed myself to be a real vampire. The thing I had learned about fantasies over the years is that they need to remain fantasies, so I made a small incision in his left arm and proceeded to feed, trying to be as human as possible about it. It wasn't hard as his blood had an odd flavour. I could see by the shape in his trousers that this was very much doing it for Klaus. I pulled away when I'd had enough. 'Klaus, really! You had Sauerkraut for dinner, didn't you!' I cried in disgust.

'Er... yes... you can taste that?' he asked, surprised.

'Yes. And I don't like it,' I said moving away from him in distaste.

'I am sorry,' he looked shocked and I knew he would be eager to please; he had taken quite a fancy to me.

'We'll put you on a Mediterranean diet for a few days and then try again,' I told him in a stern voice.

'Of course, Cameron. Anything you say,' he assured me.

'Now, go to bed and get your strength back. I intend to use you for a few days more.' I dismissed him with a wave of my arm. He got up and obeyed without question. I knew he probably wouldn't be asleep for a while in the other room; his fantasy had just come to life.

He left me by myself the next day, as he had to go to work. He'd told me he worked for an insurance company in the city and that he had done so since he'd left school. I was glad to be rid of him for a few hours as we had very little in common apart from our internet use.

For the next few days, Klaus stuck to a diet of pasta and pizza and I even got him to drink a bottle of fine champagne. I'm not sure if he trusted me alone in his apartment, but he was desperate for me to stay. Luckily for him, he had nothing I wanted.

'Let's see if you have improved, Klaus,' I said to him after a few days.

He had drunk the bottle of champagne and was getting a little touchy feely. I cut him in his other arm and a bit deeper than I had meant to. Klaus whimpered, but the sharp pain seemed to arouse him even more.

'Good boy! You have improved. Really very good!' I told him after I'd fed for a while.

I was bandaging his wound, hoping it wouldn't leave too bad a scar, when Klaus launched forward and tried to kiss me. I grabbed him by the throat and squeezed hard, then I looked into his eyes and hissed, 'You are food! You do not have the right to touch me!' Knowing Klaus, this would only make me more desirable, but I had just fed well and I didn't care.

Klaus bored me rigid and I needed to leave. By the end of the week I was able to make my escape. Klaus was quite drunk on champagne and wanted me to watch porn with him, hoping it would get me interested in him. I persuaded him to let me cut him again and he agreed, but I tasted a strange flavour on him.

'You had bratwurst!' I yelled in disgust

'I... I... it was lunchtime! How can you even taste that?' He looked at me scared and confused.

'Honestly, Klaus!' And, with that, I packed my bags and stormed out with Klaus pleading and begging the whole way to my car.

The internet. It's a wonderful thing!

Chapter 21: Roberto

George would always let me know when he was back from one of his tours and we met regularly. By the late 1990s, I noticed his enthusiasm for army life was waning. He had just come back from Kosovo and I felt there was something bothering him, but he wouldn't tell me what.

I'd been staying in Nice for a few years by then and longed to live on a yacht, which I thought would make a wonderful hiding place. The modern world was becoming very complicated with its taxes and never-ending streams of paperwork. I was constantly having to find ways of explaining my existence. However, a yacht would need a crew, and a human crew I could trust, so I asked George to come and work for me. He would only agree if he could continue doing what he loved.

'I have skills that shouldn't go to waste, Cameron. I feel I owe society,' he told me.

'Well I'm not stopping you if you want to want to go into some godforsaken hell-hole now and then and kill a few baddies,' I told him.

'I think you owe society, too,' he said.

'Me?' I was indignant.

'Well you can hardly say your existence has made the world a better place, can you now?' He looked at me sternly.

'Unfair! I fought in both world wars!' I cried in mock outrage.

'You got killed in your first battle and you only fought in WWII to stop my grandfather from ending his existence.'

'You're starting to sound just like him, miserable sod that he was,' I said glumly.

'Well, maybe he had a point. You know, you have all these

amazing abilities and all you ever do is line your own pockets and kill small dogs.'

I knew if I wanted to have a functioning relationship with a human I had to meet their moral demands. I got on well with young George because he'd had to fight to keep his darker side in check too, although he'd become calmer over the years.

'Now, this is my plan. You'll like the money side of it.'

'Money?' I said with interest. Now he had my full attention!

'I have a contact who has worked with the families of hostage victims. Often, if negotiations are going nowhere, they're willing to reward a successful rescue,' he started to explain. He outlined his plans and the role I was to play in them. It was an intriguing idea so I agreed to help him.

Our first mission in 2006 took us deep into the Colombian jungle, where Roberto Hidalgo, the 18-year-old son of a very wealthy Bogota businessman had been taken hostage by the FARC. The reward Mr Hidalgo was willing to offer for the safe return of his son was five million dollars. Getting a vampire all the way from France to Colombia was going to be a complicated affair however. We decided to set up a dummy import-export company and George hired a warehouse near Bogota which we were going to use as our operations base. Then he purchased a large crate and asked me to get in it.

'So how long is this trip going to take George?' I asked, looking doubtfully at the crate.

'About two weeks,' he said.

'I'm not staying in a crate for two weeks! I'll starve!' I cried.

'I thought you vampires couldn't die,' he mocked.

'Maybe not after two weeks, but starving is a very unpleasant experience. Can we not put a few animals in for the trip?' I asked.

'No. Customs would pick that up in no time. I could pack some frozen chicken for you, I mean we would have to change the paperwork but I could send you as frozen cargo,' he said and I saw he found the whole thing highly amusing.

'I can't eat frozen chicken, there's no fresh blood in it!' I cried in horror. 'And now you not only want me in a box, you want to freeze me too.' I was not impressed by his travel arrangements.

'You're sure you don't show up on x-ray and the like?' he asked me.

'Yes. I simply don't register. But isn't there a quicker way to send me?' I urged.

'We could do air cargo, but it'd cost four times as much,' George explained, without much enthusiasm.

'Air cargo it is then and damn the expense! I mean, really, you were planning to put me in a crate for two weeks without any food? Where's your humanity?' I threw my arms wide in a questioning gesture.

'You know, in Buffy they bury the likes of you in coffins all the time and they seem to come out ok, even after a few years. Are you sure you're a real vampire?' he asked, still mocking.

'Care to find out?' I asked, showing him my fangs.

At that, George made a hasty exit and booked our crate on the next cargo flight to Colombia. Even by air the trip was long, boring and uncomfortable and when I finally arrived in the warehouse I was hungry and irritable. I had an enormous urge to sink my teeth straight into George. He was eyeing me warily, and holding tightly on to the crowbar he'd used to open the crate.

'You alright, Cameron?' he enquired, keeping a safe distance.

'What time is it?' I asked, looking around the warehouse.

'Noon,' said George, gripping the crowbar firmly.

'Fuck! Did you get me any food?' I asked, hopeful there was something to get my fangs into.

'Not had the time to go dognapping yet,' he said, still keeping his distance.

'Go on and let me bite you,' I said. I was smiling, but I wasn't entirely joking.

'Fuck off, Cameron! I'm not your food. You'll just have to fucking wait,' he said, lifting the crowbar menacingly.

I dragged myself off to a corner to sit and sulk. George took pity and braved handing me a laptop.

'At least we have wifi,' he said, apologetically.

I felt my mood improving as I logged into Facebook. 'Ok George, I'll let you live,' I said, without a smile.

'Jeez, thanks Cam.'

It got dark at around seven o'clock, by which time I was feeling very hungry and dangerous. Finally, George got up and grabbed some car keys. 'Right, Cameron. Let's go see a man about a dog!'

We drove to a shed somewhere in the outskirts of Bogota and George said 'I assume you have eaten Spanish at some point and now speak it?'

'Dunno,' I growled. I was moody and didn't feel like talking.

He introduced me to a fat man in his forties called Ernesto. I was dismayed to find that I couldn't understand a word he was saying. *I should have bitten Joan Miró when I had the chance!* Miró had annoyed me at a party one night and I found him later, alone and asleep in one of the bedrooms of the house. I had been very tempted, but Hélène was there and I didn't want her to find me in the process of feeding.

George knew a few words of Spanish and soon the man went in to get the dog.

'What the fuck is that?' I cried when I saw a white dog being led out.

'I believe it is a bull terrier. She lost her last fight, so he's selling her cheap,' said George, not caring one iota.

'That is one fucking ugly bitch!' I said loudly.

'Easy, Cameron. Don't insult the man now.'

Ernesto didn't speak English, fortunately, so the transaction went ahead as planned and a few bank notes equating to about ten euros exchanged hands. George led the dog to the car.

'Look at all those scars! I don't like my food pre-chewed George!' I complained.

'You fucking eat what you're given, you spoiled brat!' he scolded.

I was very hungry and didn't know the lay of the land so I realised I had little choice. Soon we were back at the warehouse and I eyed up my food with distaste. The bitch took my stare as a challenge and suddenly went for me, locking her powerful jaws around my arm and biting down hard.

'You fucking bitch! Well, two can play that game,' I yelled and planted my fangs into her muscly neck. It took a long time before I felt the powerful neck relax and then the dog finally let go of my arm. Just a few more sips and she was dead and drained. George had collapsed into a chair and was laughing uncontrollably, tears streaming down his face.

'That was just the funniest thing ever! Finally one of the buggers got you back. I wish I could have captured that on camera!' He howled with laughter.

I was well fed and in a better mood now, so I took a bow and said 'Glad we could be tonight's entertainment, but next time get me something prettier.'

Owing to George's meticulous research and preparation, we located Roberto's captors within a week. The thick canopy of the rainforest made it possible for me to travel even during the daytime. To my eyes, there's no difference between night and day, it's just that daytime hurts. The fact that I could see the enemy but they struggled to see me made it very easy to overrun the rebels. We had Roberto out of there before they fully realised what had hit them.

During our trek back to Bogota, we had to come clean with Roberto as to what I was. This was to become one of the risks of the job, but we knew it would be virtually impossible to keep my nature hidden from hostages if we had to travel with them for days on end. They'd need to know why I had to keep out of sunlight during the day and why I had to find something slightly different to eat.

On that first trip, in Colombia, food proved to be quite easy. One night, I was moving slowly through the forest searching for an animal, when I heard rustling next to me. The next thing I knew, a huge jaguar had jumped on my back, digging its claws into my shoulders. *Ya beauty!*

I wrestled the cat to the floor. I thought it might not taste very good given that domestic cats taste so vile, but this animal was rather wonderful. It had an unusual, exotic flavour, almost a tad chocolatey. I didn't believe it would be right to kill an endangered species, especially a beautiful beast like a jaguar, so I let it go after a pint.

Roberto was fascinated by the fact that he was now traveling through the jungle with a real life vampire and asked me many questions.

'So you drink blood, Mr Blair?'

'Yes, and call me Cameron, please,' I said, trying to be friendly and obliging.

'So you need to kill someone every day?' he asked, looking at me with great interest.

'No, I very rarely kill. I get by on just a few pints here and there and it doesn't have to be human,' I explained. 'Actually, I had some jaguar just the other day.'

'Cameron has a taste for small dogs too.'

I shot George a dirty look at this remark.

'You eat *dog*?' Roberto said and his eyes widened.

'Now, why did you have to bring that up, George? Humans slaughter cows, sheep and all sorts of animals and here is little old me getting judged for eating the occasional pooch. And by the way, I let the cow live! I just take a pint here and there, same as with the humans and there you are making out that I'm the bad guy!' I pulled ahead of them to sulk.

'The other thing you need to know about Cameron is that that chip on his shoulder doesn't come off,' I heard George say behind my back.

'But you did kill those FARC bastards back there?' Roberto asked, hastily catching up with me.

'Yes, an extra benefit of rescuing you,' I said dreamily, thinking about the wonderful fresh local food.

'And you two live on the Côte d'Azur?' he queried.

I could see Roberto was excited. He seemed to think that George and I had just the most adventurous life ever. When we got back to Bogota, he told his dad that he had always wanted to learn French and that going to France would be a good experience before he went to university. He managed to convince his father to let him enrol in a French class in Cannes and to come and work with me and George. He fitted in very well with all the other rich young South Americans staying on the Côte d'Azur, pretending to learn French but really just enjoying their first taste of freedom.

It was after my meeting with Rashid in Monaco that I overheard a conversation between George and Roberto. They hadn't heard me coming back and were gassing in the kitchen.

'Are you going to introduce her to him?' I heard George asking.

'Not sure. I'm worried she is going to like him.'

I smiled. It was rather sweet that Roberto was worrying about his girlfriend falling for me.

'The bastard can be utterly charming. They do say it's very common for psychopaths to be very charming,' I heard George say. *Psychopath! What the...?*

'I know. I am thinking seriously of going back to Colombia, I didn't think he would murder an innocent woman,' Roberto went on, sounding serious and concerned.

'Me neither, Roberto. I don't think I can stay here, it's just so wrong. The dogs, well I'm not a big lover of dogs and he needs to eat somehow, but this woman... Anyway, let's get the deck cleaned. He'll be back soon,' said George bringing the conversation to an end.

I quickly ran back on deck and pretended I had just arrived. 'Evening George! You missed a spot.'

'Fuck off, Cameron!'

I pretended nothing had happened. So they thought I was a psychopath. Well, maybe it was deserved. I went below deck and put a DVD of *Buffy the Vampire Slayer* in the machine. That stuff always used to cheer me up no end.

Chapter 22: Marjorie

About a month after Yvette's murder, I decided to sail *The Count Dracula* into Monaco. I was hoping it'd be far enough away to keep Nanette off my back. I loved Monaco, it attracted all the right people and the parties were, at times, fabulous. It was a strange little place really, with its high rises stuck between the rocks, and the smell of money and champagne everywhere.

I was pleased to see the *Lady Zaza* was also in town. It belonged to a game old American bird named Marjorie Callaghan. Like me, she was old but with the mind of a mischievous teenager. She was the heiress to a fortune and three times divorced. These days, she sailed solo and sampled the delights of the Côte without buying the proverbial cow. Divorce number three had made her wise in the ways of bloodsucking leaches. Strangely enough, she loved me.

'Cameron darling! So pleased to see you here,' she gushed when I sailed the tender over to the *Lady Zaza* that night.

'Marjorie, darling, what *is* your secret? You look younger every day,' I cooed back.

'You are just so charming with your scotch accent,' she said, giving my chest a gentle push.

'It's *Scottish* darling, but I forgive you as you look so radiant today,' I said kissing her on both cheeks.

'Oh stop! I could be your grandmother...'

'I'm glad you're not! My granny used to knit horrible itchy jumpers all day. They were minging,' I said, grimacing.

'Minging? Oh my, Cameron you are just too quaint,' she laughed, and then she dragged me below decks to introduce me to her 'babies'.

I did love Marjorie. She was great fun and like me she was

very much into Yorkshire terriers and jewellery.

'Now. You've met Tammy, Dolly and Shania but I have a new sire – Luke Bryan, country star. Isn't he just darling?' she lifted up a fine looking Yorkie.

'Oh yes, he *is* beautiful, but what happened to Kenny Rogers?' I asked taking the small dog from her and burying my nose in its fur.

'It was just awful. When we got back to the States his fur went dull and he was very listless. My vet said he was suffering from anaemia and put him on a course of iron tablets, but I think it was too little too late. Poor, sweet little Kenny died in my arms. I tell you, Cameron I was just devastated! He was my little baby,' she said, tearfully.

'That is so sad. Strange how they can go from healthy to critically ill in the blink of an eye,' I said innocently. I did feel guilty, but he'd just been so tasty and I had drunk too much. I'd never intentionally have killed one of Marjorie's dogs.

'So little Luke here looks like he could win prizes,' I said, holding the dog up admiringly.

'He does! He is already a champion back in the USA, but this year I hope to show him at Crufts.'

I sat back in the comfortable cushions on her leather sofa. I knew that at some point the Yorkies and I would get to be alone. I'd never had a champion before and it was on my list of delicatessen items to try. I'd have to be more careful thought, and just take a few sips this time. He might win at Crufts and that would be something to chalk up!

'Have you bought anything recently?' I asked innocently, knowing she would dash off leaving me and Luke to get better acquainted.

He gave a surprised yelp when I bit his paw and quickly sucked a few mouthfuls. *Tasty you are,* I whispered in his little ear, while I pressed down with a tissue to stem the flow of blood. He was all clean and tidy and chewing a biscuit when Marjorie walked back in holding a light blue box.

'Oooh, Tiffany you naughty girl,' I cried in delight.

'I just had to have this ring. Pink diamonds! Aren't they fabulous?' She pulled a gorgeous ring out of the box.

They were very fine diamonds indeed and must have cost her a small fortune. I quickly did a calculation and realised it would probably cover Roberto's wages for the year. *No! Must keep head down! And I like Marjorie.* We talked jewellery for a while, but I could see it was close to eleven o'clock and I still wanted to go into town to get some dinner. I called my tender over and bid Marjorie goodnight.

'You must come over tomorrow night, Cameron. I'm having a few people over for cocktails and canapés,' she said, as I was about to get into the tender. I promised her I would and went into town.

I went along the next evening, but it wasn't much of a party. Most of the guests were older and there was no one there I fancied for dinner. I tried to get some alone time with the Yorkies but I didn't get them by themselves all night. Luke had started to growl at me, and barked if I came too close. A seventy-something called Gladys annoyed the hell out of me. She had *the* most grating southern accent and kept going on and on about her estate in Georgia. I suspected it probably had been great once, but since the abolition of slavery it would gradually have fallen into disrepair. I also had the impression that she was still lamenting said abolition. If she hadn't been so old and wrinkled I would gladly have sunk my fangs into her neck. I was pondering whether to call Roberto so I could leave as she loudly rattled off the names of all the important people she socialised with in New York. I hate shameless name dropping – it showed how unimportant she was – but then I heard a name that got my attention.

'You know Joseph Webber?' I interrupted.

'Why, yes honey! How in the Lord's name do you know him?' she asked me, surprised.

'I don't, but my great-grandfather worked for his father in Paris. What's he like? By all accounts his dad was a great guy. He knew how to party,' I told her.

'Joseph doesn't smoke or drink. He once told me his dad died young because of his drinking, so he doesn't touch the devil's nectar. I know him because we attend the same church in New York. He's a good Christian and family man.' She went on to tell me about his five children and 16 grandchildren and my attention started to drift again. Poor Charley, he'd have been very disappointed. I was quite sure it hadn't been the drink that had put Charley in an early grave.

I called Roberto to bring the tender round and was surprised when, a few minutes later, George turned up instead. 'I didn't think you'd be back yet,' I said surprised. He was scheduled to be at his weekly poker game in Antibes.

'Roger couldn't make it so there were just four of us and we decided to make it an early night,' he told me.

'I would have gone. You know I love a real game and it would've been better than this party,' I said grumpily.

'I wouldn't introduce you to my worst enemy, let alone my mates, you weirdo,' George said. He was laughing, but I knew he was serious.

'Boo! Unfair!' I said crossing my arms and going into a huff.

'You never take me to any of Andrei's parties, either, but I think it's better we keep our lives separate, don't you? Anyway, what was so wrong with this party?'

'It was just this woman. All fur coat and nae knickers.'

'What? One of Marjorie's old friends was going commando?' he asked me surprised.

'What? Commando?' I asked him, confused.

'Yes, as in she wasn't wearing any underpants?' George asked looking equally confused.

'Oh god, no! Now I have to get that vision out of my head! Maybe it's just an Edinburgh expression – it means you pretend to be someone, but really, underneath the fur coat, there is nothing,' I explained.

'Oh! I thought wearing a fur coat in this weather was a bit strange, but I thought maybe the old dear was a little batty,' he said, laughing. He slowed down to let me ashore.

It was still early so I decided to head into town, maybe I could persuade some girl to come back to the yacht. It wasn't usually too difficult, as who doesn't want to sit on the deck of a luxury yacht and sip champagne? I made my way to one of the night clubs and scanned the crowd for some prey.

Suddenly, I felt an arm wind around my waist and turned to find Olga behind me. Darn! I only liked to feast on a girl once and then hoped they'd leave me alone and move on if I didn't call them. I certainly didn't want Olga in my life.

'Hi Cameron. Why you never call me?' she asked, pulling a sad face.

'Hi Olga. I'm sorry, I've been out of the country for a while. Is Tatiana here too?' I asked scanning the crowd, pretending she hardly existed.

'Yes, and our friend Anna. She is Russian too.'

Anna was very pretty, tall and blonde and curvier than the other two – just my type. This was going to be a challenge. How could I not be rude to Andrei's fiancé, avoid Olga and try to get Anna back to the boat? I bought some champagne and had it sent over to their table. Sergei was there too to keep an eye on Tatiana and he looked his merry old self, only reluctantly allowing me to sit with the girls because he knew I was friendly with Andrei.

Anna wouldn't give me the time of day. I had the idea that

Tatiana had told her I was nowhere near as rich as Andrei. *What was Monaco coming to if having a yacht and being young and attractive couldn't land you the girl?* I was seeing my investment in some very pricey champagne going up in smoke and I started to get annoyed. Who did this Anna think she was? I wanted to do some very bad things to her now.

'So Anna, do you have any pets, a dog maybe?' I asked her.

'No. And I like cats.' *That figured.* Revenge would have to wait as it was getting close to sunrise.

'We go back to boat?' shouted Olga, right in my ear as the music was very loud.

'No. I need to get up early tomorrow.' I was hungry, but I wasn't going to take her with me, the girl would almost certainly get the wrong idea. Sometimes things don't go according to plan and you just have to weather it and be hungry for a while longer. I made my excuses and left.

During the next day, I searched frantically online to find out more about Anna. She was on Facebook and her page wasn't secured. She even mentioned which hotel she was staying at. As I had watched an episode of *Dexter* earlier, a plan was forming in my mind. Dexter was something of a role model and an inspiration to me at that time. I wished I could get away with leaving so many bodies in my wake.

The next step would be to get some quality tranquillisers. I knew where one of the vets from the racetrack lived and I'd be able to find some horse tranquilliser there. I broke in that night and found what I needed then I broke in to her hotel room the following night, when I was sure she had gone to sleep. I was wearing a mask and, after turning on the light, I jumped on top of the startled girl. I showed her the scalpel and syringe I had brought with me and injected her with the tranquilliser. Soon, she was asleep, and I made a small incision on her wrist. She'd been drinking champagne so I began to feel more charitable towards the girl. I drank just over a pint and then put a plaster over her wrist. I'd wanted to strip her naked and cut her cheek, but I decided that would be a bit too creepy and unkind. She had provided dinner after all.

I stripped the bed and laid her out on her back, then I wrapped her to the bed with cling film. I looked at her and her pretty face. *Silly girl! We could have had a lot of fun together. Piss a vampire off at your peril!* Then I slipped out of the hotel unnoticed.

When I spoke to Andrei a few days later he told me that Anna had called in hotel security and the French police and all sorts. She was both terrified and furious and swore that she would never set foot in France again. She took a flight back to Moscow as soon as she could.

The following week Marjorie invited me again to one of her parties and I hoped Gladys wouldn't be there. She wasn't, but the party was a disaster anyway; Nanette was there and she hounded me all night.

'Sailing your silly boat from Cannes to Monaco is hardly getting out of town,' she hissed.

'Thought it was best not to run. It might make people suspicious. I don't see your problem, though. Nothing in this murder suggests vampire.'

I was nonchalantly hanging against the railing pretending we were having a light conversation.

'I suppose that Dexter stunt in Nice wasn't you?' she hissed at me again.

'Don't know what you're talking about,' I said, all innocence. 'Darling, we should be friends. We are the same species after all,' I said, moving close to her. 'What if we were the last two vampires in the world?'

I got back a look so chilling that I took an involuntary step backwards. I wondered if I was losing my touch – two women in the past week rebuffing my advances! I was not impressed and wanted to leave. Meanwhile though, Luke had come on deck and started barking when he spotted me.

'Why does that little dog keep barking at you?' Nanette asked kicking little Luke out of her way with the tip of her shoe. 'You eat these things, don't you?'

I didn't reply. Instead, I phoned Roberto on my mobile and asked him to bring the tender round. I was in a foul mood and didn't fancy talking to anybody else. He arrived a few minutes later and I did leave the party, but I wasn't going to sail out of Monaco just yet. Bloody Nanette did scare me, but not enough to drive me away from a fun place like Monaco when Marjorie was in town. Fair enough, her last two shindigs had been flops but I was sure a third would be a charm.

'Cameron, darling,' she cooed on the phone a few days later.

'Marjorie, my gem. How are you?' I cooed back.

'Listen darling, my friend Dahlia is bringing over this medium to the Zaza tonight, you simply *have* to come!' she demanded.

'I wouldn't miss it for the world, my darling,' I assured her.

A medium! That could be interesting. She'd certainly see one dead person in the room! I wondered if the old bat would suss me out. I went over just after dark and found a group of about seven of Marjorie's friends already assembled in the living room. They had left a space for me at the large dining room table. The medium was younger than I'd expected and a rather disappointingly normal forty-something. I wanted more drama and loose, flowing hippy clothes. Even her jewellery was banal; little, plain gold hoops. *If you can't afford anything good, just don't bother dear!*

We were instructed to sit around the table and hold hands. They had put out the light and lit some candles. Suddenly, the doors to the deck flew open and the candles blew out. The medium gasped for air and convulsed for a bit. *Neat tricks!* She had brought the drama after all.

'There's a Thomas Whyte here. Does anyone know a Thomas Whyte?' she asked, eyes closed so she could concentrate on a voice only she could hear. *Bloody hell! She's conjured up the ghost of wee Tam!*

'Ask him how he died,' said Marjorie.

'He says he's a Scottish soldier and he died in 1915. He also says he has some unfinished business with a Cameron Blair.'

Marjorie shrieked at this and pointed over at me. 'It must be for you, Cameron!'

'Cameron Blair was my great-grandfather's name. They tell me I look just like him. What business?' I asked intrigued.

The medium blushed and became embarrassed.

'Erm, he's using some foul language!' she explained.

'Out with it! I'm sure you ladies have heard it all before,' encouraged Marjorie.

'He says, "Cameron, get the fuck over here you daft cunt, you're long overdue".'

There was a shocked silence then the room erupted in howling laughter. *Tam you wee radge! That was pure class!*

When we'd calmed down, we were told to relight the candles as the ghost had left. The ladies shuffled about on their chairs in anticipation. I was sure they all wanted to speak to a dead husband or cat.

Then: 'There's a Cameron Blair here, wanting to talk to Cameron.'

I saw the ladies looking enviously at me and felt bad hogging all the ghosts.

'That'll be great-grandad then,' I said with a wink.

'He wants the rest of him to come over. He says he nearly has his entire soul.'

The ladies gasped in wonder. What exactly did that mean?

'Cameron. Do you know what your grandad wants?' asked the medium, puzzled.

'I think he wants me to go to Scotland, maybe visit his grave and make peace with my family. I think his soul may rest when mine does,' I said, trying to sound sincere and philosophical. I pretended to be lost in deep thought for a moment.

Lillian, Marjorie's friend who was sitting next to me squeezed my hand and whispered, 'Yeah, I think your great-grandad would like that.'

Of course I knew what *I* meant. The twat was telling me I had slowly lost my soul. I hoped there wouldn't be any more ghosts showing up, trying to mess with my head, but the rest of the evening went to plan with various dead relatives saying little obvious things to the ladies gathered around the table. Afterwards, everyone stood around chatting excitedly with a glass of something in one hand and a canapé in the other.

The medium came over to me. 'That was very strange, Mr MacAdam!'

'You're telling me. This is my first séance. How do you see the dead ones?' I asked, as she led me away from the crowd.

'Well, I normally just feel a presence and, if I'm lucky, hear a faint whisper. Some of the time I just have to guess and make stuff up, but tonight I actually had to stop listening to the voices.' She looked at me. 'There were just too many.'

'Oh? And what did they say?' I asked calmly, but I was distinctly worried that it had been a meeting of the Cameron's victims' support group.

'There was a lot of swearing at this Cameron Blair,' she said, looking at me with concern.

'My great-grandad was a bit of a rogue,' I told her light-heartedly.

'It really seemed to be directed at you and most of them were very angry.' She looked at me, obviously trying to gauge why I attracted that many spirits.

'Well, as I said, my great-grandad and I look very alike,' I said nonchalantly.

'Did he know a Hélène?' she asked suddenly.

Fuck! She was there too! Not sure if I want to hear this. 'What did the woman say?' I said, working hard to sound casual.

'She stood out because she wasn't angry. She said she understands now and she's sorry.' The medium watched closely for my reaction.

'I don't know who this woman was to my great-grandad, but I'm sure he's sorry too,' I said, making sure my voice didn't waver. I could see that she wasn't quite buying the great-grandad story, so I quickly moved the conversation on.

'You wouldn't happen to have a Charley there as well, would you? Gladys over there knows his son and my great-grandad worked for him.'

'I don't know, there were a lot of voices there. Would you like a private session?' she asked me and I could see she was desperate to probe.

'Good heavens, no! As you say, most of these ghosts were angry. Best to let them rest,' I said laughing and moved away to talk to some other guests. I would love to have had a private session; to talk to Hélène again would have been amazing – there was still so much I wanted to say to her – but it would almost certainly have revealed me as a vampire and I wasn't willing to take that risk.

Later, Marjorie came over, still a little tearful as Kenny Rogers, her departed Yorkshire terrier, had told her from beyond the grave that he loved his mummy. I'm sure the ghost of Kenny had been there, but his bark would certainly have been directed at me.

'Cameron darling, what an evening! Gosh darn it, your grandaddy must have been quite something to have pissed that many spirits off!'

'Well, luckily we are only alike in looks,' I said with a cheeky grin.

'I'd like to have met this Cameron Blair. I do like a bad boy...' and she gave my arm a squeeze.

'I'm sure young you and granddad would have had a whale of a time,' I said laughing.

Chapter 23: Emmy

The day after Marjorie's séance, I found George on deck with a young woman. He didn't seem keen to introduce us so I went over and introduced myself.

'I'm Cameron,' I said shaking her hand. 'Who is this delightful girl, George?'

She was actually very pretty, a tall Germanic type with a healthy tan and sun-bleached blonde hair. George looked worried. *He does not want me to know this person!*

'I'm Emily. His daughter,' she said in a strong German accent.

Now this was a surprise! I'd had no idea George had a daughter. I was even more surprised that George had managed to have attractive offspring – the girl must have taken after her mother.

'You must stay for dinner, my dear, and tell me all about how our George here ended up with a German daughter,' I said eying her up with interest.

George shot me a dirty look and looked very uncomfortable. 'Not tonight,' he said. 'I have to take Emmy back to Monaco, but I will tell you all later.' With that, he shepherded her into the tender and they set off. She had obviously surprised him with an unexpected visit.

This is just too good! George managed to get a Fräulein pregnant! His grandad would be spinning in his grave – if he'd had one.

I cornered Roberto in the kitchen, too curious to wait for George's return to find out more. 'Did you know George had a daughter Roberto?' I asked.

'Uh, no, Mr Blair.'

Roberto sounded nervous and I knew he was lying. 'Any

other secrets you two are keeping from me?' I asked him in a stern voice that I knew would rattle him further.

'I'm sorry, Mr Blair. He told me not to tell you. I don't know why.' *Another lie.*

'He doesn't trust me, does he?' I asked.

'Fathers are just very protective of their daughters.'

I raised my eyebrows. 'Does she need protecting from me?'

'I don't know, Sir, it's just that... you are what you are, and... You have to speak to him,' stammered Roberto and he hastily left the kitchen.

I was annoyed. I had hoped to have earned their trust by now, but they seemed to have so many secrets and called me a psychopath behind my back. I suddenly felt very lonely. It would forever be the humans and me. I waited impatiently for George to come back to the yacht, but when he got back that evening he had a passenger with him.

'Ah, the woman that gave bleeding a husband dry a whole new meaning. How are you Nanette, darling?' I asked, helping her on board.

'Shut up. I don't want to be here a moment longer than I have to,' she replied, pushing me aside.

'But it's such a pleasure to have you on board,' I said with my most charming smile.

'Cameron, your fence has been arrested. Rashid Lal, that's your jewellery man isn't it?' she said.

This was very bad news. I had landed poor Rashid right in it. I'm not sure how Nanette had come by the information, but I knew why she'd want me to know. A vampire being found out could be very bad news for her too. Once my existence was confirmed, there would be a hunt to find more. People might well compare our behaviour and find her out too.

'You *have* to go Cameron, and quickly,' she told me.

'Do you know where they're keeping him?' asked George. I

was sure he was secretly hoping he could go and bust him out.

'Somewhere in Moscow. You wouldn't get anywhere near him,' she said impatiently.

Darn. He must have tried to sell some of the pieces to his collector. Nanette left with Roberto in our tender and George and I made preparations for me to leave. I took all the money we had in the safe and some clothes, together with the small canvas Hélène had done. I had carried that little portrait everywhere with me, it reminded me never to let anyone get as close to me as she had done and never to fall in love again. George had access to my bank accounts, so he'd be fine, but I asked him to clear some of it out in case my funds were blocked and to hide it somewhere safe.

'You and Roberto must go to the police and tell them everything apart from the vampire stuff,' I said to George. 'You both have proper wage slips and there is no evidence that the two of you are involved in any way.'

'I know, Cameron. We will be fine,' George said quietly.

'Tell me how your Emily came about,' I asked him with false cheer as I packed my bags.

He told me he'd been stationed near Bielefeld in Germany early in his army career. The locals weren't too friendly – they were fed up with all the young English soldiers stationed on their door step, most of whom didn't speak a word of German and some of whom made nuisances of themselves in the local clubs and bars. Few friendships formed between the two nations in those days, but George had been different. He didn't drink and therefore avoided the bars and clubs and he started to attend a German language class in the evening to have something to do.

'You speak German?' I asked him, surprised, knowing George's struggle with languages.

'Nah! I was rubbish at that too, but the teacher was nice.' He gave me a big goofy grin. *Wow George must have liked this girl a lot.* He told me the teacher was called Sandra Offenbach and the two of them had become friendly. After about six months, she found out she was pregnant. George did the honourable thing and married her.

She wasn't cut out for being an army wife; she didn't get on with the other, mostly British, wives and had different interests. She also hated being alone with a small child while her husband was away on exercise or an overseas posting. The marriage lasted four years. Sandra decided to end it when George joined the SAS and was posted back to England. She didn't want her husband to have an even more dangerous job and, as she preferred to stay in Germany with her daughter, they agreed to divorce.

'Are the two of you still in touch?' I asked him.

'Yes. We've always been on good terms; she just hated being an army wife.'

'Would she like being the wife of a yacht captain?' I asked him with a nudge to his shoulder.

'She has long since remarried. A fellow German teacher. To be honest, I think there was something going on between them before the divorce. Sandra always hated it when I was away on army business and I think she found comfort in this guy's arms.'

George didn't seem too upset but I thought I should offer anyway. 'Do you want me to kill him?' I asked.

'No! *Please* don't kill anyone else,' George said hastily. 'I don't mind the guy actually. He's been a good dad to Emmy.'

When I'd finished packing, we made our way up on deck and saw Roberto approaching with the tender.

'Look after that tasty daughter of yours, it a shame I never got to know her better,' I said to George smiling.

'You know I'd rather kill you than allow you anywhere near her, you bastard,' he said and I knew he wasn't kidding.

'I know, George,' I said offering him my hand, all traces of mockery gone for once. 'Take care now.'

'We'll meet up again when this has all died down in a few years,' he said as he took my hand. Then uncomfortable with poignancy of the moment he told me, 'Now bugger off!'

I got into the tender with Roberto and we set off for Monaco. 'Now Roberto, you must tell the police everything – apart from any weird vampire stuff. Just... you know, be as honest as you can,' I said as we sailed to shore.

'I will, Mr Blair,' he said still looking very nervous.

'It's *Cameron*! I can look after myself. Save your own skin and co-operate as much as you can.'

'Ok, Mr Blair.' I felt my fangs aching to push themselves out but I calmed down and told him, 'Listen, stay in touch with George, if you can, but go back to Colombia.'

'I will,' he assured me.

'At least you can take that bint of yours out on the town now,' I said with a wink and a smile.

'What?' Roberto looked confused.

'So, who is she then, your girlfriend?' I asked him.

'Erm, I have been seeing Francesca, Gianluca's daughter,' he stammered.

'Oh! Good! She seemed nice,' I said, but I had only seen her in passing and she hadn't registered.

'She is, and I want to ask her to come to Colombia with me to meet my parents,' he told me and he blushed a bit.

'Have a good life, Roberto. I hope we'll meet again and you'll forgive me,' I said as I offered him my hand.

He was taken aback. 'I... I... It's all good, Mr Blair,' he stammered, as we shook hands. I went on shore and watched him sail off.

I had made a right royal mess of things. Why had I allowed so much human involvement in my life? It had never gone well. As Roberto sped back towards *The Count Dracula* I realised I would miss this life; I'd really had the most wonderful time in the south of France, but it was time to go and it was time to grow up, be more responsible and become someone else again.

Chapter 24: Serge

As Roberto piloted me towards Monaco, and I left my fabulous life behind, I thought about the demons I needed to put to bed. I needed to grow up a bit and deal with things and, if I was to decide my future, I knew I had first to look at my past.

For many years I had, from time to time, felt a presence in my life. I couldn't quite pinpoint it but I had the impression that it was another vampire. I'd been surprised when I discovered Nanette's nature as the impression had led me to think I had a 'vampdar' that told me when I was in the presence of another – but Nanette hadn't registered. I had begun to imagine that the presence I felt couldn't be just any old vampire; it must be my maker. I had always been curious about how and why he had made me, and the fact that I had felt his presence over the years made me determined to find him. Who was he and why did he still have an interest in me?

I'd had the foresight to send Roberto to Cannes on the train to retrieve my BMW, so now it was there waiting for me on the quay in Monaco. I pondered where to go next. Paris was always a good place in a crisis so I programmed the GPS to where I needed to stop for petrol and daylight hideaways. I wanted to stop off at a hotel along the way and try and contact Nanette via one of the chatrooms. She may have been unnerving, but she was the only person I knew that had met their own maker and I needed to know about her experience in order to track down my own.

I was about to start the engine, when there was a knock on the windscreen.

'Emmy!' I was surprised to see George's daughter. 'Hi what are you doing here?'

'Mr Blair. I'm so glad to see you. I need some help.' She looked worried.

Oh no you don't! If you think I'm going to piss George off and have some SAS-trained, super-motivated vampire slayer on my back, you have another think coming!

'Listen, dear. Whatever problem you have, trust me, your dad is the best person to turn to!' I said starting the engine of my BMW.

'But you know my dad. He says you're his oldest friend so you know he is a bit of a... erm... as you English say... a bit of a *nutter*.'

'Well, A: I am not English and B: your dad is not a nutter. Please trust him and tell him what your problem is,' I said revving the motor impatiently.

'It's just that a boyfriend stole all my stuff and I told dad it was a mugger. I really want my stuff back and I know he is hanging out in St Tropez. I am worried my dad would beat him up,' she said.

'Sorry, dear. Really not my problem,' I said lightly.

'But Cameron! *Please!*' she insisted.

'It's Mr Blair to you, dear. Now, I am in something of a rush and I've got to dash.'

I saw her tearing up, but even those blue eyes and golden locks couldn't wipe the image of George wielding a wooden stake from my mind.

'Look. I have to go now, but if your dad ever *really* can't help you, send me a message on Facebook. I'm Cruftslover.' I wound up the window and drove off. I didn't look back.

I headed for the motorway, hoping to reach Lyon before sunrise. I found a hotel with free wifi for the day and monitored the chatrooms for some Nanette activity. I had to be careful in case my internet traffic was being monitored, so I just posted a message and hoped it would work.

I didn't have to wait long for a reply.

MacFangs: To the one that drains old suckers, the others that made us have not been eradicated. Below what caused Troy's downfall we shall meet.
QueenofFangs: Do you want me to come to Paris, or Helen? I think they were equally guilty.
MacFangs: There's a place called Helen?
QueenofFangs: There is one in the USA, in Georgia.
MacFangs: Yes, go to that one.
QueenofFangs: So I assume it is Paris?
MacFangs: I was trying to avoid plastering that all over the internet, but yes.

No date, no time, but I knew we would find one another somehow. I was surprised she'd agreed so readily to come all the way to Paris knowing how much she hated me. I drove on to Paris the next night and abandoned my car not too far from an entrance to the catacombs.

The Parisian catacombs had been a good hideout on many occasions. I'd hidden some stuff from the 1920s down there, but with all the artsy happenings and rediscovery of Paris's subterranean I had read about, I doubted it would still be there. As I re-familiarised myself with the subterranean network of tunnels, I found that the place was overrun with people and it was hard to find a quiet spot. Sometimes I'd come across an illegal rave in one of the rooms or stumble on a tour group going around all the interesting graves. There were also a lot of artists frequenting the tunnels creating colourful art on the walls with their spray cans. I even spotted a few sculptures on my travels. One day I got talking to a dreadlocked hipster and asked him what had attracted him to the catacombs.

'No police here, man,' he explained, posing in front of a rather good mural, 'I can just get on and create my art.'

'There are quite a few of you down here now, do you not want your work to be seen by a wider audience?' I asked him.

'They call us cataphiles and I get a good-sized audience. And they are like-minded,' he told me. 'There's a great community down here with performing artists, sculptors and painters like me.'

We talked about art for a while and he showed me some of his friends' works. Some of it I liked very much. He told me his name was Jonas and before he left he invited me to one of their get togethers at the weekend.

I met Jonas and his friends a few days later at their weekend gathering where we discussed art and listened to music. It was good, and reminded me a lot of my time with Hélène and the Paris of the early 1920s, but this time there was loud techno music and people kept checking their phones and iPads even though they couldn't have had any reception down there. I left when they started smoking joints and wanted me to. I wasn't going to make that mistake again.

A short, dumpy girl with a dirty anorak and messy hair followed me out. 'Hey! You'll get lost without a light,' she shouted after me.

I hadn't stopped to think that my not needing a torch would seem odd to a human. 'Oh, it's OK. I don't live far from here and I could find my way blind,' I told her.

'Can I see where you live?'

Crap. I'd made myself comfortable in a less frequented room, but it was rather out of the way and she'd be astounded that I was able to find my way there in the pitch dark.

'My place is still a bit away. Are you sure you want to leave your friends and follow a complete stranger into some dark tunnels?' I asked.

She hesitated and then said, 'I'll ask my friend Linda to come with us.'

Soon, Linda, Anaïs, some torches and a bottle of wine joined me for a private party chez Cameron. I didn't like Anaïs – she was a tad grubby and she was stoned. Linda I liked a lot more as she was clean and not too stoned by the looks of it. I slipped a sleeping pill into Anaïs' drink and hoped that I was Linda's type. I was more groomed than the rest of her friends, but hopefully living underground in the catacombs would give me enough street cred to get into her knickers.

Anaïs quickly fell asleep and to my delight Linda didn't mind and she crawled closer. She was pleased to speak English with me as she said she still found speaking French difficult and tiring and late at night she'd rather gave it a rest. She told me she was there as an au pair for a year and hoped to study French the following year in her home town of Sheffield. Soon we were making love, quietly so as not to wake her friend. It wasn't great, as she didn't want to get naked in the cold underground room and the floor was hard and uncomfortable. I think we were both a little disappointed at the end of it.

She lit a cigarette and poured herself another glass of wine. The conversation was a bit awkward and banal and after a while she asked, 'Do you have somewhere I could brush my teeth?'

I gave her a bottle of water and she disappeared into a tunnel with her torch. With her gone for a while I was able to sink my fangs into Anaïs. I needed to be careful not to drink too much as the girl had smoked a lot of hashish and god knows what else.

Linda came back, lay down next to me and got ready to go to sleep. I cuddled into her and got ready for the drugs I'd ingested to take their effect. I had vivid nightmares. Nanette chased me around the catacombs with a stake and I could have sworn she was standing right next to me at one point. I must have yelled out loud, as Linda sat up and switched her torch on.

'Are you all right?' she asked, alarmed.

I told her it was just a nightmare and checked my watch. It was only four in the morning, so I told her to go back to sleep. She moved herself over to the other side of the room and soon drifted off. When I felt the effects of the drug wearing off, I switched on my laptop. I couldn't get an internet connection this deep below ground, so I had to make do with some games I had stored on the computer.

I woke the girls up at nine o'clock and offered to walk them back to an entranceway. Linda was pretending nothing had happened between us, as I think I was probably meant to be her friend's date. I stopped in the tunnel when I saw the daylight ahead, kissed them both on the cheeks and said I'd see them around. They disappeared into the daylight and I turned round to go back to my room.

Suddenly, she was just there. Nanette had found me! In over 300 kilometres of tunnels she'd just walked right up to me.

'So what do you want, dog breath?' she asked.

'Hi Nanette. Would you like a tour?' I offered with an inviting sweep of my arm.

'Cameron. Make it short. I'm really not in the mood for your stuff. I can't believe I came all the way to Paris to talk to you. I have a good mind to stake you and do everyone a favour,' she said, none too pleased.

'Wow Nanette. I just dreamed that you did exactly that, but anyway... I wanted to talk to you about your maker. Can you tell me about him?' I asked her.

'I'd rather not,' she said walking back in the direction of my hideout.

'Hang on a minute. It's morning. How long have you been here?' I asked her and she looked at me with those weird golden eyes and grimaced.

'Too long. And I don't think I will ever erase the image of your pale, naked bottom from my memory.'

'Eeeuw! You were watching?' I cried in disgust.

'I thought your use of a sleeping pill was inspired. I might try that one. The girl really didn't feel a thing, not even when I bit her too!' she said, walking on.

'Does the hashish not affect you?' I asked.

'Oh, it did! I think we vampires really can't cope with drugs. You only bite a junky once. I slept the hashish off in one of the tunnels. Now why do you need to talk to me?' she asked, as we reached my hideout.

'I think my maker is following me.'

'Have you seen him?'

'I can sense him. Now and then I just feel he is there, watching me.'

Nanette sat down and thought for a while. 'I think maybe it's only our makers we can sense. I didn't sense you until you became such an idiot and started to give the game away. Apart from my maker I've never sensed anyone else.'

'Tell me. You met and staked your maker didn't you?

'You heard that story then?' she asked me suspiciously. 'I never told you.'

She couldn't have been happy that I knew that story, she had carelessly divulged it in a chatroom. Once I'd realised QueenofFangs was Nanette, I'd remembered it.

'I need to know my maker. Your story might help me find mine,' I told her.

'Why do you want to find the bastard?' she asked.

'Bastard indeed. I've never understood why he made me and then just left. I'm also starting to agree with you, that I'm a bit of a nuisance and that there probably shouldn't be any more of me,' I said.

'First sensible thing I ever heard coming out of your mouth,' she said emphatically.

'Who knows how many this vampire has created?'

'The thought of you having idiot brothers and sisters running around Europe is making me feel quite nauseous,' she said with utter distaste.

'Apart from you, I don't know any other vampires. I need to know how my maker has coped over the years and why he has looked in on me but not made contact,' I went on.

'So. Are you going to kill him?' she asked.

'Don't know yet, but does the wooden stake in the heart really work?' I asked her.

'Well, I tried it and the next thing I knew there was a little heap of dust,' she said.

'Do you think it would be frowned upon by the others?' I asked.

'Don't know, don't care,' she said with a dismissive wave of her hand.

'So what wood did you use?' I asked.

'For heaven's sake Cameron, I grabbed the first broom stick that came to hand. I didn't stop to see what type of wood it was,' she said impatiently.

'Please. Tell me about your maker,' I asked her again.

She sighed. Then: 'Serge made me because I reminded him of his wife. In 1845 he had managed to piss off a vampire by I don't even remember what, but you know how petty we get when somebody annoys us.'

'I do! I nearly set fire to a woman once for stealing my scooter,' I said.

'Why didn't you?' she asked me mockingly. *Has she just accused me of being a soft wuss?*

'Well, I thought it was a bit extreme so I made her steal her parents' dog instead.' Nanette gave me one of her looks filled with loathing and then continued her story.

'The vampire came to his house, killed his two small children and his wife, made him watch their murders and then made him a vampire to make him live with the memories for all eternity.'

'Wow! So did he ever go after his maker?' I asked.

'He hunted and searched for this vampire for 25 years, but never managed to find him. Serge was rather pathetic you know. He would catch prey for me and let me have the first bite. He insisted on calling me Marie-Louise and kept telling me that now we would be together forever and that I was safe. After five days I couldn't take it anymore, so I staked him,' she told me calmly.

'Poor guy,' I said in mock compassion.

'I think I did him and the world a favour. He had gone quite mad by living so long. He wanted to recreate his family and was stalking a family that had a child the same age as his oldest son. I mean, I wasn't going to be looking after a vampire child for all eternity! I believe vampires do age and that they go a little peculiar over time. Bit like you really,' she said.

'I don't think that's true! I'm as sharp as I used to be in the 1920s' I said, outraged.

'Then maybe you just weren't that bright to start with, but you do have some weird habits,' she said lighting a cigarette.

'Have you ever even tried dog?' I asked her.

'We've all been hungry,' she said. Suddenly I saw her face change. The façade came down and she looked vulnerable. 'I need a favour Cameron,' she said softly. I was surprised, but now I understood why she had come to Paris. As much as she disliked me, I was the only person she could reveal herself to. I was the only person that she could trust and that could help her.

'Harold wasn't as stupid as everyone thinks. He never did marry me,' she told me. 'When he dies I will, as his companion, inherit just 100,000 euros. The kids will get everything else.'

'Doesn't sound too bad for a nursing job with food and board included,' I said looking at her with interest. She was very different now.

'I still use my real paperwork. I'm called Wided Medjnoun and according to my passport I should be 53 years old. Once Harold dies I want to disappear and start a new life with a new identity. I think he has just a few weeks left,' she told me.

'So you need an introduction to my contacts?' I asked.

'If you don't mind,' she said looking at her feet. I realised that the hatred had come from envy and jealousy, the fact that I was independently wealthy, living it large, apparently without a care in the world and being dependent on no one. Then I had wrecked it all by one stupid murder! She would have killed to have my life and she was sure she wouldn't have been so stupid. *Wided, you are still a young vampire. Wait until the human blood makes its changes and then greed will take you over too!*

I promised I would call my contacts that evening and set up a meeting for her to get some new papers. I asked her to stay till nightfall and told her my life story. Then reluctantly she told me hers. I knew she'd ended her human days as a prostitute, but not much else.

She told me she had left school at sixteen even though her teachers had said she was very bright. By the age of eighteen she had married a man called Ali Medjnoun, a second cousin who wanted to move from Algeria to France. Both sets of parents thought the two would be a good match.

Wided hadn't yet realised how pretty she was, but Ali had, and he jealously guarded his new wife. He controlled her every move, not even allowing her to go out and work. The couple didn't have much money and arguments soon started. Her great misfortune was to discover that she couldn't have children and Ali grew frustrated at her inability to bear him sons. He was a cruel man and would beat Wided and lock her in the house while he went out to work. At age 25, Wided couldn't stand it anymore and she ran off to Marseille.

Unable to hold down any legal, paid work, as she didn't want her husband to find her, Wided soon caught the attention of a local pimp, Sahid. He took her in and gave her a place to stay, but he also raped her and made her work in his brothels. She was held captive with some other unfortunate girls for many years until one day Sahid got into a fight with another pimp and was gunned down in front of his brothel. Not knowing what else to do, and now in her 30s, Wided decided to stay on the game.

Without a pimp, or a brothel to work from, she ended up working in some of the most dangerous parts of Marseille, picking up sailors on shore leave. These were the hunting grounds for the likes of me, and poor Wided met her end there. The vampire that made her was quite taken by her beauty and, as she'd explained already, wanted her to be his companion, but by this time Wided had had enough of all the evil bloodsucking bastards in the world, so she put a wooden stake through his heart. Wided died with him and Nanette rose like a phoenix from the ashes. She reinvented herself as a confident woman who used her beauty to get what she wanted and never cowered from a man again. You would mess with Nanette at your peril.

We parted that night knowing each other inside out. We'd never be friends, but I knew now that I could trust her and call on her if I needed to.

***

In the past, I had tried to trace my maker by talking to others about theirs. Most of the stories were absolute nonsense. Amongst the Goths, it was mostly a very childish competition about whose maker was older and who had the most historically interesting background, but often I would stumble across a so-called expert like Vampanillo78. I got talking to him in an internet café later that night.

> Vampanillo78: You really know nothing about vampires MacFangs. 1845 is not an old one; I was made by a real old one who had been made during the Spanish inquisition.
> MacFangs: How?
> Vampanillo78: He sucked my blood and then I drank his ancient blood.
> MacFangs: Sorry, I mean why you?
> Vampanillo78: Because I am special.
> MacFangs: Aye, you're special alright.
> Vampanillo78: Thanks MacFangs.

I had one interesting lead. I knew my maker was blond and rather tall, so I posted a question on one of the forums.

> MacFangs: I heard about this tall, blond vampire that was active in the Great War. Has anyone heard a similar story?

An interesting reply was soon posted.

TruthseekerNL: There is some evidence that the Germans in 1938 experimented with using vampires as secret weapons.

MacFangs: Evidence, really?

TruthseekerNL: There is this photograph doing the rounds on the internet showing a Polish soldier, and he seems to be fighting off something invisible attacking his neck. He looks absolutely terrified. According to witnesses this was a vampire that was tall and blond, but of course he isn't visible on a photo.

MacFangs: When was this picture taken?

TruthseekerNL: It was in September 1939 during the battle of Bzura that 2 Polish soldiers claimed one of their comrades was killed by a vampire. As the Poles lost the battle and had to retreat, there was no physical evidence. But the soldiers stated that when darkness fell this German soldier attracted them, bit and killed one of them and then just disappeared into the night.

MacFangs: Have you heard of any other such stories Truth?

TruthseekerNL: There are a lot of accounts by German soldiers too, about two possessed allied soldiers attacking and killing German troops, mainly during the Ardennes offensive, but I don't think this is your guy as the two were described as being dark haired. Ya beauty! George Senior and I are an internet sensation!

MacFangs: Amazing stuff. Do you know if there have been any other sightings of a tall blond vampire after World War 2?

TruthseekerNL: There have been two more, both in Berlin. One was in 1973 when East German border guards heard the alarms going off, but could not spot anything on their CCTV screens. When the patrol went out they just spotted a tall blond man going over the wall and disappearing into West Berlin.

MacFangs: And the second?

TruthseekerNL: Really quite recent. In 2010 they found the body of a woman with her throat cut in an apartment, but the forensic scientist noticed that the blood puddle was far too small and that the victim at the time of death could only have had about 2 litres of blood. The average human holds about 5 litres. I think this is due to a vampire attack but the German police put it down to maybe a ritual killing, where the victim was bled at another location, then moved to the apartment. Anyway, a man was seen leaving the apartment and he was described as tall and blond.

MacFangs: Thanks Truth, you really know your stuff.

TruthseekerNL: Yeah I hope to catch one of them one of these days, I think there are two active in the south of France and this one in Berlin.

What? Fuck! How the hell...? That rattled me. Maybe hanging around with the glitterati hadn't been such a good idea after all.

MacFangs: How do you know about these two in the south of France?

TruthseekerNL: There are all these stories from paparazzi photographers in Cannes who swear they took pictures of a dark-haired woman and a young man, but when they looked at the pictures later, there was no image of them.

MacFangs: Wow, spooky.

TruthseekerNL: I know! I've already booked my flight to Nice. I have to check this out.

MacFangs: Well good luck, when are you going?

TruthseekerNL: I'm going in a few weeks. I know the

Cannes festival would be better but I really can't afford the hotels and the flights around that time. I hope they are still in town.

Now this was interesting and very unsettling as well. Nanette would be well miffed if she knew an internet nerd was on to her and, worse, he had already booked his flight to Nice. I decided to send her a quick email, vampires being hunted down wasn't in anyone's interest and I might need her again.

The last story Truthseeker had told struck me as particularly interesting. It was so similar to my own murder of Yvette – like father like son, I supposed – and it made me even more determined to find my maker. He sounded like a chap who had 'lived' through some tumultuous times and could give me valuable insight into how to survive as a vampire, but before I could embark on that mission, there were a few other issues to be addressed.

Chapter 25: Pablo

After two weeks in Paris, I needed to leave. The French police had wasted no time in tracing Rashid's movements in Cannes and when a witness said he had seen him going to my boat and linked it with my disappearance, an arrest warrant was issued and the story was plastered over the papers. I'd been debating whether or not to do something about Rashid before going north so when I finally plucked up the courage to ask Andrei for a favour, I was afraid I'd left it too late. I contacted him, with some trepidation, on a burner cell phone.

'Andrei? It's me.'

'Cameron, Jesus Christ! You're wanted for murder! You're all over the papers!'

'Can I still trust you?' I asked.

'Did you do it?'

'No, but it doesn't look good. A man I've done business with was arrested with some jewellery from the murdered woman.' For the time being I would have to lie to Andrei. 'Listen Andrei, how much influence do you have in Moscow?'

'I know people,' he said, cagily.

'Can you meet me in Paris?' I asked him.

'I am there next week. Usual hotel,' he told me.

Andrei liked to stay at the Ritz on the Place Vendôme, so we met there in the lobby the following week. We walked towards the Tuileries garden and found a quiet spot to talk.

'How can I help?' he asked.

'Could you get a man out of a high security prison in Moscow and out of Russia?' I asked him bluntly.

'Is this the businessman you want to disappear?' he asked.

'Yes. I think if we can get him to Afghanistan, he'll be able to stay hidden,' I told him.

'Maybe, but it is going to be very expensive,' he said leaning back on the park bench looking thoughtful.

'Don't worry, I will make it worth your while.'

'I can have him dealt with in prison, stop him from talking. It would be cheaper and simpler,' he offered.

'No, Andrei. Don't worry about the money.' I pulled out a small canvas. 'As I said, it will be worth your while.'

When Hélène had told me she'd once sat for Picasso, I had made enquiries. Picasso told me he had sold the painting he'd done of her in 1923 to a wealthy lawyer in Paris. It didn't take me long to find the lawyer's house, but it took a year before I had the confidence to break in and make the painting disappear from his office wall. I'd hidden it in the catacombs, hoping to give it to Hélène for her 26th birthday, but she'd taken her own life a month before. I'd been pleased to find it still in its hiding place in the catacombs all these years later. I'd thought about retrieving it as I saw the prices of Picasso's work go up and up over the years, but it had been meant for *her*, so I couldn't bring myself to retrieve it to just sell. Now there was a purpose for this small painting; a gift intended for one friend could help another.

Owning a Picasso was Andrei's dream. Better yet, this one would probably be seen as an undiscovered work as it had disappeared so long ago. Andrei was speechless.

'Where...? How did you get this?' he stammered.

'It was stolen in 1925, but I don't think there's any record of its existence,' I explained.

'How did you get it?' he asked.

'Not important. You can say you found it at a flea market and thought it was a fake. You paid fifteen euros for it.'

'So it is real? You had it authenticated?' he asked, turning the painting over and studying it from all angles.

'Yes.'

'Do you know who the portrait is of?' he asked, unable to take his eyes off the canvas.

'It is of Hélène Bruchard. She sat for him occasionally.' Andrei gave me a quizzical glance. I leaned back nonchalantly, not letting on there was anything special about that. His eyes quickly went back to the painting.

'Wow, it is just stunning! So, I am to understand that if I get your man to Afghanistan you will let me have this painting?'

'If you can get Rashid Lal out of prison and to a safe place, yes, the painting is yours.'

'And are you ok, Cameron? Do you need money or a place to stay? I have a very nice place in St Petersburg if you want to hide out there for a while,' he offered.

'Nah, I'm ok. I know my way around Paris and I don't think they'll find me here. I also have a few other things I need to do,' I said.

Andrei gave me a large wad of cash anyway and I took it. I had just promised to give him a picture worth a few million after all. As we parted company Andrei promised he would do what he could, but it would not be easy. Rashid was still being held in Butyrka prison, one of Moscow's largest but also oldest prisons, awaiting extradition to France. It would be an unpleasant place to be. I'd read that it was very overcrowded and that in summer it could get very hot. Being a Pakistani national in an overcrowded Russian prison would be dangerous and I wanted my friend out of there as soon as possible.

A week later it was all over the news that Rashid Lal, suspect in a murder case, had – allegedly – just walked out of Butyrka. It was reported that he had taken the place of an Afghan prisoner that was to be released that day and had managed to walk out without the mistake being spotted. There were accusations of prison guard bribery, but no evidence was found and Rashid had since disappeared off the face of the earth. The painting of Hélène now takes pride of place on the living room wall in Andrei's house in St Paul.

***

I had accessed my emails and Facebook account a few times in different internet cafés, and was worried that if my internet activity was being monitored, it would be obvious by now that I was in Paris. In the old days you could just have gone to a port and bought a ferry ticket, but now everything needed to be booked and paid for online with a credit card. Even with a false passport, getting out of France was going to be difficult.

Then I stumbled across a solution. I noticed a Dutch lorry delivering flowers to a shop in the heart of Paris one night and it struck me that it would probably be a regular delivery. The next time it came, I was packed and ready to jump on board. I wedged myself under a shelf and settled in for the return trip to Aalsmeer. The driver would probably go and pick up his next delivery there in the early morning from the flower auction warehouses.

I had read somewhere that it was the largest flower market in the world, but when we got there I was taken aback by the sheer scale of the operation. I would easily be able to nose around for a bit, as most of the traffic of carts full of flowers was automated and I wouldn't show up on CCTV, but finding a consignment on its way to Scotland would be difficult. As luck – or maybe misfortune – would have it, I found a cart destined for Glasgow. I followed it and managed to get into a Glasgow-bound lorry undetected. *Ach well, the good thing about Glasgow is that there's a road to Edinburgh.*

Chapter 26: James

It was time to confront my past head on. I had looked after George's family all these years, as I'd promised, but maybe my own needed me more. I'd been back to Edinburgh in 2007, but I hadn't wanted to know what had happened to my parents and brothers in case it was too painful. I hadn't been ready then, but now I decided to deal with all the unanswered questions I'd asked myself over the years.

George had already done a fine piece of research in 2007 in case I'd changed my mind and had given me a CD with what he had been able to find out on it. Now I looked at it for the first time. My brother Hector had been only two years younger than me, so he'd followed me into the army soon after I set off for France. I'm not sure he'd ever have found out that I'd deserted as he was killed at the battle of Arras in 1917. Reading that hit me hard. He had followed in my footsteps and my worst fears had been confirmed.

My little brother James had been six years younger luckily, so although he too had signed up, the war was over before he was able to see any action. He'd stayed in the army, obviously wanting to prove that – unlike his eldest brother – he wasn't a coward; he must have been itching to see some action. When I read that, I wished again that I had stayed dead. Maybe then my wee brother would have chosen a different career. It must have broken my mother's heart to see her last son march off.

James got his wish for action in 1920 when his regiment was posted to Ireland and he fought in the Anglo-Irish war, which ultimately led to Irish independence. There followed a number of overseas postings with the Royal Scots that took my wee brother to Egypt, China and finally Hong Kong. In his late thirties he had married a local girl in Hong Kong and they'd had a son in 1939. James had steadily worked his way up the ranks in the army and by the time the battle of Hong Kong started in 1941 he was a regimental sergeant major and had quite a comfortable life. But that all changed after the Japanese attack and subsequent surrender of the British.

My brother spent the following four years in a camp as a prisoner of war, which must have been horrific. His wife and young son managed to escape and hid with her Chinese family. Amazingly though, all three survived and were reunited after the war. James took his family to Edinburgh where he bought a house in Morningside and he stayed in the army until his retirement. He and Mei-ling, or May as she was known to everyone in Scotland, must have found it hard settling in Edinburgh. It must have been an alien place to her.

James had died in 1975 aged 74 and Mei-ling followed in 1985 aged 70. Their son, Hector, still lived in the same Morningside house and was now a retired accountant aged 72. I had to meet him so I decided to pose as a journalist writing for *The Scotsman* and called him to arrange a meeting. He agreed to let me interview him at his house at 5pm. It was winter, so it would be dark enough. *Interview with a vampire* I giggled to myself as I hung up the phone.

And there he was, standing in front of me, an elderly Asian man that was my nephew. It was an emotional moment when I walked into his hallway and saw the pictures of my family. There was an old picture of my brother Hector in his uniform that must have been taken just before he went to the front, a picture of my parents looking old and grey and a wedding picture of James and May looking very exotic. There were also family members smiling back at me that I didn't know.

'So you're writing an article about the Royal Scots then? My father spent his whole life in the army you know,' Hector said, leading me into his living room.

'Well, not so much about the Royal Scots, more the soldiers that deserted,' I explained.

'How dare you!' he said angrily. 'My father didn't desert!' and he turned to lead me straight back out again.

'Oh no! No, I'm not here about your father.' I said hurriedly, holding up my hands apologetically. 'I'm here about your uncle, Cameron Blair.'

'I think you're making a mistake. I only had an uncle Hector, but he didn't desert either, he died in the Great War,' he went on angrily, blocking my way in.

'My research shows that a Cameron Blair was born to the same parents as your father James, in 1895,' I explained hastily. 'So your father never mentioned he had an older brother?'

'I had no idea my father had two brothers. He never ever mentioned a Cameron to me,' said Hector, looking puzzled and he sat down.

'Did you know your grandparents?' I asked, taking a seat too.

'No. They were dead by the time we came to Britain. They both died in the 1930s,' he said. *Good*, I thought. At least they hadn't had to live through another world war.

'Did you get married, Mr Blair?' I asked my nephew.

'Yes. My wife died last year, but we were married for 48 years and we have four children and eleven grandchildren. And I'm delighted to say that my first great-grandchild is due in a month,' he said smiling at the prospect of becoming a great-grandfather.

'Wow! That's quite something. And they are all happy and healthy?' I asked.

'Yes, yes, they are all doing fine. My youngest isn't working just now, but he's a clever chap so I'm sure he will find something soon,' he said without any noticeable concern.

'Ok, well it looks like I disturbed you for no reason. I'm sorry I had to let you in on the family secret,' I said, getting up to leave.

'Don't worry, but your story might be a difficult one to write. I think there will be a lot of families like mine, who'd rather not mention a son or brother that deserted. It's not something you want to tell your children,' he said as he walked me to the front door.

'I know, but you'd think that after all those years your dad might have mentioned something,' I said as I took a last look over the family photos.

'No, sorry. I'm afraid I can't help you any further,' he said as he opened the front door and shook my hand.

I left feeling rather empty. I'd just been wiped from the family tree, never to be mentioned again. Deep down, I couldn't blame them. I took the number 23 bus up to Princes Street and sat on a park bench for a while looking at the castle that was lit up for the night. So what now? I didn't get much time alone with my thoughts as a sixty-something woman plonked herself down next to me.

'Ye can say what ye like about Edinburgh, but it is a beautiful place. I always like to come here and just sit and look at the castle and the Christmas lights while I wait for the seven o'clock train to Glasgow.'

That figured. An Edinburgh lady would never sit next to a stranger and start a conversation. I decided to humour her. 'You're from Glasgow then?' I asked.

'I was born in the Gorbals and I've lived in Glasgow all my life. Just came through for wee a bit of shopping. I come for the Jenners sale every year,' she explained in a broad Glaswegian accent.

'Got any good bargains?' I asked, pointing at her bags.

'Oh aye! I got a smashing wee top for fifteen pound!' She

proceeded to pull a hideous red blouse out of her bag and I spotted she'd found some equally ghastly shoes to go with it.

'That'll be perfect for a night out,' I said, trying to sound impressed.

'I love going to the bingo now and then, and you know how women are, always need something new on. It costs a bloody fortune, so it does. I'm Helen by the way,' she said.

'Pleased to meet you Helen, I'm Cameron.'

'That's a proper Scottish name. Ye from Edinburgh then?' she asked.

'Aye, I was born here, but I've been away for a while.'

'I bet it's good to be back,' she said, giving my leg a friendly squeeze.

I didn't know what to say to that so there was a silence. She looked at me and put her hand on mine.

'Are ye having problems son?'

What the hell, I might as well discus my sombre thoughts with a complete stranger. 'I found out that while I was away my family decided to eliminate me from their lives. I just saw my nephew and he had no idea I existed,' I started telling her.

'Aww, that's no right son. Did you have a fight with your brother?' she asked me.

'No. I made a bad mistake that brought shame on the family,' I said.

'Did you marry a Catholic?' she asked, raising her eyebrows.

'No! Good grief, they wouldn't have minded that. I didn't marry,' I said hastily.

'Are ye gay son? My eldest is gay and at first we were shocked and upset too, but I've met his partner now and he's a great lad. I'm sure your family will come round too,' she said giving me a tender look.

'I'm not gay.'

'What *did* you do then? You dinnae ken me, but I'm no gonnae tell anyone ye ken,' she asked.

'I ran away from the army. I'm a deserter,' I told her, looking at my feet.

'Were you in Afghanistan?' she asked

'Yes.'

'Did you get court-martialled?' she asked.

'No. I'm still on the run.' I said with a wink. She seemed to get quite angry at this.

'Well, you have to turn yourself in son. I can understand your family not wanting to know you. How can they forgive you when you haven't faced up to what you've done?'

'I'm a coward, aren't I?' I said, looking at my feet again.

'Do you think they can tell your nephew that Uncle Cameron joined the army and when it got hard and scary he ran away?' she continued angrily.

'Well, going to prison won't change anything,' I said, leaning back on the park bench sulkily.

'Maybe not, but for your family it would be a sign that you admit you made a mistake and are trying to make amends.' Suddenly she looked at her watch and jumped up, hastily gathering her belongings. 'Help ma Boab, I'm gonnae miss ma train. Good luck to ye Cameron. I think you need it.'

'Thanks Helen. It was good chatting to you. Have a safe journey.'

She dashed off in the direction of Waverley station and I decided to go to one of Edinburgh's nightclubs as I was starting to feel a bit peckish.

Helen's words kept milling around in my head. It was a bit late to turn myself in – and that would never have been an option – but was I a coward to just selfishly go on, not doing any good to man or beast and thinking only of what I wanted? Was it maybe time to stop? I'd been about for a long time. I generally tried not to think about the people who had come in and out of my life and concentrated instead on my latest desire and not letting anything get in the way of my obtaining it.

I knew where I had to go next, but first I was in need of a good meal.

Chapter 27: Hedwig

The next day I spotted an Italian lorry making a late delivery to one of the shops in town. I managed to climb on board unseen and settled in for the journey south. I was hoping the driver was heading for the Newcastle crossing, as I planned to travel to Berlin and thought I'd be able to find another lorry heading in that direction on the ferry. But that's where my luck ran out. We made another two stops along the way, picking up pallets of Scottish whisky, then there was a very long drive south that meant we must be heading for the Dover-Calais crossing.

On board the ferry, I managed to swap to a German horse box with some sheep in it, things were starting to look up. The sheep were an unusual breed and probably on their way back from an agricultural show. I later looked them up online and found they were called Heidschnucke. They looked quite cute with their black faces and long, grey hair. If I ever had a farm again I'd certainly get a few. They were nervous and tried to get out of my reach, but eventually I had one of the fluffy jumpers pinned to the ground. It wasn't as good as cow or dog and it kicked and struggled through most of the meal, but afterwards I was well fed and bursting with energy. Damn this was going to be a long and boring ride.

As the sun began to come up, I covered myself with my coat and some straw as best I could. There was a large gap above the door and sunlight would soon be flooding in. Good for the wee beasties, but not for me.

It was a very uncomfortable ride, but fortunately it was winter and when we reached our destination in the early evening it had just gone dark. So what now? I didn't want to be caught by farmhands with pitchforks so I decided that the only course of action would be to make a run for it as soon as the door opened. It must have been quite a sight, me covered in straw and sheep muck dashing out of the horse box surrounded by bleating startled sheep. I heard the farmhands calling after me, but I just kept running. When I stopped and looked around, I found that I was in a quiet rural area. The land was flat so I guessed I was somewhere in the north of Germany, but I had absolutely no idea where.

I needed a bath and some clean clothes and preferably a car. Logistics were just so much easier when you could kill people – I could have gone up to one of the remote farmhouses, eaten the inhabitants and relaxed in a nice warm bath. There would probably have been a nice German car in the driveway and a feisty farm dog to have taken along for the journey too.

I decided to do the decent thing and just steal a car. I could always find a hotel for the day and have a bath then. I spotted a nice BMW parked next to a farmhouse and to my delight the keys were still in the ignition. The lights in the farmhouse were out so I gathered the owners had gone to sleep trusting their neighbours and not suspecting any criminals were likely to be in their remote neighbourhood. I pushed the car down the drive to the road before I started the engine and drove off.

I soon reached a motorway and managed to get my bearings; I was just south of Cologne and still about 570 kilometres from Berlin. Now, German motorways are something else: straight and wide and no speed limit so this late at night and with no traffic I was sure I would get to Berlin before daybreak. *Come on baby, let's see what you can do!* I pushed down the accelerator and soon I was doing 185 kilometres per hour. It was exhilarating and probably the most fun you could have legally. I sped past Hanover and Braunschweig and after about four hours Berlin came into view. My maker had last been spotted in Berlin, but would he still be there and would I be able to find him? I parked the car and found a hotel for the day. *Woo hoo! Free wifi and a bath.*

I couldn't wait to go online and see what was going on. I tracked down the article about the woman in Berlin who had been murdered and was missing a few pints of blood. I also found the address of the apartment where she'd been killed. It wasn't much to go on, but I had to start my search somewhere.

I spent the night walking through the streets, starting at the apartment and working in a spiral pattern outwards. It was a quiet residential area and there weren't many people about. Suddenly the hairs on the back of my neck stood on end. I turned round and saw a tall, blond man coming out of a building. He stopped and looked directly at me. *What was I to say? What should I call him? Dad? Maker?* We both stood, staring at each other, and then I started to move towards him.

'Hello. I'm Cameron. I think you made me,' I said looking at the taller, blond man. He looked about 23 and seemed shy and awkward.

'I knew you would come for me eventually. I'm Carl-Heinz…' He held my gaze and then he asked hesitantly, 'Are you here to kill me?'

'I've thought about it, but with you being older and able to sense me it might be difficult,' I said, feeling very awkward too.

'Oh,' he said, keeping his eyes fixed on me.

'Can we just talk?' I asked.

'Of course. Do you want to come up to my apartment?' he asked and I nodded. He led me into a grey building that must have been constructed sometime in the 1960s.

So there he was: my maker – living in a one-bedroom apartment in residential Berlin. I looked around and already knew I had little in common with him. I wouldn't have chosen the ghastly flowery wallpaper and pink velour furniture. It looked like an old lady's apartment. I studied him: he was very tall with blond hair and blue eyes. *He'd have made a great poster boy for the Nazis if they just could have captured him on camera.* He was dressed in nondescript jeans and a sweatshirt and could have been any quiet university student studying something serious like maths or theology.

'Tell me, why did you make me and then just abandon me? It's always seemed so senseless. I mean, you must have had a reason to do it?' I started off resolutely.

'I wasn't a free man then, and it took me a long time to get my freedom,' he said looking sad and resigned. I imagined he was unhappy about me turning up. He hadn't wanted me in his life before, so why would he want to see me now? But I wasn't going to go away until I had some answers, so I leaned back in my chair, got comfortable and waited for him to speak. He took a deep breath and started telling me his story.

Carl-Heinz had been born there in Berlin in 1875. He had, like me, a normal and happy childhood, but unlike me he'd been a very bright student and had won a bursary to study medicine at the Friedrich Wilhelm University, these days known as the Humboldt. There, he'd studied under Professor Lindtman, a specialist in haematology. Carl-Heinz had admired his professor and was delighted and honoured when he'd received an invitation to dine at his house. Lindtman had caught a vampire, a young woman – well really just a girl as she was only fifteen when she was made. Lindtman believed in vampires and had suspected there was one in his neighbourhood and not a very careful one at that. Hedwig had been so young when she was made that she really didn't know how to live as a vampire, she just felt the hunger and attacked the first thing that came along, be it human or animal. Lindtman had hunted the streets at night looking for this immature vampire and had soon found her feeding on a stray dog in a back alley. She'd been dressed in rags and was filthy, more wild animal than human. When she saw him she had tried to run away, but he threw a fine net made of silver mesh over her and stopped her in her tracks.

'I'm sorry, girl. I know it hurts, but I really don't mean you any harm,' he'd told her in a soft voice.

She'd screamed and fought hard against the mesh that was burning into her skin.

'Stop fighting and I will free you,' he'd said, trying to calm her down.

She didn't hear him. She was like any trapped animal fighting for survival, but eventually she tired and slumped to the floor crying in frustration and defeat, and waiting to die.

'Now, now. I will help you as long as you don't attack me,' Lindtman had told her as he peeled the net off her and hugged her to him. She'd tried to crawl away at first, but when he lifted her up she had put her arms around his neck and rested her badly burned face against his chest. He'd carried her to his home and stayed by her bedside all night, stroking her hair. He'd told her not to worry and that he would take care of her.

Hedwig had accepted her master gladly. She'd been out of her depth living on the street, and here was someone who was kind, supplied her with food and clean clothes and accepted her for what she was as long as she obeyed him. He'd also convinced her to let him experiment on her and she accepted the tests without question.

Lindtman had developed a drug that made vampires easy to manipulate, but as Hedwig was already mostly in his control he'd needed another test subject. When Carl-Heinz came to dinner, he found that he himself was the main dish.

The professor had watched as Hedwig drained the young student of his blood, and then made her cut her own wrist so that Carl-Heinz could drink her blood and come to life again.

All night he'd paced around the corpse, taking notes and photographs. At about two o'clock, Carl-Heinz had stirred and sat up. The professor gave him a shot of serum and the student became his professor's next test subject and slave. He'd needed a vampire with more fight in him to see if the drug really worked.

'And did it?' I interrupted him.

'It did on me.'

'Didn't anyone miss you? Wasn't the professor a suspect in your disappearance,' I asked him.

'Lindtman was questioned and when he said I'd left the dinner alive they believed him. He was such an eminent man they never treated him as a suspect. He even visited my parents a few times to see how they were doing. On the surface he was a very caring and considerate man. I think he thought that what he was doing was necessary for the progress of science; sacrifices had to be made.'

'It sounds like you're still fond of the guy.' I found it hard to believe how he could have been.

'He was like a second father to Hedwig and me and, thinking back, he was much more humane than some of the other scientists I had the misfortune to encounter. But excuse me, Cameron, where are my manners? Have you eaten yet?' Carl-Heinz asked.

'Not recently. What does one eat here in Berlin' I asked, excited.

Carl-Heinz took two doctors' coats out of a wardrobe and showed me a hospital ID badge.

'I managed to get hold of this, so I've been visiting a few patients in hospital,' he said without a hint of irony.

'Lead the way!' I said, enthusiastically. He gave me a strange look, I don't think he'd expected such youthful exuberance. He too must have wondered why we were so different.

The hospital was large so two more men in white coats didn't attract attention. Carl-Heinz had been coming here for a few weeks and had come to know the wards. One or two of the nurses even gave him a friendly nod and an 'Evening, Herr Doktor'. He did look like a medical student or young doctor. We visited a lady with Alzheimer's who was restrained as she'd been trying to pull out her drip, but we made sure it went back in properly. Then we visited a coma patient who had so many holes in his arms that a few extra punctures wouldn't show up. For dessert, we made a visit to the blood bank.

'Thanks for dinner, Carl-Heinz,' I said, as the blood rushed through my veins making me feel energetic.

'Don't mention it. It's rare to share a meal with someone,' he said, deadpan.

We agreed to meet again the next night and I went back to my hotel and settled in for the day. I was hyper on human blood and wanted to share my day with someone so I decided to go online and post Hedwig's story on one of the vampire forums. Soon the venom started to appear.

Mangateeth: Stupidest thing I ever read, if this were true we would have vampire armies by now.

I'd have to ask Carl-Heinz about this – maybe we did...

LadyVamp267: Stop posting all this nonsense, you obviously know nothing about vampires, they are all powerful and would never be captured by a mere human to be used in experiments. I am sure this Hedwig would have ripped his throat open.

Then Truthseeker came on.

TruthseekerNL: So you found your German vampire then?
MacFangs: I think so.
ThuthseekerNL: Is he in Berlin?
MacFangs: I don't know, I just managed to establish contact with someone.
TruthseekerNL: Shame, I didn't have much luck in Cannes finding my two Vamps, I'd like to meet you and find this guy.
MacFangs: Oh dear, I hope you had a nice holiday anyway.
TruthseekerNL: It was ok, Cannes is very touristy and the beaches are too full. Why is this vampire talking to you?
MacFangs: I think I know his original identity, I think he is a relative, a cousin of my great-grandfather.
ThuthseekerNL: Wow that would be awesome, can you tell me his name?
MacFangs: Not yet, he could be telling me a pack of lies.

Then Ladyvamp267 butted in again.

Ladyvamp: MacFangs He is always full of s**t, I wouldn't go all the way to berlin for that c**t, F**kwit sometimes even pretends to be a vampire.
MacFangs: You kiss your mother with that mouth Lady?
Ladyvamp: F**k off you puny human wannabe.

I decided to play a bit of poker, not wanting to give Truth any further clues and because slanging matches are only fun for a little while.

Chapter 28: Carl-Heinz

The following night, I probed further and asked Carl-Heinz what the professor had wanted to do with his two tame vampires.

'The professor was a pure scientist,' he explained. 'He had been fascinated by vampires for many years and wanted to know everything there was to know. He ran a lot of tests on us, something he couldn't have done without the drug. As a haematologist he wanted particularly to study the blood and how it changed us.'

'Did he ever intend to publish his findings?'

'He once told me the world wasn't ready yet for our kind and he wasn't going to publish until he had a foolproof method of finding, capturing and controlling vampires.'

'And didn't he realise the military potential?'

'*He* didn't, but in 1903 he took on an assistant, a cousin that he thought he could trust.' Carl-Heinz continued the story. The professor knew the two vampires had a connection and could sense each other's presence so he was working on a device that could detect a vampire. With both the vampire research and his university work, the professor had badly needed help and looked to his younger cousin, Albert Lindtman for assistance. Albert was also a haematologist and the professor, thinking that a cousin and fellow scientist would make a trusted partner, let Albert in on his secret experiments and introduced him to his two vampires. Albert immediately saw how the military might exploit his cousin's work and if the professor had looked closely he would have seen the look of pure greed rather than the hunger for scientific discovery in his cousin's eyes. Albert knew an official in Berlin with connections to military research, so in

1908 the two vampires were moved to an old hospital outside Berlin and the professor was forced to retire and given a pension. As far as Carl-Heinz knew, the tracking device was never developed further.

Hedwig had by this time started to show some worrying side effects, like a sort of Alzheimer's, and she had become very forgetful. When the professor left, her symptoms worsened and she became aggressive as well, reacting badly to all the strangers who wanted to inject her with this, that and the other. They stopped the drugs, but it was too late. Hedwig forgot what she was and how to feed, and even the simplest things such as dressing herself became tasks she no longer knew how to do. As she was still so dangerous and could kill someone with great ease, they decided to put her down like a sick animal.

'Did you know all this was going on?' I asked him.

'I was walking in a haze most of the time, doing whatever I was told, but I do remember that they got me to do their dirty work on Hedwig,' he told me looking very sad again.

'They made you kill your maker?' I asked, shocked.

'Yes,' he said, his voice flat.

'How did you do it? Stake? Beheading? Or are there other ways?' I asked with interest.

'Does it matter?' He looked at me with incomprehension. I don't think he got many visitors, and he didn't quite know what to make of this eager, restless young man, that wanted to know all the gory details despite it being clear that it took him great difficulty to talk about these painful memories.

'Sorry. I'm just interested in how we can die. I watch and read all about these things and it's hard to separate fact from fiction,' I explained.

'It was beheading. It is very quick. I used a sharp sword, standard German army issue if you need to know,' he went on, slight irritation creeping into his voice.

'Thanks. Sorry to push you on this, but do you think they used this as another test to see if the drugs worked?' I asked.

'I'm sure of it. We were no more than lab rats to them.'

'Did you have any side effects?' I asked.

'Mine weren't as bad. Apart from the occasional splitting headache, I was just in a daze, one day blending into the next. Even now, my memory is still very good. Playing chess keeps me sharp,' he said proudly and asked if I played.

You can't get me to sit still long enough to read a good book, let alone for a snoozefest like chess! 'No, sorry. I don't,' I said with an apologetic smile and asked him to continue.

They forced Carl-Heinz to make another two vampires. One went quite mad on the drugs and just stood in a corner crying. When they took him off the drugs, he became dangerous and vicious and managed to kill one of the guards. They darted him with the drug and disposed of him when he reverted to a blubbering mess. On the other vampire, Otto, the drugs seemed to work. He calmly did what was required of him and seemed an ideal testing subject. But Otto had them fooled all along. The drug had actually had absolutely no effect on him and at the first opportunity he ran off never to be seen again.

'Do you think he's still out there?' I asked surprised.

'I am sure he is. He is a clever fellow and knows how to survive,' Carl-Heinz told me with conviction.

'You're his maker, you'd be able to sense him. Haven't you ever felt his presence?' I asked him, intrigued.

'No. I think he got as far away from Berlin as possible. I have never seen him again.'

The team decided to try again and two women were found for Carl-Heinz to turn. One, Anna, had been imprisoned for killing her two young children by drowning them in the bath and she was sentenced to death. No one would know that this murderess would get a second life as a vampire. The other, Elsa, had been sentenced to death for poisoning twenty of her neighbours by baking cakes with rat poison. Neither of these girls were sane to start with and the drug didn't make things any better. Like Otto, Elsa pretended to do well on the drug, but she got impatient and after a week of treatment she snapped and rampaged through the facility, killing five guards and medical staff. Carl-Heinz was sent in with a stake to deal with her, but she didn't go down without a fight.

'I lost a finger in that battle,' he said, showing me his left hand with his middle finger missing.

'It doesn't grow back then, once a limb is off?' I asked, astonished.

'We are not lizards, Cameron. We heal quickly, but once a limb is severed it doesn't grow back,' he told me impatiently.

'Good to know,' I said cheerfully. 'Continue CH.' He gave me another look. *Probably too early for the CH.*

Anna had complained about headaches straight away and was not as willing a subject as Carl-Heinz had been. After a few weeks she developed memory problems and it looked as though she was going to go the same way as Hedwig. They got Carl-Heinz to dispose of her before things deteriorated too badly.

'A stake this time. I think it was oak, but I can't be sure,' he said, pre-empting my enquiry with a disapproving look.

They made no more vampires after that, but decided to keep Carl-Heinz alive. War was now looming large and they wanted to use him on the battlefield.

'So this is when they got you to make me and god knows how many others!' I said, shuffling excitedly in my chair.

'That was the idea. I would turn an allied soldier and hope he would go back to his trenches and cause mayhem.'

'Did it work?' I asked.

'Not at all. You know it takes a few days for the bloodlust and the realisation to set in. After that it is anyone's guess what will happen. The first soldier I turned went for the German trenches and caused quite a few problems for us. It took me three nights to find him and kill him again.'

'Whoops!'

'I know. They waited and deliberated until 1915 before they tried again,' he said.

'And that was the great German success of Cameron,' I said raising my arms in triumph. He gave me another look, but I got a faint smile too.

'Yes, not the debâcle of the previous attempt but just futile. I made another a week later and I took him behind the allied lines hoping he would go for the first human prey he saw. I even tried to brainwash him, but again he went for the German lines and had to be dealt with,' he went on.

It was decided that vampires were just too unpredictable and dangerous to be created so they just used Carl-Heinz as a soldier. He was a pretty good and indestructible one, but the dream of a great vampire army fighting for the Kaiser had crumbled. When the war was over, no one knew what to do with Carl-Heinz. A completely tame and obedient vampire was too good to be killed, but the team of scientists at the facility had been depleted and by 1921 only Albert and his assistant were on the payroll. Germany was suffering financial meltdown and there was absolutely no money for any more research. Most of the time Carl-Heinz was left undrugged and just stayed in his cell while Albert and his assistant worked on other projects.

'You must have been bored out of your mind,' I cried in horror.

'It wasn't too bad. They gave me books to read and it was

nice to have my head clear again. The worst thing was I could remember everything as clear as day,' he said sadly.

'Did they not trust you to be out of your cell? I mean, you were a scientist too. You could have worked,' I asked.

'They'd had so many bad experiences with the vampires that they were happier just to keep me locked up and out of the way. You know, to them I was no more than a gorilla or something; some human qualities but a wild animal that could kill you in an instant after all,' he explained.

'Did you ever wonder why the drug worked on you but not on the others?' I asked him.

'Of course. I don't know for sure, but I have always been a quiet character, without any rebellion or aggression,' he told me. 'I think that was the difference.'

I was just about bouncing in my seat. At last I was going to get answers to some crucial vampire questions and I was making myself quite dizzy trying to decide what I wanted to know first. 'I have so much to ask! They experimented on you, so what did you discover? Do you know if garlic can kill?' I was just bursting with curiosity.

He filled me in on a few facts and myths. Garlic was toxic and gave you a nasty rash but was not deadly. Holy water and crosses did nothing at all; he thought that had been invented by the church to accentuate their role in the good versus evil of the vampire myths. Oh yes, and a virgin's blood is no different from that of a non-virgin. He finished by telling me that sunlight was indeed deadly. We called it a day at that point and I went back to my hotel agreeing to meet again the next night.

When I arrived the following night, I dived straight in, eager to pick up the story.

'And then the Nazis came along.' I asked shuffling in my chair excitedly, ready for some more juicy information.

'Indeed. Fucking Nazis. Bunch of fanatics that ignored all previous research and decided that I was the only good vampire, as I was a good Aryan boy. They ignored totally the fact that Anna had been blue-eyed and blonde too.' Carl-Heinz was angry. Nazis apparently weren't his favourite either. I wanted to ask if he thought they'd tasted funny too, but thought better of it.

The Nazis cranked things up a notch; suddenly the place was crawling with scientists again. A lot of racial and psychological profiling was done on Carl-Heinz and volunteers with a similar physique and intelligence were recruited. It was a bloodbath and of the 25 test subjects only one was allowed to stay alive. The rest either went mad or became too dangerous and unreliable to keep.

One, a fanatical party member and mathematics student called Heinrich, had been an ideal candidate on paper. He seemed to react well to the drug and carried out all the commands he had been given, but Carl-Heinz had his suspicions. He believed that the drug had had no effect on Heinrich and that, like Otto, he was pretending. It didn't really make much difference, as Heinrich's goals were the same as those of the research team.

Carl-Heinz and Heinrich did not get on. Heinrich loathed the older vampire who only obeyed orders because he was drugged and did not share his fervid vision. When war broke out, the two of them were sent east on strategic missions that put their night vision and stealth to use with devastating effect in Poland and later in Russia.

'You know, there's a photo of either you or Heinrich circulating on the internet,' I interrupted again.

'No, that can't be.'

'I know we don't photograph. It's more a shot of a Polish soldier fighting off an unseen thing around his neck. That's how I got on your track,' I told him.

'I have to see that. Maybe I will remember if that was me,' he said shrugging his shoulders.

When the war turned and the Soviets started advancing, the two vampires were sent out almost every night on their deadly missions until, one night, Carl-Heinz returned alone.

'Do you think Heinrich ran off?' I asked.

'I doubt that, you could not get a more loyal soldier than him. I hope that the Soviets killed him as he was a truly evil vampire.'

'Do you think the Soviets had knowledge of vampires?' I asked.

'I know they did. They eventually caught me too and they were ready for me with a silver net.'

'Did they have the drug?' I asked him.

'No. As our troops pulled back, we got close to Berlin and the facility, but by this time the drug no longer worked so well on me and my head was clearing,' he said. He explained that his officers had ordered him to torch the facility with himself inside, but he'd managed to escape. He hadn't wanted to be captured by the Soviets, but they were already advancing on the facility and seemed to be ready for him. They didn't have the drug, but knew of it and were keen to develop it, so once again Carl-Heinz disappeared and for a number of years was kept in a laboratory near Moscow.

Chapter 29: Heinrich

I asked Carl-Heinz to tell me about his missions with Heinrich on the eastern front, but he was reluctant to talk about them.

'You have to understand. Heinrich was a truly nasty character with a sadistic streak. I mean, he was evil even by our standards. I have killed a lot but I was drugged and went about it in a mechanical way, and later on I just killed for food – no need to torture the unfortunate human – but Heinrich, he wanted to wipe every Soviet and non-Aryan off the planet. He just enjoyed killing,' he told me with distaste.

'Were you at the siege of Leningrad?' I asked, pushing for more information.

'Of course, and also at Stalingrad as it was strategically so important. It was one of our jobs to run along the streets trying to draw the snipers out. Well, mostly it was me drawing fire and Heinrich going after the sniper. It wasn't pleasant; he never killed anyone quickly. I can still hear the screams.' He tailed off. 'I really don't want to talk about it Cameron,' he said, closing the subject.

'Sorry Carl-Heinz. I won't bring it up again,' I said apologetically.

My curiosity had been roused, though, so I turned to my historical expert. TruthseekerNL had given me his email address, as our conversations had often been disturbed by some know-all goth. He was actually called Stefan Sluis and lived in the Dutch town of Gouda. During the day he worked for the council, but at night and weekends he spent his time on the internet looking for vampires. He was one of the leading lights in the vampire conspiracy community. I emailed him with this latest snippet of information.

Hi Stefan,

I've learned that there was another vampire working for the Nazis. A sadistic motherfucker going by the name of Heinrich. Apparently he was involved with the sieges of Stalingrad and Leningrad. By all accounts he never killed quickly, so there must be some accounts of mutilations etc. Have you got any information? I've been reliably informed that he was captured and killed by the Soviets.
Thanks,
Frank

I had told Stefan that my name was Frank Olsen and that I lived in Denmark. I didn't want him to put two and two together with regards to the murder of Yvette Jaunet; Cameron McAdam had been released as the name of the main suspect and much had been made of my champagne lifestyle. I'd even spotted some footage of my yacht on Sky News. The fact that there was no photo of me and they'd had to make do with a sketch artist was majorly frustrating the press. I hadn't seen myself in a mirror of late, but I knew the sketch didn't look much like me. Carl-Heinz had looked at it too and told me I was much better looking in real life. I suspect the witnesses subconsciously wanted me to be more villainous-looking than my pretty-boy baby face made me.

Stefan soon wrote back:

Hi Frank,

I have been looking into the siege of Leningrad lately and I came across an interesting witness account from December 1943. According to a Soviet soldier they would sometimes come under attack at night and find one of their comrades either with their throat cut or mutilated in some horrendous way. Mostly they didn't spot the perpetrator but sometimes

they spotted one or two men running back to the German lines. Some soldiers believed that they had their shots on target but the men kept going as if the shot had missed them. Then one night this Soviet soldier heard his comrade screaming in agony close by and he made his way over to help. A German soldier had him lifted up against the wall and was carving him slowly with a hunting knife. He shot the German at point blank range, but he just turned to him and smiled, and then began to run towards the German line. Suddenly another man came out of the shadows and took this German's head clean off with one blow of his sword. Before the headless body fell to the ground it crumbled and only a pile of dust remained. The other man then dropped the sword and held his hands in the air. A barrage of gunfire erupted from the German side but the soldier was lead safely back to headquarters apparently unharmed. After that nothing more was heard or seen from that German soldier. So Frank, do you think this was your vampire changing sides? The account sure sounds like your Heinrich. I would really like to meet you in Berlin and see if we can find him. As it was a relative, do you have a photo?
Stephan

I wrote back to thank him, but I really didn't want to meet and I could hardly send him a photo. I was surprised that Carl-Heinz hadn't wanted to tell me about Heinrich though. Killing him had certainly been nothing to be ashamed of.

Chapter 30: Lyudmila

At first, I respected Carl-Heinz's wish not to talk about Heinrich and what they had done together, asking instead about what had happened to him in the Moscow laboratory.

'So, did the Soviets treat you any better?'

'Hah! No. Much worse,' he said bitterly, clenching his fists. 'I was locked up without books and often injected with stuff that made me very unwell.'

The memories seemed to pain him, but if what Stefan had told me was true and Carl-Heinz had gone over to the Soviets voluntarily, why would they have treated him so badly? I didn't know what to make of it all, because Stefan was usually so accurate in his findings. I had a feeling Carl-Heinz was lying to me, so I continued my interrogation.

'Did they have any other vampires?'

'They made me create about ten others and they experimented on them too, but without success. They could force us to do things with their silver tools, but they never discovered the control drug.'

I decided to risk his displeasure and confront him with Stefan's information. 'I recently came across the information that Heinrich was killed by a German soldier with a single sword blow. I think you beheaded him before surrendering to the Soviets.' I watched closely to gauge his reaction.

'Where did you hear that?' he spat out, furiously.

'My Dutch friend, the vampire historian.'

'You people and your blasted internet.' He turned away from me angrily.

'CH, why did you keep this hidden? Killing Heinrich was probably the best thing you could have done,' I said.

He turned back and looked at me in silence for some

moments. I could see he was weighing up how to respond, but he eventually told me why he had done it – and why he was so ashamed. By the end of 1943 the drug had started to wear off and he'd begun to remember all the things he and Heinrich had done. He had seen the suffering of the people of Leningrad and wanted no further part in it. He had also seen the courage and determination in Leningrad and believed he was fighting on the wrong side.

'They were suffering so much. People were dying of hunger in the streets, but still they held out for more than 800 days,' he explained.

'Ah, so you hadn't heard of Stalin then,' I piped up, smiling grimly.

'Exactly. As soon as the Soviets found out what I was, they tried to use me to their own ends, of course. When I refused to kill any Germans, they carted me off to the facility in Moscow.'

'What did you think they were going to do?' I asked him.

'I know *now* that I was stupid and naïve,' he answered, looking rather sheepish, 'but back then I just thought they would be grateful if I came over to their side. I thought they would let me decide how I wanted to help them. I thought they would use my night vision skills and my ability to draw fire without being killed.'

'So what did they get you to do in Moscow?' I asked barely managing not to sound too interested.

'The secret police rather liked to use me. They would lock me in a room with a suspect that they wanted to get to talk. They preferred a room with lots of mirrors, letting it slowly dawn on the suspect what he was locked in with.'

'Fear of the unnatural is a powerful tool,' I said gleefully. *Wow! Inspired torture!*

'Yes, it worked very well. Mostly, they started talking

before I had a chance to feed,' he went on.

'Were you allowed to kill them?' I asked

'Mostly yes. After the confession I was led back to their cell and left in there until I had drained the person. If I refused, they would just leave me in there until the hunger became too strong,' he said and I could see that the memories still troubled him.

'Nasty!' I cried, smiling at the sheer evilness.

'I don't think Stalin's secret police are remembered for their kindness,' Carl-Heinz continued drily.

It seems the Soviets had never trusted Carl-Heinz though. After all, not only was he German, he was a vampire and he had changed sides. He told me he was only allowed out of his cell to do their dirty work and they made few efforts to communicate with him. They didn't think it necessary to provide him with intellectual stimulus so there were no books or newspapers.

'It must have been very frustrating and boring for you.'

'It was most of the time, but then there was Lyudmila,' he said, sitting back in his chair and musing.

'Tell me more! Was she pretty?'

'She had the kind of body you can only get after years of eating cheap meat, potatoes and cabbage washed down with vodka,' he said without humour.

'Oh dear. Not a love story then,' I said, disappointed.

'It was a long time since a woman had showed me any kindness and I did like the fact she had a very ample bosom,' he told me, and then there was a shy smile. *My word! 136 years old and still shy about girls!*

Lyudmila, it turned out, had been one of the guards and one of the few in the facility that spoke German. They discovered a mutual love for chess and after her shifts Lyudmila would bring a chessboard down so they could play, with Carl-Heinz having to reach through the bars to move his pieces. The other guards hadn't liked that she fraternised with the prisoners and didn't trust them speaking German. Carl-Heinz was able to understand what they were saying about her when she moved out of earshot and he heard the dirty tricks they were planning to play on her.

'I often asked why she risked it, and she said that she had never got on with the morons in the first place. Her father was German and it had never been easy for her,' Carl-Heinz explained.

'So you probably didn't get much alone time with her,' I asked, hoping for a dirty story.

'No. Apart from the odd stolen kiss and quick feel of her breast, we didn't get up to much. But as I said, we shared a love of chess and she made good conversation, she knew a lot about German culture. They didn't give me books so she often came and sat with me in her lunch hour to read to me.'

'Very touching. Do you think she loved you?' I asked

'I'm not sure. I think it was the same for both us; there just wasn't anybody else who would give us the time of day.'

Carl-Heinz and Lyudmila were not trusted and it was about six months before she was allowed into his cell, where the guards made sure she was locked in with him. After Stalin's death in 1953 enthusiasm for the vampire project waned and funding began to be withdrawn. Lyudmila was worried she would be moved elsewhere, but she needn't have been. The vampire project became a graveyard for scientists whose careers were going nowhere and they moved it for a while to a remote region of Kazakhstan.

'Well, Lyudmila told me we were in a remote region. For me it was just another cell in another facility,' Carl-Heinz explained.

'Why did they move you?' I asked

'They started to do experiments with radioactivity and discovered that radiation had no effect on vampires, apart from the fact that we stayed radioactive for about two years and had to be kept in absolute isolation.'

'So, vampires could be quite useful for going in after a nuclear accident like Chernobyl,' I said, my mind racing with ideas of vampires carrying out disaster recovery. *I could make a lot cash cleaning up nuclear spills.*

'I suppose so, but they were thinking more of reconnaissance after a nuclear strike. They still needed the drug though, to make sure we would come back – a radioactive vampire on the loose is even worse than an ordinary one – but they never managed to develop it.'

'Did you glow in the dark or get any super powers,' I asked, getting wildly carried away.

'I think you have read a few comic books too many, Cameron,' he said, with the kind of look you'd give an annoying kid brother.

But I could be relentlessly childish. 'So, did you and Lyudmila ever *do* it?' I asked.

Carl-Heinz looked at me with disappointment in his eyes, I was obviously not up to the same intellectual standard as busty Lyudmila had been and I despaired of him ever being comfortable enough to share the sordid details of his life with me. I decided we needed a session of male bonding to get him out of his shell.

'Ever learn to drive CH?' I asked him.

'Never had the need, I take the U-Bahn.'

'So you live in a country where there's no speed limit and all these wonderful fast motors and you can't drive? CH, you haven't lived!'

I declared that we should go out right then and remedy the fact so we wandered to a quiet area and I found an older

Mercedes without an alarm system and showed Carl-Heinz how to break in and get it started. Best to start with something older and less powerful, I told him. We took the car to a quiet street and started what became nightly driving lessons. He was a quick learner and had, like me, excellent night vision and reflexes. After a few nights I had him doing 160 kilometres an hour on the motorways around Berlin. I thought he was enjoying it, but with Carl-Heinz it could be hard to tell.

Back at his apartment after one of the nightly drives, Carl-Heinz asked me to move in so we could continue our talks during the day. He'd started to trust me and had maybe even begun to like having a lively, young vampire around. Once I was installed, he continued the story where he'd left off.

By the 1960s, the project's funding had been cut again and there were very few people left working in the facility. Lyudmila had achieved promotion by the sheer fact that she was the only one that had worked there for so long. She had become the night supervisor and she allowed Carl-Heinz to come out of his cell in the evenings.

'One night, she came into my cell and told me that the guards, Ivan and Piotr, had both called in sick. She embraced me and we started kissing. I stopped and asked her who else was there. She had undone my trousers and murmured "no one".' He paused. 'I killed her quickly and fled while I could.'

'Poor Lyudmilla!' I cried, in mock horror.

'Come on Cameron. You know killing comes easy to us and frankly by that point I would have killed a naked Greta Garbo!' he said forcefully.

'You could have shagged her first!' I cried in disbelief.

'It was the first opportunity I'd had to escape and I wasn't going to miss it,' he said drily.

He was right, I think I would have done the same. Killing does come easy to us and I hadn't felt regret, guilt or shame since I'd made my first human kill. If it didn't throw up so many questions and launch investigations I would quite happily eat and kill every night, but we vampires quickly learn that killing is a slippery slope and if you want to live amongst humans you have at least to pretend to live by their rules and fly under the radar. My problem was that I liked human company and conversation, so I was keen to remain among them with all the problems that brought. Maybe now I knew some other vampires, I'd be able to live without humans, but I couldn't see that hanging out with Nanette would ever be an option.

It was 1969 when Carl-Heinz finally managed to escape from the facility and, having spent most of his vampire life in captivity, he had to learn from scratch how to survive without attracting any attention. He learned quickly and relished his new freedom, eventually getting back to West Berlin in 1973.

'Yes that story is online too. East-German border guards were spooked by a tall chap going over the wall but not showing up on CCTV,' I told him.

'I suppose I have to admit that the internet is a wonderful invention, so much knowledge at your fingertips,' he said, nodding his head.

'How do you get by without human help,' I asked him, 'without credit cards and ID papers? How do you even get internet connection?'

'One of my neighbours has an unsecured network just now, but I have learned as I stole the latest gadgets how to get by. Internet cafés are good too, but not much use during the day,' he explained.

'And this flat. Is it yours?' I asked, looking around at the hideous decor and hoping it wasn't.

'The apartment? No, it belonged to my last victim, an old lady. I stalked her for weeks and knew she had no visitors.

She divulged her pin code before I killed her, so when that dries up I will move again,' he said.

'Don't you mind? You get a place just right and then you have to move again,' I asked, still fearing the worst.

'Just right? Look around you, Cameron. Does it look like I did much to the place?' he asked, smiling for once.

I hadn't wanted to say anything before, worrying that my maker really did like the floral wallpaper. I was relieved to find he had some taste after all, but we'd have to do something about his clothes. He told me he didn't care too much where he stayed. After the years of confinement he preferred his almost nomadic lifestyle, but he was not willing to leave Berlin.

'You know, Cameron, I think I always enjoyed books more than the company of humans,' he said and I looked at him with disbelief, before deciding it was probably true.

'I am surprised you came back to Berlin. It can't hold many happy memories for you.'

'No, it does,' he assured me. 'I was very happy as a child here and to be honest I didn't know where else to go.'

'But Berlin must be a totally different place now from the city you grew up in.'

'Of course, I was shocked to see how much damage the bombing of world war two had done and then this big wall in the middle of the city. My first weeks back were a little unsettling to say the least. But now I like the fact that Berlin is constantly changing. There is always something new to look at and it is a very lively place,' he said and I thought he looked content with his life.

One thing now puzzled me though. 'I thought you'd looked in on me on occasion, but thinking back now that was before 1973, so it couldn't have been you.' I had been sure it was him I'd felt, but now I didn't know who it could have been. 'I just wonder, do you ever feel the presence of other vampires?'

'I do,' he told me.

'Are there any others here in Berlin?' I asked intrigued.

'I haven't felt anyone else for a long time, not until you came to visit.'

'There's this woman in the south of France,' I told him 'and I had no idea she was a vampire too until she confronted me.'

'Sorry, I can't explain that. By the way are you hungry too?' he suddenly asked.

I chummed Carl-Heinz on his hospital round again that night. I'd begun to think of him as an older, nerdier brother. He had been totally institutionalised by his years of confinement and was a very different character from me, but I enjoyed his company all the same. I had the feeling Carl-Heinz was still uncomfortable with me posing so many questions but the awkwardness he'd felt at first was lifting and he'd definitely warmed to me. As George had said – I was a psychopath, but I was an utterly charming one!

'Did you make any other friends apart from Lyudmila?' I asked him one day.

'There is Dmitri.'

'Another Russian?' I enquired.

'He is my chess buddy and he is Belgian. He told me he lives in Ghent.'

'Internet chess?' I asked, but I already knew the answer.

'Yes. He is very good, but I have managed to beat him a few times,' he told me proudly.

'You really are a nerd!' I said emphatically, but Carl-Heinz didn't seem to think this was a bad thing.

Chapter 31: Baz

Carl-Heinz invited me to stay with him for a few days more as he wanted to show me the city. It was winter and he absolutely wanted me to see the Pergamon museum's archaeological treasures. As soon as night fell we headed over to Berlin's Museum Island and got in before last admissions. It was impressive, with its large reconstructions of ancient buildings.

'It is one of my hobbies, archaeology,' Carl-Heinz explained. He looked very comfortable and quite in his element walking around the exhibits. He really could have been just any university student.

'Do you not fancy travelling, CH, maybe seeing Rome?'

'I'm not as adventurous as you. I like knowing where I'm going to hide for the daytime – I wouldn't know what to do in Rome,' he told me.

'Italians are very tasty. You wouldn't think it, but a hint of garlic in their diet enhances the flavour of a human immensely. Let's go out on the town tonight,' I suggested 'and get a couple of girls drunk on champagne. It'll be my treat!'

'Are you missing the south of France, Cameron?' he asked me with a smile.

'I'm not saying Berlin is bad, but yes, I do miss the climate and the food. But as you know I can't go back for a while,' I said, thinking nostalgically about my boat and the life I had left behind.

'Where are you going to go next?' he asked.

'Not sure yet. I was considering Rome myself. If you wanted, we could go together.' I really thought that Carl-Heinz could do with broadening his horizons.

'No, I don't think so. I'm old and rather stuck in my ways. I think it was all those years stuck in a cell, I'm just not comfortable straying too far from home.'

'Apart from Lyudmila, did you ever make any actual human friends?' I asked.

'I tend to steer clear of humans apart from at mealtimes. I don't trust them anymore.'

When we got back to the apartment I found that Emmy had left me a message on Facebook.

> Cameron,
> My dad has been arrested and is being held in Nice prison on suspicion of murder. They think he murdered that woman in Cannes. Can you please help?
> Emmy

I wrote back to see where she was and she got back to me immediately to say that she was still in Germany, but was trying to get a flight to Nice. I asked her to wait so we could go down to Nice together.

'This is your friend George's daughter?' Carl-Heinz asked, concerned.

'Yes.'

'It could be a trap to lure you out,' he warned.

'It could be,' I said quietly.

'Does she know you are a vampire?'

'I don't think George has told her. I don't think he wants me anywhere near her,' I explained.

'I'm not sure what you are going to be able to do, Cameron. I mean, believe me, you do not want to be caught. I do not understand why you want to help this human.' He grabbed me by the shoulders, giving me a questioning stare.

'I got him into this mess in the first place,' I said trying to avoid his gaze.

'Get him a good lawyer, that is my advice,' he said releasing me.

'Thanks for putting up with me Carl-Heinz. It was really good to meet you,' I said shaking his hand.

'Be careful, Cameron,' he said. 'I do hope to see you again someday,' and I could see that he meant it and was genuinely worried about me.

The car was still where I'd left it. It must have been reported stolen by now, but it hadn't been spotted yet. I drove the 400 or so kilometres to Paderborn fast. Realisation dawned, of course she lived there. George had been stationed close to here when he was in the army. Emmy had a small one-bedroom apartment in town, but I thought it best to get a hotel room. I called her even though it was well past midnight.

'You could have stayed here,' she said 'the couch folds out.'

'I think a hotel is better,' I told her. 'I do have to tell you a few shocking things about myself.'

'I'll come over then,' she offered. 'I can be there in about half an hour.'

'It isn't too late for you?'

'Nah, I'm a bit of a night owl anyway,' she said and then hung up.

Emmy arrived at the hotel about half an hour later as promised and came to my room. She looked stunning even though she was just in jeans and an old t-shirt with her blonde hair loosely tied back.

'So, how is George doing?' I asked.

'I only spoke to him briefly. He was quite down. There seems to be a lot of evidence against him,' she said anxiously.

'There can't be. He didn't do it!' I told her, forcefully.

'I know, but still, we are all worried and I don't think Nice prison is that great.'

'It's not as bad as the one in Marseille, but it's still no picnic,' I said, worried.

'So, shall we start the drive down tomorrow morning?'

I looked at her for a while. Should I tell her, or should I just disappear and let George fight this one alone? There couldn't be any evidence against him after all.

'What evidence have they got?' I asked.

'They found some blood on Dad's shoe that matched the DNA of the dog that was taken.'

Damn! It was my fault, then. I had taken Cleo on board to have later in the day, and George had disposed of the little corpse. It would be pretty damning evidence. I took a deep breath. I would have to come clean.

'Listen Emmy...' I began, tentatively. 'It was me that killed the woman... but I'm not going to let your dad take the rap for it.'

She looked at me in complete horror and instinctively moved away from me.

'But you're so rich! Why would *you* need to rob and kill her?' she asked, shocked.

I sighed and then just told her everything, about her great-grandfather, my life with George and the murder itself. Emmy didn't say a word throughout and when I was done it had already started to get light. Before I could stop her Emmy got up and ripped the curtains open. I screamed as the light hit my face and ran into the bathroom. She came in after me.

'I had to see if it was true,' she said, looking at my blistered face.

'But why the face? I would have put my hand behind the curtain if you needed proof,' I said petulantly. There were blisters all over my face and neck.

'It will heal won't it?' she asked, still studying me. I decided to spring my fangs if she needed proof that badly. She jumped back, but still couldn't take her eyes off me.

'Yes, it will heal, but it still hurts,' I whined, childishly.

She went back out and closed the curtains then she gathered her things and got ready to leave.

'So, you'll pick me up just after dark and we'll head south?' she asked, calmly.

I was pleased she'd taken the whole thing so matter-of-factly. Anyone else might have freaked out and screamed the hotel down. She might find things a little harder to take when I needed to feed though. As luck would have, it a stray dog came up to me that night as I was walking to the car. It was about the size of an Alsatian, but of no particular breed. I suspected there was a bit of golden retriever in there and maybe some husky. A sizeable dog that should keep me going till Nice.

'I didn't know you had a dog!' Emmy said, looking pleased and surprised when I picked her up from her apartment.

'I don't. It's my travel food,' I said, looking at her intently, challenging her.

'You can't eat this dog!' she cried, horrified. 'Look at his little, floppy ears!' She reached back to the dog and scratched him behind his ears and he wagged his tail in delight. I don't think she believed that this really was my packed lunch.

'Emmy, don't get attached. I *am* going to eat Fido,' I said.

'Don't be silly, you can't eat a dog. Everyone loves dogs,' she said smiling, and she put her seatbelt on.

I sighed and drove off. I was going to break her heart but she had to know what I was if we were going to travel together.

'I am going to call him Baz, after my favourite director Baz Luhrmann,' she said gaily.

'I'm going to call him Breakfast after my favourite meal,' I said, without mirth.

I drove fast knowing that as we were nearing the French border, I would soon have to slow down to a measly 130 kilometres an hour. I spotted a rest stop and parked the car well away from any others.

'You'd better have a wee walk and stretch your legs,' I told Emmy.

'Ok. I'll take Baz too,' she said, opening her door to get out.

'Baz stays,' I said, grabbing the dog and pulling him on to my lap.

'Oh, no you don't!' she cried.

'Emmy,' I said sternly. 'Go and have a walk!'

She got back in the car and stared hard at me then screamed as I sank my fangs into the dog's neck. She got out and stumbled away from the car. After my meal I found her sitting on a bench with her head in her hands. I sat down next to her.

'How could you? That sweet dog!' she sobbed.

'Would you rather I bit a human? Are you offering?' I asked her drily.

'You are not a very nice man! I don't understand how you could be my dad's oldest friend,' she said drying her eyes.

'Believe it or not, we stop each other from becoming far worse people, and your dad doesn't like dogs,' I explained.

'Could you promise not kill any more dogs on this trip?' she pleaded.

'I certainly couldn't! What is it with you humans? You didn't bat an eyelid when I told you I was a vampire, even though you knew I must have killed countless humans. But, oh no, don't kill the poor little doggie!'

She looked up at me. 'I suppose you're right,' she said quietly. 'It is the lesser of two evils.'

'Anyway, I haven't even *killed* this one... yet. He's going to be my sustenance till Nice,' I said light-heartedly.

She got up and ran to the car, got in and flung her arms around Baz's neck hugging him tightly. He growled when I got in.

'Right. I'll drive until daybreak then we swap,' I said, starting the car.

'Stop! We have to get Baz some food and water and he needs a walk,' she pleaded.

'Ah! Not a bad idea,' I said, turning off the ignition. 'If we feed him, he'll last longer!'

She immediately started to cry again and buried her face in Baz's fur.

I rummaged around for some money and something to make a lead out of so the traumatised dog wouldn't run off. Emmy stopped crying and wiped her eyes while I fashioned a lead from one of my ties.

'That dog better be here when I come back, otherwise you'll be on the menu,' I said, and squeezed her arm until she cried in pain. She believed me, though I knew I would never hurt her. *Well, not* much *anyway!* I went to see if the service station had any dog food and Emmy took Baz for a walk.

It was late once Baz had been taken care of, and Emmy was quite tired, so she crawled into the back seat with the dog for a sleep and I got into the boot with my laptop. I would only get four hours on it before the battery ran out and the rest of the ten hours of daylight would be boring and uncomfortable. *If Emmy thinks I'm evil now, wait till I get out of a car boot after ten hours of being folded up and bored!*

Chapter 32: Jean-Claude

We had booked an apartment in Nice online, one that accepted pets and had a parking space. It was also close to the prison so Emmy could visit her dad. We agreed that if she looked after the dog I would only eat occasionally and, big dog that he was, he should survive for a while. She came back from her first prison visit looking glum.

'It is a horrible prison, old and overcrowded – and I think that Dad has been in a fight,' she said sounding depressed.

'Then I feel sorry for the other inmates,' I said trying to cheer her up. 'We can't leave George in there, it wouldn't be fair on them.'

She wasn't amused and stroked Baz absentmindedly. 'I asked his lawyer to visit us here tomorrow night, so we can discuss his case,' she told me.

'I did manage to get a guy out of a Russian prison once. Not sure if Nice would be that easy though. I read that there have been about eleven escapes from French prisons by helicopter. Not sure if my mate Andrei would let me use his helicopter for that,' I pondered aloud.

'And then my dad would have to be on the run for the rest of his life. I don't think I like that option. By the way, he says that this guy Roger is holding some cash for you. He managed to withdraw about 50,000 euros before they blocked your account,' she said.

This was excellent news! I could always do with a bit of extra cash and I'd be able to give Emmy some to pay for the lawyer. I got in touch with Roger and we arranged to meet in a café in Antibes.

'Terrible business, this. I can't believe they suspect George of murder,' said Roger when we met in the café.

'I know. We're doing everything we can to get him out,' I said as we sat down at a table and ordered beer.

'I'm surprised you came back – they're looking for you too. Good thing you don't look anything like that sketch they have of you,' he said.

'Have you been to see George yet?' I asked him.

'Yes, once. It's a depressing place that, but if anyone can handle himself in a prison it's George.'

Very true. I'd always wondered how my man George would do against Andrei's man Sergei. *Not sure who I'd put my money on...* I bought Roger a few beers and then I took the bag of money from him and headed back to Nice.

Maître Delorme visited us the next evening. I'm sure she was good at her job but she didn't think George had a very good chance of avoiding a lengthy prison sentence. She didn't know who I was as I'd just introduced myself as a family friend, there to lend Emmy moral support. When she left, I packed a bag and told Emmy I would be gone for a few days.

'Where are you off to? I thought you came here to help!' she said, obviously disappointed.

'I did and I will. There are just a few things I need to do, or rather want to do, and you don't want to be there when I do them,' I assured her.

'Promise me it won't involve dogs,' she said, and gave me an appealing look.

'My dear, it most certainly will!' I said brightly.

She wasn't pleased, but by now she knew me well enough not to persist. I wasn't going to go out without just one more Yorkie and maybe a bichon frisé if I could find one. It was time to paint the town red and I couldn't have Emmy there to see it.

***

Back on the seafront in Nice, I drank in the familiar smell of Mediterranean blood and money. I booked myself into a hotel and walked the Promenade des Anglais that night, hoping to find an old lady walking her Yorkshire terrier. At last, I spotted a young woman talking on her mobile phone while dragging a Yorkie along. She was in a hurry and was stomping along so fast in her high heels, the wee dog was struggling to keep up. I overheard her saying that she just had to bring Claude home and then she would get in her car. She told the person on the other end she'd be there in half an hour.

She was so preoccupied with texting and walking that she didn't notice me following her into the building. She lived on the first floor and I lingered on the floor above until she left, then I quickly opened the front door with my tools and picked up a surprised little Claude, who was waiting behind the door hoping it was his mistress coming back. I had a quick look around the apartment, but this girl didn't have much of value so I sat down comfortably on her sofa and enjoyed Claude. After, I wrapped him in a bag and took him to the nearest bin.

And now for some champagne-soaked floozie!

Going to a nightclub in Nice would be risky, but it was winter and I didn't expect any of my acquaintances to be about. I soon got talking to a French girl called Charlotte. She was quite short but had a great body. She told me she was a dancer, but was working at the airport to make ends meet. She and her friends put on quite a show on the dance floor and she wanted me to join them. I don't dance anymore; since swing and rock and roll I hadn't really kept up with the latest trends. She soon came back over to talk to me.

'I work at the check-in desk, so it isn't often I get a night off,' she told me.

'Well let's make the most of it then. Do you drink champagne?' I asked.

'I *love* champagne,' she purred.

She agreed to come back to the hotel with me and there I had my wicked way with her. She had a small tattoo on the inside of her wrist that would hide the puncture marks well. I knew she had to look good for her job so marks on her neck wouldn't do.

I let her sleep till about seven o'clock, then gently woke her and asked her to leave, saying I had to get ready for work too. She was scratching her wrist as she got dressed.

'Bloody winter and there are still mosquitoes,' she said, irritated.

'Terrible, those wee monsters. Here let me get you some cream,' I said, pulling out a tube of ointment from my bag. She kissed me and asked me for my number. I gave her a fake one as I didn't want to meet her again. I never bite the same girl twice after all.

After five days of debauchery and indulging in all the things I enjoy most, I went back to see Emmy.

'So, how many dogs and humans died for you?' she asked, looking none too pleased.

'I don't see the problem,' I retorted, 'I've seen you eat meat. What's the difference? Just because you give it a name doesn't make it any less of an animal. Here humans and I agree: animals are food!'

'I suppose you eat cats too?' she asked.

'Ah, no! I would like to, but they just taste incredibly vile!'

'Well, thank god for that!'

'When god created cats, he said "and let there be cats and let their blood be as rancid as their characters are evil!"'

'Wow, you *really* don't like cats,' she said and seemed to find me highly amusing.

Turning serious, I sat her down and laid out my plan. I was going to surrender myself to the authorities, but it would have

270

to be to the secret service and in total secrecy. Emmy was to set something up with the head detective and would only phone me if she was assured that she was dealing with the right person.

'Are you sure this is what you want to do?' she asked me. She looked at me intently, but a little suspiciously, as though wondering if I was up to something else.

'I think so. They might put me to good use and treat me well. Foreign legion vampire fighting for the good of France and all that,' I said cheerfully. But I was dreading what was ahead. Carl-Heinz's experience was not a good omen. I knew I probably wouldn't be treated well, but I couldn't see any other way to get George out of prison.

Emmy hugged me and told me there must still be some good left in me.

If you only knew what I want to do to you, you wouldn't think that, dear girl! 'Your great grandfather never forgave me for turning him into a vampire. I think this makes us even now,' I said.

I'd rented an apartment in Lyon for a month as I needed to keep my distance from Emmy. I was sure the detectives would have her followed as soon as she came forward with the information that she knew where I was. After about two weeks, I got her call.

'Hi Cameron. I think I've got the guy you want to talk to.'

'Have they agreed to release George once I surrender myself?' I asked.

'Yes. They said they would, as you are their main suspect anyway,' she told me.

'Have you told them what I am?'

'I haven't. I don't think they would have talked to me if I had. I'll give you Jean-Claude Bernard now of the DCRI,' she said and soon a male voice came on the line.

'Monsieur Cameron MacAdam?'

'It's Cameron Blair actually, MacAdam is the false identity I've been using,' I said, wondering if this man could be trusted.

'That explains why we found that you died in 2003.'

'You won't find Cameron Blair either, but I will explain that when we meet.'

'You are confessing to the murder of Yvette Jaunet,' he asked me.

I asked him for his number and if I could call him back. I wasn't ready to let them trace me yet. I got in my German stolen car immediately, ditched my phone and drove north. The DCRI headquarters were near Paris so I knew I'd be heading there eventually. First I needed some guarantees.

I called Monsieur Bernard back after a few days. 'Have you released George Baxter?' I asked.

'We are not going to do that until you surrender yourself.'

'As a gesture of goodwill, could you move him to Grasse prison?' I knew this was a new prison and conditions were a lot better there.

'I can do that. He will be moved in the next few days. Now, Monsieur Blair. Are you confessing to the murder of Yvette Jaunet,' he asked me again.

'Can you guarantee that no one will know of my capture apart from Emmy and George,' I asked, questioning whether they would stick to the bargain.

'Why would we keep it a secret and deny the Jaunet family justice?' he asked me, annoyed.

'I think I could be useful to France,' I told him. 'I'm someone that you would certainly want to keep in the dark. I am sure you have the ability to provide proof of my death, which should resolve a few things.'

'The police are already very unhappy that we are getting

involved in this case, they think it is to cover up a diplomat trying to get away with murder. Who exactly are you, Monsieur Blair?'

'Listen, I'll call you back in a few days when George Baxter has been moved,' I said, bringing an end to the conversation. I wanted them to jump through a few hoops before I gave them any more information.

I texted Emmy and asked her to post on Facebook once she had visited her dad in a new location, then I ditched my phone and drove on to Paris. She replied after two days and I made contact with Monsieur Bernard again.

'Thanks for moving Mr Baxter. Have you got things in place to bring me in?' I asked.

'Yes. We have manufactured something for the police that will say you died in Argentina a few weeks ago, but that you confessed to the murder beforehand. We have found an Argentinian lawyer to verify the confession, which is written in your handwriting.'

'You are a clever, sinister lot there at the DCRI. Well done,' I said, amused.

'So, Monsieur Blair. Are you confessing to the murder of Yvette Jaunet?'

This time he got his answer. 'I murdered Yvette Jaunet in her apartment in Cannes by cutting her throat with a scalpel. I then stole her dog and her jewellery and took them to my yacht where I killed her dog too. George Baxter is only guilty of disposing of the dog's body, he did not know it was Ms Jaunet's. I told him I had hit the dog with my car, but that it had died soon after I got it on board. I have a few other murders to confess to too, but we will keep that as a treat for later.'

'If this is all a hoax, we will make sure Monsieur Baxter ends up in the Baumettes in Marseille and we will charge his daughter with wasting police time,' he said.

'I am deadly serious, Monsieur Bernard,' I told him.

'Where are you?'

I told him I was in Paris and arranged for him to pick me up. Later that night I waited for him by the Eiffel Tower. As I got in the back of the large black sedan and shook Jean-Claude's hand I had a strong feeling of impending doom, but I knew I had made the right decision.

Since I'd gone off to war, and died for the privilege, I hadn't done a single selfless thing. I'd disappointed my family and then gone on to leave a trail of death and general misery, culminating in the incarceration of probably my only true friend.

But it wasn't really George that had made me care. I liked the grumpy old bastard, but hardly enough to surrender eternal freedom. No. There was somebody else who needed to live her life – and she deserved a father. It was time to stop and let this generation be.

After all, *living people should live their lives and dead ones should stop making a nuisance of themselves!*

Cameron is back!
in

Blood Ties
Language in the Blood, Book 2

by Angela Lockwood

After meeting his maker on the battlefields of the First World War, Cameron Blair has spent almost a century coming to terms with his new vampire identity. Along with a taste for human blood and lapdogs, he has acquired the linguistic skills of his victims and learned to survive in the shady underbellies of Europe's great cities.

The end of Language in the Blood sees Cameron facing a dilemma when blame for one of his kills gets laid at his best friend George's feet. Cameron discovers a deeply buried vestige of humanity and surrenders to the French authorities - a decision he soon regrets as it becomes clear they don't have quite the same heroic role for a vampire agent in mind that his own vivid imagination does.

For more information about Angela Lockwood, Cameron Blair and the Language in the Blood series, visit:

http://www.cruftslover.adzl.com/

https://www.facebook.com/CruftsloverAkaCameronBlair

Other books by this author available on Amazon:

Something Short

by Elspeth Morrison and Angela Lockwood

Something Short is a collection of short stories from French and Scottish shores by two female writers; Elspeth Morrison and Angela Lockwood. We meet a variety of interesting and amusing Scottish characters in Begonia, The Wee Baldy Man, The Pop Star and a mad scientist in Animals, but also some personal experiences in dealing with arthritis and depression in Begonia and The Goldfish Bowl. The stories are short but impactful and we hope they leave a lasting impression on you.

You're Not Alone

An Indie Author Anthology

by Ian D. Moore and Friends (Angela Lockwood, contributor)

An international group of indie authors, inspired by the personal grief of one, decided to collaborate in the spring of 2015 in a project to create this multi-genre smorgasbord of original short stories, all with the same potent theme – relationships. Some are heartfelt, some funny, some poignant, and some are just a little bit scary – much like relationships themselves. All are by authors fired by the shared enthusiasm to give something back in aid of Macmillan Cancer Support. Cancer touches us all. It has in some way affected those who have contributed their time and talent here. This is our way of showing that we care.

Indie authors carry forward a revolutionary shift in publishing, which allows the author to be creative director in their own work. There are many exceptional, experienced and acclaimed writers who have decided to take this bold step in publishing. In producing this anthology we have also had the inestimable assistance on board of artists, graphic designers, and bloggers – all of whom have a place in our acknowledgments. You, the discerning reader, are the other vital part of this equation. By buying this book you are supporting the work of indie authors, as well as discovering their worth. You are also supporting the charity to which we have chosen to dedicate our work.

100% of the royalties earned or accrued in the purchase of this book, in all formats, will go to the Pamela Winton tribute fund, which is in aid of Macmillan Cancer Support.